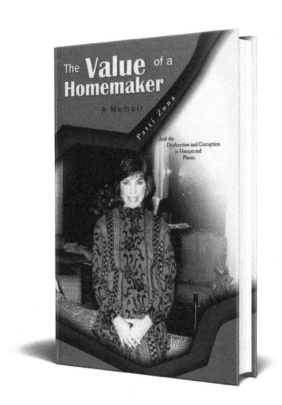

*THE VALUE OF A
HOMEMAKER*

Also, by Patti Zona

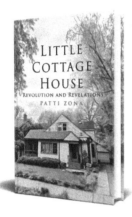

Little Cottage House   *Bohemian Momé*   *Patti Z. This is Me*

"Patti Zona is one of the most honest and forthright voices to read today. Her insights into society's missteps are the kind of ideas that should be shouted from rooftops! Thank goodness she has the gumption to bravely point out that the emperor has no clothes."

Red Gallagher

THE VALUE
OF A
HOMEMAKER

a memoir

WWW.PATTIZONA.COM

978-621-434-047-7 (paperback)
978-621-434-048-4 (hardback)
978-1-952874-53-6 (eBook)

Printed in New York by:

OMNIBOOK CO.
99 Wall Street, Suite 118
New York, NY 10005
USA
+1-866-216-9965
www.omnibookcompany.com

For e-book purchase: Kindle on Amazon, Barnes and Noble
Book purchase: Amazon.com, Barnes & Noble, and
www.omnibookcompany.com

Omnibook titles may be purchased in bulk for educational, business, fund-raising, or sales promotional use. For more information please e-mail **info@omnibookcompany.com**

Designed by: Gian Carlo Tan

CONTENTS

DEDICATION

My wish for my book to be read with an open heart and mind is that it will instill a quest for more knowledge of the unspoken and unknown. That those questions will be answered and encouraged for understanding and enlightenment, for when those simple quests are recognized for their importance and honored, then we all can benefit from that knowledge.

We all have a certain responsibility in life, that is, a gift instilled in all of us. For some, it has been buried or squelched, not allowing the best to come forth, either from ourselves or from others. When that happens, then we have a special challenge to conquer that fear or oppression; for to do nothing only perpetuates and eventually magnifies any problem creating an even larger quagmire.

For this reason, I dedicate these writings to all women who have struggled against obstacles and uncertainties and have persevered for all humanity—to all the young mothers and not-so-young mothers to recognize the importance of a role that nurtures the mind and body and replenishes the heart in body and of the home . When I realized I would write a dedication, I would wake up in the morning with the song in my head, "This Is Dedicated to the One I Love." I want to add "To the *Ones* I Love" and care so deeply about—family, children, the reason and purpose, dear friends, and new friends, who are unconditional, supportive, encouraging at times when needed, but will offer their abundance of insights and wisdom from their own experiences and journey. We learn from each other.

I also want to dedicate this book to not just a few good men, for there are so many more who will surface when faced with obstacles that they have been thrust into. They will do so even they are unaware of the ramifications or consequences that will test them, and some men even when being aware of those that will be affected. In those times, the right and honorable decision and action will have to be made. Therefore, I write in the hope that women and men will unite to help bring a healthier, and brighter, future for our children and for all humanity.

Acknowledgments

Sister Paulissa, I poured out my heart to you, I also wrote numerous pages for validation and understanding, not only for myself, but also as a comparative. I would learn there was nothing to compare with, as the outcome would already be known . . . thus just another formality, for what purpose one can only surmise. One of your last words that would come back to me was that I wrote beautifully and I could be a novelist. I realized later, that writing is sometimes the only recourse we have when our voice is unheard. So, thank you.

I want to thank all the people that were involved in this process in one way or another. I especially want to thank all who were so encouraging, and excited with hopes that this book would be recognition of the real reason and purpose, and that is families . . . valued and treasured for their importance. For all my dear friends, old, new, and my rediscovered friends too, I always say you are a gift. For my family, my sisters and brothers, nieces and nephews, I am so proud of you. And, of course, to my own children, life does take unexpected and unplanned courses and we can only do and be the best, not just for ourselves, but also for society and future generations. May this book be read to inspire something better.

Preface

I *AM GRATEFUL FOR THE* support and encouragement, sometimes fervently given, for it has been so long in the making. From the beginning of this project, my intent has been constant, and that is to try and make a positive difference for all. That is a huge undertaking, for I was a wife, mother, a homemaker—with many talents and abilities that would help me through those difficult times as a means of expression and a release.

I started writing for understanding and also to document the experiences that I underwent for so many years. At the beginning, I wrote in free hand, for I rebelled against the computer until I realized life and these proceedings were too vast for pen and paper. I bought my first computer in 2001. I should have taken a class, but I felt I had limited time. Through much trial and error, and lost writings, I could see the makings of my book take shape and form.

Many times, I would write in the wee hours of the morning, for there were fewer distractions. It was not unusual for me to write five to seven hours at a time, with a few breaks, but not every day, as my work was emotionally exhausting. Sometimes, however, I would awaken in the middle of the night with a particular memory, insight, or just in plain anguish and a need to express. I should have been painting or creating masterworks, but my life did take a turn of a more serious nature.

At the time, it was as if I was trapped in a continuous, taunting, and unending dream, but in actuality, I was only reflecting the reality of events, that was not of my making. I would not have a voice; my words were dismissed and or unheard. The people whom I trusted to protect me had their own agenda that would profit themselves. I knew if this was happening to me and, was allowed to continue, there would be a downward spiral that would have a far-reaching impact—setting standards and precedents that would eventually erode and trickle down. More importantly, I would not be heard. However, I learned and discovered that I could write.

Prologue

*S*HE SAW HIM CHANGE FROM a loving, devoted, husband and father to someone she no longer knew. This book is about corporate structures, the demands they make, the complete loyalty that is required, often at the cost of the family. This is also about the ultimate betrayal, and how people in position of power are not what they seem. This is a book about a single woman fighting the corporate giants for the recognition of her role, significance, and worth as a wife, mother, and homemaker and her longing for it to be valued.

This is also about seeing and experiencing corruption in courts, and in high places, and daring to unveil the unspoken, unknown, truths and realities. This book will also touch on power in the wrong hands and its destructive consequences that many times set precedents and standards that can be far-reaching.

Her husband was a banking expert. After their separation, her life would change dramatically in many ways that were beyond her control. Her ex-husband would not be content with just a divorce, and would find legal ways, as well as using his money, position, and connections to harass her for years. He used the courtroom to vent his anger and frustrations and they assisted with his merciless and unwarranted appeal that would continue for ten years. Divorced, annulled, appeals turned down repeatedly—she survived amidst all the turmoil and deception and now it is time her story is heard . . .

The Mask of Despair

*S*OME THINGS HAPPEN IN LIFE *that we would prefer to forget, but instead we are relentlessly taunted for years—enduring—as if testing the human will, endurance and fortitude.*

There is no escaping the drama that was forced upon Patti Zona. Her life would change in ways that were beyond her comprehension and become so disturbing, that she sought answers to her questions and attempting to understand during restless nights and even while sleeping. The nightmares would continue for years, with somewhat different scenario, but always with the same theme: searching for an escape that could not be found.

The man wears the mask—a mask of deception, but she senses his weakness and shame. She has deep feeling for this man, mingled with great sadness and disbelief, for there is no communication or understanding. They are both in agonizing despair that empties them of words, not knowing how to approach the other. He reaches out, but she sees his uncertainty, for he is torn between two worlds: one that included her and the other that would destroy her.

She looks at him. His mask is removed. She searches his face for a sign of emotion, some feeling, but there is nothing. She pulls away and steps back, for she has this chilling fear and starts to run. She stops and looks back. She can see his anguish, his tears. Her heart breaks. She searches his face one last time. He smiles meekly at her and raises his arms in shameful resignation. She steps back. Suddenly, he is a stranger to her now.

In this dream, there were people surrounding her, silently observing. It was night. The sky was black with a smattering of stars. The air was clear, for it had freshly rained. The streets were wet and shining, with the reflection of streetlights. The streets were tree-lined, inviting. Yet I am running from something unknown, yes, it's me in those nightmares.

That is when I see a slender man standing on the street corner, his head down as if he had been crying. I stopped and gently touched his shoulder to comfort him and he looked up. His face is sad, but it frightens me. He was a mime. I could not understand, so I ran.

I kept running until I came to my house on Mill Pond. I walked up the steps and opened the door. I went inside. I felt a sense of relief. I walked through the foyer, and saw the soft amber light coming from the den. I stood at the door, looking in and saw my husband standing, with his back to me. I wanted to tell him of my strange experiences, to reassure myself by telling him. But as he turned around, one-half of his face was masked, like the character in the 'Phantom of the Opera'.

He came toward me. My instincts told me to leave quickly. Again, I looked back. His mask was gone. His face was expressionless. I had a chilling fear that I could trust him no longer.

I never knew that *this dream* would be an omen of things to come. One that would be part of my journey in life, that would teach me in ways, that would not be gentle, desired, nor ever wanted. My life would change in ways that would go beyond comprehension and would be allowed to continue for years as if testing the limitation of endurance, draining me emotionally, physically, and mentally. What made it worse was the fact that it was so unnecessary, serving no purpose, but to hurt and humiliate. I often still wonder why he was allowed to use his power, connections, and position to torment me, for I was the mother of his children. Where was our protection of our rights?

Because we were married for so long, I felt our divorce would be done with dignity and respect. Of course, there would be a great period of adjustment. After all, we had been married for twenty-eight years. That is a lifetime. But the years of climbing the corporate ladder had taken its toll on our family; for its demands were constant, eventually driving a wedge between us, until we felt like strangers. I married him, but he was now married to his work. That was his main passion that consumed him and left nothing of himself to give to his own family. He was involved and was known as the banking expert when it came to doing mergers and acquisitions—a euphemism for hostile takeovers.

This would cause a major transformation in my husband, for the work was constant, difficult, and demanding to the point that he would immerse himself in his meditative tapes to relax and eventually he would do self-hypnosis to numb his conscience and his feelings in order to escape the regrets of his actions. To me, this just did not seem healthy or right, as we need to rely on our senses to guide us, not to numb or remove them. Unfortunately, he traveled so much that he truly was becoming a stranger to me and to our children. If he did have a problem with alcohol or drugs, there would have been a diagnosis to assign, an intervention to try, a whole community to support him and our family with weekly meetings and daily devotions. But the addiction he developed just enhanced his performance in his career, his addiction was well rewarded, and he would always be well compensated. And that "high" would be so intoxicating, he would be unaware of the devastation would take place in other areas of his life, even if it meant sacrificing his family.

Even to this day, I still have a restless urgency for an understanding and closure, for consequences of this painfully touched every aspect of my life for too many years. Many times the devastation would catch me by surprise. I never got use to the emotional brutality that ensued. It would be so unexpected each time his actions reflected not only reckless disregard for my well-being, but also the ruthlessness toward me as if I were an object to be conquered. Because this was about money, power, and position, my husband would test his limits in the courtroom, using all his tactics and loopholes that he learned in the ruthless world of mergers and acquisitions.

When this first began, I naively thought "surely the courts will protect me," for his actions were blatantly obvious, and it was clear that I had been wronged, and was vulnerable. I had no family here and my last child was now in college in Colorado. So after a couple of decades as a devoted homemaker, I was adjusting to the inescapable pain associated with an empty nest as well as a divorce. Yet, I was never allowed to experience fully the depth of those transitions in my life. I was the wife and mother, the homemaker that would not be valued or treasured, but erased. Rick was lashing out. He would not, and did not have to, account for his actions any longer. He was a man now entitled and could and would buy his exemptions at any cost, knowing no boundaries or limitations. He was allowed in his corporate world, the courts would assist as if a game, and when I thought he could not hurt me any longer, he would use the church to absolve his sins and erase his past and my existence. For that, I thought I would truly break for it was as if I had lost my identity.

CHAPTER 2

Innocence Lost

*O*VER THE COURSE OF ACQUIRING his success, Rick forgot that he was fortunate to be surrounded by a loving family that was always there for him. How lucky can one be to have loving grandparents, aunts, uncles that helped pave the way, cousins that were there to help build those treasured memories, and such loving parents? His parents became like my own.

After our marriage, his parents embraced me not only as a daughter in law but grew to be as a daughter. I felt loved, protected and wanted with this new family. Rick's mother taught me to cook, how to fold laundry the way she did. I thought she was an expert. She taught me how to iron, how to put the creases in the right places. When I felt sick in the morning, my mother-in-law lovingly would make Rick's salami sandwiches but also teaching me in the process how Rick liked the little peppercorns taken out. I would stand back at a distance for the whiff of the salami would make me queasy, and then we would add the mustard on the fresh Italian bread. In the beginning, I was a bit intimidated by Rick's mom, but that didn't last for long for she became my mentor, my dearest friend and truly became as a loving mother for me. I felt blessed, safe, and protected by her. I was so thankful.

Now most young couples would have a hard time living with in-laws or parents for any length of time. But we were different in that respect. I was very young but still determined to learn how to be the best wife possible. I was to be a mother and that was going to be a tremendous responsibility, and I wanted to be prepared to do it right. Being surrounded by this wonderful nucleus, vibrant Italian family was a gift to me. I soaked up all they had to offer and thrived in their presence. I grew to love them, and I know they loved me as their own daughter. I could see it and feel it, and I wanted to make them proud and never worry about having this new young girl come into their home and their life. The transition to motherhood, daughter-in-law, and wife was transforming. My whole life shifted.

Rick's life hardly skipped a beat. The major change for him was that he now had a bigger incentive and determination to finish college. This gave him even more reason to stay focused on getting a good education. It is true that being married at an early age has some disadvantages. But we had family to call upon when we needed them. They helped us get on our feet and get off to a good start. For a little over two years, they did not ask us to pay rent. They did expect us to do our share and make good advantage of our situation, so that one day we would have our own home. During this time, and actually even before our marriage, Rick had several part-time jobs. He worked at the local drug store and malt shop in Crete, at a newspaper stand selling papers and magazines, and he worked at the post office delivering mail. He seemed to thrive in these roles, and seemed proud of an honest day's work. He would go to his jobs with enthusiasm and come home with even more enthusiasm. We both were happy and secure in our protected little world.

I would love to walk down to Seahausen's, our local drugstore/malt shop, and visit Rick. To me he seemed so mature and worldly. He would point out all his duties and what they would entail, and I was impressed. But I also secretly thought it would be fun to have a little job like that myself. He would make me a malted milkshake, and if it weren't too busy, we would catch up on both our days, while sipping my delicious malt. Sometimes, I would stay until he closed, and we would walk home together, as this little store was only about four blocks from our home with my wonderful in-laws.

Rick also worked occasionally for a few hours at the little newspaper stand, he seemed to adapt with each experience, and it kept him busy. I remember he worked for Mr. Denunzio, a nice older man. He happened to have only one arm. I was always curious and wondered what and how this injury happened but felt it was too sensitive an issue to question. I wished I had now because I am sure he would have liked to tell his story. But I was again impressed with my young husband's initiative. I do not know how he met him but every one seemed to be connected in this little town. That was such a long time ago.

We lived with my mother-in-law and father-in-law for a little over two years. Rick was able to focus on getting his degree in accounting, meanwhile keeping his part-time jobs without the stress of providing for the normal expenses of independent living (e.g., paying rent, utility, or grocery bills) and still having all the comforts of home. What money he earned, he would put toward our future home and education.

When I turned seventeen, I was just a high school girl, but pregnant with our first baby. Back in the 1960s, it was unheard of for a young girl who was pregnant to attend school with her classmates. I talked to my high school principal and told him my situation, and that I as still determined to finish my junior year with hopes to graduate, for education was always important to me. Perhaps people sensed my genuine sense of kindness and compassion, because the principal allowed me to continue. It was known that I was the only married girl in high school, but it was agreed that I would not talk about this in school as it might promote this kind of unwanted behavior.

My life would change at a very young age. I realized that I had to grow up and accept all the responsibility that was thrust upon me. I was secretly going to have a baby. There would be no fanfares for me or school dances. I would never have the experiences of the typical teenager. When I think back about my situation, I am amazed and impressed with my classmates' attitude toward me. The majority of the kids just accepted, never making a big deal over my precarious situation. There was one boy that would make some comment that I would usually try and ignore. But there were also a few boys that expressed their regrets that I was now married. Surprisingly, I had never really dated that many boys, as my father was very strict and vigilant. Rick was the only one who did not seem to fear my father. He could be very bold, but with me, he was sweet and gentle. I felt somehow safe with him. I was impressed with his patience and I trusted him for I had known him since I was fifteen.

I was not allowed to date until I was sixteen and that was only on Fridays or an occasional Saturday, and I had to be home before midnight. Because Rick accepted these strict rules, I was impressed with his integrity and patience. That was not always easy as first love is sweet and tender that eventually grows into intense yearnings not yet experienced. I was so innocent and unworldly, maybe that is one of the qualities that I was so attracted to Rick.

Thinking back, the dynamics of our relationship changed during that period of time. When Rick went to college his feelings became more intense, wanting to really make love. But, I was torn. I felt I loved him. After all he was brave, loyal, and I trusted him. But I was still nervous. He never forced himself, but yet I knew his frustrations and I felt for him.

We made love on my seventeenth birthday; that was my gift to him. I remember thinking, "*this is my birthday.*" How dumb could I possibly be? The first time was not what I expected or really wanted. However, I just conceded to Rick's wishes and ended up paying a very heavy price. I became pregnant and would give birth to a son on his father's birthday. I remember the shock, the shame, and fear that gripped me. From that moment, I felt my life change profoundly. I felt so alone in a wilderness of uncertainty and regret. For me, I felt this was mine alone, my own problem, my own quandary, from which there was no escape. I would have to go away, somewhere unknown, have a new name, get a new identity. I could not even imagine having a baby. I still had to finish high school. If I had a baby, how could I do that? Would I get to keep the baby or would someone else take the baby for me? I did not know. I had no idea of what it was like or what to expect. I was so frightened and alone.

I knew I had to tell Rick, for he had the right to know. I also knew that I would have to tell my parents. I felt so ashamed. I had let them down and now I felt I was heading for the gallows, with no redemption. I deserved to suffer the consequence of my actions; at least that is what I thought at that time.

I remember telling Rick that we needed to talk. He picked me up from school and we took a walk, which is one thing that we rarely did. I don't know if he felt something also, maybe the same fear or possibility. I will never forget his reaction when I told him that I thought I was pregnant. He stopped and he looked at me and just said so matter of fact, "We'll just get married." Just like that. So simple. That was the solution. I was stunned. I knew then—like I did from the time I first met Rick—that he was courageous, not afraid of anything or anyone. He offered to be there when I told my parents. I told him no and that I wanted to do that myself, for I did not want my father to hurt him and I knew he could. I did tell Rick that he should tell his parents and he agreed.

He took me home in the late afternoon, when my father was not yet home from work. I remember thinking it was better to tell my mother first, for I did not want her to witness the rage my father might have against me. She cried when I told her, but it was also one of the times she held me and I felt her sorrow and her concern. For some reason our house seemed unusually quiet, which was rare. When my father came home, my mother told him that I wanted to talk to him. I am sure he could see or feel her distress. We went into the dining room. I never sat down, but my father did. I really felt I was on my death march, that this was the end, and I hadn't even begun to live my life. I gathered all the strength and courage I could muster and I told him that I was going to have a baby. He rose from his chair. He was livid and I thought he was entitled to feel this way. He went to strike me, but then he stopped in mid-air, turned, and walked away. I knew then he would not hurt me again. I also knew in that moment that I was an adult, no longer a child.

16

Rick kept his word and he did tell his parents that night. I learned later that his father told him that he did not have to marry me. Nevertheless, Rick told them I was the girl he always intended to marry. That detail stays with me despite all that has happened, and fueled a place in my heart that will always love him. I hadn't even anticipated being married yet. I had my own dreams and goals that I felt should be pursued in their natural course. I had envisioned myself finishing high school and any other extended education that I would need in order to pursue my dreams. As I could remember, I would say, "When I grow up, I am going to be a singer, dancer, artist, and missionary." Well, I was almost grown up and I did have many gifts and talents that came easily and naturally for me. I felt fortunate and thankful that I had more of a creative spirit that wanted to grow and experience. And I was confused about how my life would unfold, as these parts of me would need to defer to the very real demands of parenthood that were looming.

Rick was of a more practical nature, but he also had a playful side. I liked that combination. I liked the fact that he did follow his dreams. He wanted to be an accountant. To me that seemed solid and practical. I felt our differences complimented each other. I had talents and was creative, but I also had a lot of common sense, sensitivity, and a certain amount of wisdom that kept growing. In that wisdom there was also an unusual childlike nature that still comes through even now. Since I had so much to learn and accept at that time, I let the people around me make my decisions for me until I felt confident in my own right. Little would I know that our lives together would take such unexpected and incredulous turn during this period of change that would transform us all.

CHAPTER 3

COUNTRY CLUB

*L*IFE IN THE *COUNTRY CLUB* neighborhood in the beginning offered so many hopes and promises for my family. This Edina neighborhood where we bought our house in 1979 had an interesting history. Years ago, when these homes were built, in the early 1920s, the buyer or family would also include a membership to a country club, Edina Country Club. Thus, this incentive was a great concept in housing for couples wanting to establish a home in a desired neighborhood. This would bring families together to relax, play, or entertain socially, business, or personal, all in walking distance. This little neighborhood was well thought-out, including a four- or five-story redbrick schoolhouse that really caught my attention. It brought back a feeling of nostalgia. It stood as a symbolism for bright futures for all the children: well cared for, nurtured, and loved. The streets were named alphabetically: Those running north and south were Arden, Bruce, Casco to Drexel, then Wooddale, Moorland, Edina Boulevard to Browndale Avenue. The streets that would run east and west were Sunnyside Road, in the middle were Bridge Street, and then Country Club Road, all connecting and encompassing this inviting little neighborhood.

We would eventually buy a pretty little Mediterranean house at 4516 Casco Avenue. It was a pleasing textured tan stucco home, with cocoa brown shutters and the original red terracotta tiled roof. The front door was arched with the same color as the cocoa brown shutters, looking warm and inviting. Every home in Country Club had its own uniqueness and originality. I liked that aspect of this well thought out community. We would move in our new-old house just days before Christmas, so actually in 1978 but really going into the new year of 1979. This would also be the coldest winter, we as a family had ever experienced.

When we first looked at this house, it was in the early fall of 1978. The colors were brilliant with touches of the green still holding amidst the reds, oranges, and yellows. The leaves on the tree-lined streets served as a beautiful canopy that could not but capture your eye and attention. The sidewalks would be a carpet of fallen leaves; so many that raking was a futile attempt, for the trees were magnificent and grand and filled with abundance of leaves, running their own cycle of life. All the homes offered their own charm and personality bringing together the perfect neighborhood. This would be our new home even if for a short while.

I loved that house. We had the best neighbors and probably one of the friendliest and most interesting streets in Country Club. But unfortunately, it was one bedroom too small for all five of us, for it only had three bedrooms and our boys were growing up needing their own rooms. I could understand that. It also had only one bath upstairs and a quarter bath on the main level. Rick at that time was way too frugal especially with his growing family. Another important issue was the fact that the closets were so small, while our children were growing. We needed more space. Rick many times would surprise me in his decisions. The thought that we could have bought a four-bedroom house just four houses up from us, but Rick did not want to spend the extra twenty thousand dollars—that was maddening to me. Rick was rather frugal about expenses. But later in his years that would change for himself.

Although this house was small, it still offered coziness, like a small den off the living room, surrounded by large windows framed with rich dark wood. I called this room the reading room with just enough room for two small beige sofas at each end and a small table between. The kitchen was tiny, but it had a built-in breakfast nook with a bench that would open up for storage. When Monica would have her little friends over, maybe a breakfast of pancakes, they would sit at the little table visiting while I would be singing little songs while preparing their meal. I remember little Kim laughing and saying, "Mrs. Zona, you sure are entertaining." We all laughed. I hoped my pancakes were appreciated as much as the entertainment. My fondest memories will always be the fact that I could always be there for my children. I always wanted them and their friends to feel welcomed and invited and to me it was always important for me to know their friends too.

I also had acquired quite a few paintings through the years. I would use these paintings throughout the house. We had a wonderful staircase with a landing halfway up. I would hang some of my most prominent works facing the entry below and on the walls going up the stairs, I hung my paintings of various themes. When anyone would come to the wonderful arched doorway and into our little entryway, they would see the tiny tiles that were laid out one by one in various shades of browns, tans, and beige, for the tiles were original too. No more than two people could really fit in that tiny foyer, but when they walked into the room, they would be drawn to my paintings. It looked rather impressive for not too many people had their own original works of art cascading up their stairway! Since I was a stay-at-home mom, it as my way of contributing something that money and status could not. It would be fun to give the history of each. Many would be impressed. Since I had painted ever since high school and continued doing so as a pastime in my marriage, my intentions were to continue painting even when we moved to Minnesota. But that would prove to be impossible for the demands of my family were needed and necessary and would take precedent for me.

As beautiful as the fall was in Country Club, this first winter would have its own majestic presence. The beauty of a freshly fallen snow, sometimes windswept into interesting shapes and forms that only nature can provide, smooth plains of snow that would lead to gentle peaks against a fence or wall, watching the snow fall covering the slippery ice underneath so you had to tread carefully. There must have been a sudden deep freeze during the last autumn rain of the season, for some of the houses facing the coldest and windiest force were incased with a layer of ice. The snows continued until I wondered where we would put it all, narrowing the streets and walkways. Some of the trees would buckle under the burden of the weight of all the snow and ice, lending unique new shapes. I wondered whether they would survive this awesome winter. Then the snows would stop. Fortunately, there would be many bright sunny days and sometimes a profound stillness, making the air so calm. Maybe it was the wall of snow that prevented the breezes going through. Early in the morning there would be this incredible quiet as if nature itself was hibernating, until the strongest and the bravest ventured from somewhere or maybe it was just the most curious making their presence known. This was to be our new home. What would tomorrow bring?

In the warmer seasons, much of the allure of our neighborhood was the fact that the Minnehaha Creek ran alongside the backyard of some of the homes off of Sunnyside Road, Browndale Avenue, and Edgebrook Avenue. Minnehaha Creek was a well-known favorite for canoeist, sometimes offering in some areas of the creek small rapids, but better known for its sauntering, scenic beauty. The canoeist could actually canoe for miles, for this creek started at Grey's Bay in Lake Minnetonka and winding its way to the Mississippi River intertwining through countryside, parks, and those fortunate enough to have it flow through their own backyards. They eventually would have to portage their canoes in some low-lying areas, certain water rapids and occasional waterfall, for instance the Minnehaha Waterfalls another well-known historical park in Minneapolis.

Eventually we would buy a house on Edgebrook and Browndale that was on one portion of the creek known as Mill Pond, another historical site. This part of the creek had widened into a beautiful small lake that many times in the winter would be the perfect place to ice skate, walk the frozen creek or cross-country ski. On the Mill Pond area would also be the start of some rapids that you could see and hear from our house so during the winter thaw one would have to be careful not get too close to the rapids. Throughout all the seasons this wonderful creek provided the perfect surroundings for the visionary poets, writers and artists, and would always capture the attention and imagination of children of all ages to play and explore to their heart's content, building fond memories even amidst the storms. To me it seemed idyllic.

I remember not too long after we moved into our house on Casco Avenue having two young visitors that lived down the street from our house. We were still getting settled, boxes that still needed unpacking, and finding space for everything was proving to be quite a challenge. When the doorbell rang and I went to answer, I was pleasantly surprised to see two teenage girls at the door. They introduced themselves and then explained that they had heard we were new in the neighborhood and wanted to meet our two sons. They were not home at the time. During this dialogue, out of the blue, one of the girls asked me if I was divorced. I was rather stunned by that odd question and I told her so. I then asked her why she would even ask such a question. She answered, "Well, many people are divorced that live here." Wow, I didn't quite know what to say. I was so astounded! I remember saying, "I am married, and I do not have any intentions of ever getting a divorce." And I concluded that conversation with "And I think that is the strangest question I have ever been asked." I do not know what compelled them to ask such a jolting question or even if they could comprehend the magnitude of that question. But it was obvious that divorce had impacted their life somehow. I felt they must have been searching for acceptance and understanding. That first encounter would always come back to haunt me.

I was left feeling a little uneasy and I didn't know if it was for those young girls, for their casual acceptance and attitude or for my own hidden fear. What did we get ourselves into? What was going to happen to us now that we were so far away from all our family and friends? I put this strange interlude out of my mind for at that time, I really felt secure in my marriage, never doubting my husband or myself. I knew marriages had their ups and downs, but we had been married long enough and had been through enough that I felt with each difficulty that we went through and conquered, it just made us that much stronger, more durable and lasting. Yet I realized that this time the challenge was not just for myself or my husband. We were uprooting our sons at a rather precarious stage in their lives. They were teenagers of fourteen and sixteen. For them, it might not be as easy and for that to me was a bit unsettling. I knew that for this transition to work would require attentiveness, working together and being there for each other. After all, for now all we had was each other.

That is what I wanted to believe—that our love for each other was forever, changing and growing through the years, but always solid. Learning from each other, wanting and bringing out the best in each other, for ourselves, and for our children. It was shortly after we moved to Minnesota that we learned Rick was to be made partner of Ernst and Ernst (Ernst and Young) As Rick had predicted, our life would change, but shouldn't this be a good thing? Life has a way of changing ever so gradually and we get so caught up in the busyness of our lives. Rick was proving his worth as a new young partner. I was busy with the demands of three children, all the complexities of two teenage sons and all the other demands that were necessary to run a household.

We found, this wonderful little neighborhood, seeming so idyllic and inviting, offering everything that any family would need or want and all at our fingertips. What we would learn and experience would be our own unique and complex experience. This was a transitional period not just for my husband, but for our family as well. This also could and should have been a time of recognition and awareness, along with the tremendous responsibility for and from all concerned and all involved. There is a cause and effect.

One of the biggest reasons for moving to Minnesota was for the schools which were proclaimed to be the best, especially in Edina, offering the best in education, music programs and, of course, sports. We definitely were drawn to this neighborhood, for all of the wonderful possibilities it provided. But when it came right down to it the main reason would be for my husband's career, which of course would affect our family as well. But again, without the added incentives of fine schools and inviting neighborhoods, we probably would not have chosen to live here; for there were other opportunities not only for my husband, but for myself as well and for our family without making this move. We did give this transfer careful consideration, knowing our sons were teenagers, and having a young daughter. Hoping this would be the best choice for our children, for all of us.

Looking back, I can't help wondering if this was just being a façade, the seduction, the temptress that would lure young families into its web of humiliation, pain, and suffering? We did not know then and would not know for a long time, for it was all so insidious and beguiling with hopes and promises that would not be kept. Broken promises. Broken vows. Words that were thoughtlessly spoken and would eventually become meaningless. Ambiguity and deception seemed to be a part of every transaction with Rick that would later play out its real intent or purpose. There is a reason and purpose and cause and effect, which would eventually be exposed, unsuspecting and unwarranted and certainly not deserved.

I often wonder what the founders of these beautiful cities and communities would think of the progression through the years. Would they be proud of what they see, or disappointed in what progress has provided in the name of success, bigger and better? People running away from the cities, from their little neighborhoods to get away up north or some place offering peace and tranquility, away from all the business, congestion and to breathe in the fresher air, all feverishly preparing and thinking of their next getaway, forgetting to live in the moment, for their thoughts are always someplace else and you can see it and feel it. Proudly bearing their badges of honor and pride that they wear so well. This has become a symbol of the success, the big beautiful home, the country-club style, but always striving for even more greener pastures. What was on the other side of the fence that might be bigger and grander? How could it be acquired? There would be a need to impress and eventually arrogance would take over their persona, replacing the genuine warmth and friendliness of one's character. Life would become a charade, a game or a conquest, when tempted and going to the extreme and excess, forgetting the original purpose. Would our founding forefathers look back in a quiet contentment and pride or saddened by our misplaced values and what we have replaced? I wonder.

When we moved into our little neighborhood I wanted to believe that this would be a most positive move for our family. Rick promoted this move to our family as Ernst and Ernst had, by sparking a keen interest for himself not only for his career but the added bonus for his family. Rick's family was always the initial motivating factor, giving him the incentive and purpose to succeed. Rick expounded on all the virtues that Minnesota had to offer, the high quality of life, the unsurpassed quality in education, the natural beauty of the many parks, lakes, and streams that we would enjoy as a family. We would take sailing lessons, which seemed to spark an interest in our sons. We would join the Edina Country Club, would be just across the street from our house. How lucky can you get?

Life is a learning lesson but sometimes it takes so long to understand and comprehend the magnitude of our decisions. For a family of five, each at different stages and with different personalities, it is impossible to know how the effects will play out, for awareness and timing is very important. But always the crucial component in any kind of meaningful success is the unity of family—solid, unshakeable, always dependable. Family is the foundation of existence that should be valued, not forgotten, or ignored in any process of life. Isn't that what we are taught or have we forgotten? This should have been a move that we would build and grow as a family. But instead all the extra trappings were used to replace our family as if an illusion.

Within a few months of moving into our house on Casco Avenue in 1979, Rick would learn that he would be made partner of this prestigious CPA firm Ernst and Ernst. This would be bittersweet as he would be the only new partner in Minneapolis, which caused a lot of resentment amongst the staff. Rick was very distressed about this. This time should have been a time of celebration, instead was hardly acknowledged by his peers. I felt for my husband and tried to comfort and reassure him. I remember how confusing it was for our sons. They were teenagers and having to adjust and fit into their new school and community, trying to find their niche in this new place, which would not embrace so readily. Nothing was familiar. The music programs were already set. No need for another first chair in trumpet. You have to prove your worth. Credentials and previous experience seemed to be unimportant. My sons felt for their father along with their own disappointments and fears. It was a confusing time and I desperately tried to fill the void, for I was a wife and mother and I felt all of their pain along with my own.

I actually thought that with this strange new beginning we would return to South Bend or Chicago. We could easily pick up where we left off. Go back to the familiar, stable and secure. Instead, Rick embraced it as a challenge, and became more determined to prove his worth and value to this firm to the point that he could not see the needs of his two sons. Monica at six was adjusting beautifully in her school of Wooddale. That was a blessing. Life should be this joyous and carefree. She was fine, while her brothers were having their own challenges at a time when they needed their father most. I was trying to know and be it all. I knew our family was unique. We were the youngest parents. That was bad enough but I looked much younger than my years, which presented different challenges. It would be awkward meeting the new partners' wives, for I definitely was the youngest, but I would eventually win them over, because I genuinely liked them. I didn't care if they were young or old, short or tall, round or skinny as a rail, as long as they had a good heart, a certain amount of intelligence and substance and good solid convictions. If they didn't have that or care to learn, I gave them the benefit of the doubt and a prayer of hope.

I will always treasure my memories and friendships with our neighbors on each side of us. Since I was a young wife and mother, I valued the wisdom of my treasured friendships through the years and that would never change. My dear neighbor Barb and I would take many architectural walks in the neighborhood. She was the epitome of grace and dignity. She was so knowledgeable that I would soak up our conversations as a sponge, whether our conversations be about philosophy, gardening, politics, or religion. I felt that Barb represented everything that was proper and wholesome. We also played tennis together for several years with her lifetime friends, rotating different partners each week. It was a great way to meet new friends.

I could have adapted quite easily if it were just myself. But I always had that invisible tethered bond of maternal responsibility and now it seemed to be working overtime. It was uncanny. I could see the effects on our sons through this transition and I felt for them, but oddly enough Rick seemed to be oblivious to everything and everyone around him, for he was too immersed in his own needs, making his own quagmire. Where did he want to exert his energies, time and attention—his family or his company? It was a real dilemma for him. It was very difficult to admit that maybe this was not the time or place for uprooting his family. But he did make a choice and that was to prove his worth. That would be his conquest, his mission. For he always knew that his family, would accept and be there unconditionally. He wanted to be the sole provider for his family for that was a natural in his Italian background. Rick made this subconscious decision not knowing or thinking of the consequences.

He would prove his worth. He would be recognized, admired, and rewarded for his hard work and his sacrifices. The problem was there was nothing he wouldn't do to prove his worth. This conquest became a way of life and main focus that would consume his thoughts, time, and energy when our sons needed guidance. It bothered me to see this transgression. I resented the fact that any company would uproot families and not prepare or give them the necessary time to adjust and acclimate to the unfamiliar, the unknown, or unexplored. We were a family that was whole, but Ernst and Ernst would drive a wedge, chipping away deliberately methodically, grooming this new young partner who was able and willing and would be insidiously seduced. Challenges can be exciting, especially when one realizes the stakes are high, the goals are attainable and so good for building the ego, recognition and worth.

The prize should never be greater than the cost of the loss, especially the loss of family, friends, and the loss of integrity and honor or the loss of self. Tempting fate, trading true values for the loss of ones conscience or soul. I thought and believed at one time we were better than that. Our ideals and standards were strong, solid, unshakable. Nothing or no one could come between us. For me it was almost sacrilegious. Where were the limitations or boundaries that would protect the families? My family! Starting anew, we were alone, removed from everyone dear and everything familiar. How dare any company tempt or demand at such a heavy price, when all we needed was a little more time together as a family, especially during this period of adjustment?

Our children finished the 1979 school year. Monica adjusted, having been accepted by her little classmates. I would walk her to school and be there at the end of her day to greet her, talking to her teacher and meeting her new little friends. It will always be a cherished memory of that special time. However, our sons were unhappy, sometimes sullen, sometimes angry. We learned of upcoming changes to the high-school. Edina East would be merging into Edina West. My oldest son would be graduating his last year of high school in yet another school, creating the largest graduating class ever. There would be over a thousand kids in his graduating class! The graduation was held outside to accommodate family and friends. He was the new kid who always stood out. Because Mark's name ended in a Z he would be the last kid to receive his diploma. After all those names were called, the anticipation grew in intensity, almost electric. When Mark's name was called, the applause and acknowledgments were deafening.

Finding our son amidst the throng of other elated family and friends seemed impossible. But it was amazing. It was as if a parent and child could not be separated for there was this invisible connection and awareness. When we found Mark, he just beamed. It was hot and noisy and the crowd was exuberant. I wanted so much to know his thoughts, his experience and to see him beaming with pride reassured me and touched my heart. He was my first child graduating. I wanted to protect and guide him, give him the best that a family could provide that would allow him to spread his own wings and experience the joy and gifts of life with pride and dignity. He was my scholar, my gentle child wanting to find his own path. Later over dinner, Mark exclaimed that when his name was called and the crowd just roared, it was as if everyone was cheering for him. That was what he chose to believe, not because he was the last kid—that just stood out.

Not only would we learn that Edina would merge into the largest high school, we would learn that Wooddale grade school would be torn down and used as a park. All the children in the neighborhood would now be bussed to the little school of Concord. Many of the neighbors along with myself petitioned to save this wonderful little school but to no avail. Our words were not heard, for the decision was made and there would not be any more discussions or consideration. Progress.

CHAPTER 4

DISILLUSIONMENT

THOUGHTS OF OUR FIRST SUMMER in Minnesota keep coming back. I could see the needs of my children. I also felt the neglect and absence of my husband, not just for me, but especially for my sons. This was the age of changes. Our sons were trying to assert their own independence but needing the guidance and influence of a loving father. Rick just could not provide the one thing that we all needed the most from him. We needed a little time together, and reassurance that our family was his priority.

They say we should pay attention to our instincts, listen to that inner voice, and pay attention to that feeling that nags and pulls in your waking hours and persists in your fretful dreams. I brushed aside all the signs, dismissing them as I dismissed my fears of conquering the mountain. I would prevail. After all, I was the dutiful wife, taught to please. I wanted to think that this was just another natural course in our journey. Each journey a little more challenging, but always offering lessons in life. I have always had an innately curious nature or inquisitive side. Fortunately, I had a certain amount of common sense that people were attracted to, including my husband. He valued my opinion in many matters of importance. In that respect we were a team—relying on each other's strengths, complementing the differences.

I realized that this move to Minnesota might be a mistake. The timing wasn't right for our family. Our house was lovely, but not quite suited for a growing family of five. Even the ominous winter of nature itself seemed to want to alert us for what was in store, and that we were not really prepared. Rick's bittersweet promotion to partner that fueled a fierce determination to succeed, forced him to neglect his own family. I felt it wasn't too late to turn back. I just did not feel comfortable with the turn of events, how things transpired. There was a difference in attitude and mentality here. A sense of misplaced pride, a closeness and contentment within, not necessarily open to new ideas or the newcomer, always subjected to the test of time, scrutiny and selective consideration. I did not believe that this was the time in our marriage for a summons of such inquiry. Our sons were growing up too fast. To me, it was time that my husband took a more active role in raising his children, especially in this transition, for his sons were growing up needing more of a male influence and direction, understanding and support that only the father can give at this stage in their lives. If that was not possible for Rick to do, the alternative was at least to let him know our desperation.

How could I convey the depth and gravity of all this to a man who was so important in our family, but so consumed and unaware? I wrote that letter out of frustration and desperation, wanting the magnitude of our situation to be taken seriously. I wanted Rick to realize that his presence as a husband and father was more important than any amount of money.

January 31, 1980

Dear Rick,

I'm not happy—it's making you unhappy and disgusted. I don't want to live our marriage like that. Like this. I don't know what to do. I do know I want the kids, and I feel they need me. Duane might prefer to be with you. I don't know. I want the arrangements to be made to suit both of us, and if it is friendly it will work out better for all of us.

Since you are so busy, the arrangements shouldn't be that difficult and you will probably see the kids more than you do now. You say that I am the cause of the type of relationship with the children and that I know is true—but I needed your help and support. It is so easy to be critical, and sometimes I just get too tired and drained and confused to know what to do. Believe me, I know you've tried to please me and the kids too and I probably have been very demanding. I'm sorry. I guess as the kids get older it does get more difficult. There are just so many different and conflicting emotions to deal with. I just feel we both need to step back and really think about our problems and try to resolve them, either together, maybe even apart.

I guess it is hard to comprehend the life ahead. I did so want our marriage to work, mainly because I owe you. You did help me for seventeen years, but now I feel we are just hurting each other. Rick, I never wanted riches, just security, someone to really care for me and treat me with love and tenderness. I have never been able to deal with harsh treatment or behavior. I couldn't as a child, and I won't as an adult, not from my husband and certainly not from my children. If I cause that type of behavior then there must be something in me that must provoke those feelings in others.

Sorry that I have to write this, but as you say, you are tired of hearing my complaining voice. Plus, I really cannot say what I really mean it is much too difficult. I'm not very good at verbal expressions, as you well know.

I only want the best for both of us. At least you have a fine career, and I shall look to my future too. It's scary, but I refuse to live a miserable, loveless marriage. Please, help me to make this work for both of us and for our children.

Patti

* * * * *

January 31, 1980

Dear Pat,

I'm very distressed that you are not happy. It is a difficult and confusing time for both of us. From the tone of your letter, it does not appear that you have any love left for me.

You should not blame yourself for the relationship with the children. You have done a tremendous job. You're absolutely right about the lack of support in raising the kids. I haven't done my job in this regard. And it has placed a huge unfair burden on you.

It is unfortunate that we have to resort to writing to each other instead of talking. It does say something about our relationship.

I feel badly too that you think you owe me for helping you for seventeen years. I don't want you to feel indebted to me. You're not. My job has taken so many hours (years!) away from you and the children. It is I that owe you.

Just as you are torn by conflicting emotions, so am I. I love you and the children very much. I feel that my job has cheated us all. Yet at the same time I also feel married to the firm. It is painful and frustrating to think of leaving the firm especially when the financial rewards should now start to become substantial since I have just become a partner. But perhaps fate would have it that I should leave and start a new career outside of public accounting.

I don't think we should do anything rash or hasty. After all we have been married for seventeen years. Also, I believe our separating would hurt the children a great deal.

You're right that we have to step back and try to work out our problems. I'm not sure I know how to begin. But let's try to analyze the various courses of action from the most drastic and immediate to other possible courses of actions would be:

1. *Divorce—that is a very serious and drastic measure. It should not be taken lightly. It would drastically affect our lives and the lives of Monica, Duane, and Mark. It is a very scary thing. And although you may think of me as a ruthless scourge, we would also need to consider the financial ramifications. It would be impossible for me to maintain two households at the same standard of living. You, the children, and I would all suffer financially. It is an irrevocable step, which I believe is inappropriate at this time and should only be considered as a last resort.*

2. *Separation—there isn't much difference between divorce and separation. My comments above about divorce apply equally to separating except that it is not irrevocable. However, I believe a separation would most likely end in divorce.*

3. *Marriage Counseling—or some type of family counseling. This would involve participation by both you and I, and possibly the children. Although I know this is the most sensible approach, I have my inner distrust for counselors. Perhaps, it's my ego—but I would like to think that marriage counseling is not necessary.*

4. *Other Courses of Action—we could try to work out our differences without outside counseling. We could seriously discuss my changing jobs, with the viewpoint of my spending more time with you and the children. Perhaps it's too late for that. I don't know. I guess the more I write and think, the more obvious it becomes that I need outside counseling, but I just don't want to face up to it!*

Pat, I believe we should try to make this work. But if you have decided that you do not love me, that you are too tired, and that we do have (in your words) "a miserable loveless marriage," then it is probably too late and we would only prolong the agony. Let's try to make the right decision for all of us.

Love, Rick

* * * * *

He wrote me back that he loved me and he loved our children. He asked me to be patient and that things would get better. He was doing this for us, for our family ...

I don't know why I saved these letters, written not on pretty stationary that one would treasure, but letters on yellow legal paper. Legal paper. Seems ironic now. Maybe subconsciously this paper represented the importance of being heard, taken seriously as Rick would any important business matter. But there was a big difference here. We were the family and all I needed was reassurance that Rick was committed to our marriage, our family. I wanted to believe that our love was stronger and more important than his career. Rick and I did talk about what we wanted for each other, the importance of being a family together, and taking time to know and enjoy our children, to be there when needed. I remember him telling me to be patient. Things would get better. He was doing all this to secure our family's future.

What could I do? I did not want to tear our family apart. I always believed it was important to do what you love in life, bringing out the best qualities, being inspired and having a passion, a zest for life. What greater incentive than a loving family? I knew we were the biggest incentive in Rick's life. I told him that I did not want him to be driven at the expense of losing his family. He assured me he would not let that happen. I wanted to believe ... So I stayed.

CHAPTER 5

RECOMMITTING

I RECOMMITTED AND TOLD MYSELF I would give my husband the chance to redeem himself. I did love him and I did not want to be the one to make the call to break up our family. What would be the reason? The fact that he wanted to provide for his family, was that good enough? There just had to be a healthier balance. Many times if there was a problem at work, maybe a sensitive issue, sometimes even a moral issue, he valued my opinion, my input. That meant a lot to me, but it wasn't unusual for me either, for even as a young child I had good judgment or common sense. Maybe that just came with the territory, being the third child or the middle child of six. Nor was it unusual for my siblings or friends to really depend on my sense of knowledge for direction in life. That can be an awesome responsibility for a young person, even an adult. But many times I was the person that people would come to for advice or just vent their problems or frustrations.

It baffled me that not everyone had the same amount of common sense. Were they not listening or seeing what was going on around them? Did they not take time to think or question certain actions that seemed suspect and maybe not proper, sometimes allowing dire consequences? It felt validating to me that my husband indicated that he valued my opinions, my thoughts, encouraged me to stay, work things through for us, and our family. When I read Rick's letter, I had several mixed reactions. I felt his turmoil. I also knew there was a certain amount of truth and serious issues to consider. But the main motivation for me to stay "was knowing" that Rick did not want to lose his family. He loved me. We were too important, too valuable in his life. I could see it in his face and hear it in the tone of his voice. I would do my part and I trusted my husband to keep his word.

We knew we would have to make some rapid major adjustments in our family. Rick began making a real effort to make time for his children. It warmed my heart to observe this, and melted much of the resentment that had developed to see him trying so hard. He even joined a father and daughter organization in the neighborhood, involving a meeting once a week that he and Monica seemed to enjoy. Our sons were not as easy to appease, but that was not unusual for teenagers that have been uprooted and trying to fit in. As wonderful as our neighbors were, our house we bought just was not big enough. The boys needed their own rooms. Rick decided we would sell our house on Casco Avenue and buy a house that would accommodate the needs of our family. We put our house on the market ourselves and sold it within a week. Now we really had to work fast. Now Rick did not want to move out of our little neighborhood of Country Club, which limited our search. At this time, there were not many houses on the market.

One Sunday as we were taking our usual walk in the neighborhood, for it was a great place to walk, we noticed a house for sale on the Mill Pond. It seemed like the perfect house for our growing family, entertaining guests, etc. This was a white cedar shake house, surrounded by big beautiful trees, flagstone steps leading up to an open veranda front porch, with flowerboxes of flagstone the length of the porch. The roof of the house was of aged cedar shake and on top of the chimney was a weathervane of a horse made of black iron. I liked the detail. The land was raised higher than the surrounding houses, giving it a distinctive quality. A white picket fence came up to one side of the house, following the contours of the gentle slope of the land. There were many trees on that side of the house, and looking down, one could see the Mill Pond of Minnehaha Creek. Thanks to Mother Nature, the grass was a rich vibrant green. Off center in the front of the house stood a huge old oak tree, standing sturdy and brave through the many years, shading the house on the hot summer days and shielding as a fortress on the bitter cold winter days and nights, standing magnificently on guard to provide and protect.

Seeing this house instilled in us all kinds of wonderful possibilities. We knew our sons would like living on almost their own lake. Immediately, we knew that if the price was right, this would be our new home. So I memorized the phone number and gave Rick, its address. As soon as we got home, Rick called the realtor and the next day we met with the original owner. He was a very nice, distinguished, older gentleman—at least ninety-one years old—George Wells.

His wife had just passed away and I could see and feel the loss in his demeanor. I felt saddened for this wonderful man. He loved this house where he left vintage magazines, some very historical books, as well as some *Old World Encyclopedias* and several books of *Who's Who* in America and Minnesota in which he was acknowledged. I felt, "he should be surrounded by family during this time" I could tell he had a stoic sense of pride, not crumbling under these impending decisions and eventual loss of his independence. But the sadness lingered.

We bought that house on the corner of Edgebrook and Browndale, overlooking the Mill Pond of Minnehaha Creek. For weeks after we moved, we would find Mr. Wells sitting in his car, looking at his house with longing. Sometimes, I would invite him in, or give him a glass of lemonade, and we would talk.

He would tell me about his family, especially about his wife. She liked to sleep in the bedroom downstairs on Browndale, and he would sleep upstairs facing Edgebrook and the pond. I told him when we were settled I would like to have him over for dinner. He said he would like that, but he was on a rather bland diet. I told him that that would be no problem, and that I would be happy to prepare whatever sounded good to him.

Since my invitation, I had not seen Mr. Wells for several weeks. So I called the assisted-living home, where he resided, and they told me that he had quietly passed away.

I hope it gave Mr. Wells some comfort to see his beloved house, for so many years, becoming our family's home-for many loving years to come. It was my hope. A new home to mark the new stage of our family, including Rick's recommitment to us all.

Even though we moved only a few blocks, it turned out to be our most strenuous move. For some reason Rick decided that we could incorporate this move as a wonderful bonding experience for the whole family. Everyone would contribute, for he took off three weeks while we all would scrape old paint, wash all the old window sills, put on primer and then paint walls, ceilings, etc. Rick was very good at delegating tasks that he felt appropriate. Many times we worked at this house from early morning to midnight. When I had any moment to spare between houses, I would pack boxes again. It was ongoing, draining and physically exhausting for weeks. Rather than fostering closeness, it added additional strain on the family as whole.

We worked practically nonstop. I developed a severe migraine that lasted three days. One day while painting, trying to disregard my throbbing headache, Rick asked me if I would stop to go pick up some more paint and other items at Sears. I felt I had to do it all, and just stop suddenly and go shopping. I was a mess, paint in my hair, on my legs and arms, my head hurting so bad that I just go—too exhausted and hurting too much to rebel. While driving to pick up the paint, I tried to quiet my thoughts, and I said a prayer of relief. I just resigned myself to get through this whole ordeal. The person at the store was so nice and helpful. I'm sure I was a pitiful sight. On the way back to the house with all the supplies needed, I felt an incredible calm and my headache just melted away. I was so thankful, a little shaky but thankful.

When all the furniture was in place and the last of the boxes in their designated location, just waiting to be unpacked, my headache returned with a vengeance. Rick and the kids were going to get some dinner, but I was so immobile with excruciating pain, plus waves of nausea sweeping through my body, leaving me practically delirious, I could not possibly go. I needed rest at this time much more than a need for nourishment. With the house suddenly quiet, I was finally able to sink into an exhausted state of sleep. It was not unusual for me to experience bad headaches. It was not unusual either that I would become very sick, which ironically would offer a relief from the pain, but also contributed to a sense of disorientation and weakness. There was no option but to rest. The amazing thing is after being so incredibly ill, I could rebound it seemed so quickly. I would be so thankful to be free of pain, and that horrible nausea that I felt I could do anything. Maybe this would be the last of my headaches.

The deep heavy sleep took over my exhausted body until Rick and the boys came back from their dinner. Rick quietly came into the room to see how I was doing and if I felt well enough to eat. I told him I was still too sick, but I just needed to rest a while longer. I continued to drift in and out of sleep. During this time, Monica spent the day with her friend Molly. Molly's mom brought her over early that evening. I felt terrible that my body would betray me at this time. Rick offered to give Tuny and the girls a tour of our house even amidst this unorganized state. It was strange, moving in at such a fast and furious pace for those weeks, and now that we moved in I got so sick. I was upset that Rick put so many restrictions on this move. I also resented the fact that he could walk away from all the chaos, close the door without a thought of the results of some of his decisions.

I unpacked with the help of the kids. There were lots of closets and storage in this house, so that made things a lot easier. Within that first week, we really accomplished a lot, for we were eager to make this comfortable and inviting, so that we could relax and enjoy our new home. I finally began to feel a sense of accomplishment and hope for the promise this new chapter of our lives held.

That following Sunday, for some reason, Rick went ballistic. I do not even know if there was any specific reason, or just a momentary madness. Seemingly out of the blue, he stormed downstairs, pulled out the FOR SALE sign that was in the garage and plunked it in the front yard for every passerby to see. Wow, I had no idea what was going on in his head! The kids and I were stunned by this bizarre reaction. I did not know if it was the house, his work or an accumulation of disappointed events and the enormity of it all. We were dumbfounded and scared.

We all were pretty quiet, waiting for the storm within to cease. I really wanted to give this house a fair shake. The thought of packing up again just did not seem feasible. We let Rick stew and simmer in his own thoughts. Several hours later gathering up all his courage and pride, Rick walked out the front door, onto the front lawn and yanked the sign out of the ground and put it back in the garage. We all looked at each other with a sigh of relief and waiting for what would happen next. Rick walked into the room and looked at his family with a sheepish grin on his face. We all act so differently to stress. Some will get sick. Others get angry. Had he gotten a glimpse that the major upheaval and relocation to "just the right house" perhaps wouldn't bring the solution to what ailed us? Would it demand more of him than he had anticipated? Eventually we learn from our trials and errors . . . we hope.

GALLERY I

Just learned we would have our third child.
Rick loving and protective and I'm feeling so loved and fortunate.

Home at last. May dear mother in law Diva, me and my wonderful father in law
Alfred on the frozen tundra. Always and adventure.

Me, Rick, my mother in law Diva and Monica eager to cross country or just walk to frozen trail on Mill Pond.

Our family getting ready to cross country ski on the frozen Minnehaha Creek. Rare to get the whole family together and kitty too. She decided not to come. She prefers the piano and a sunny spot.

*Our Siamese kitty Sonya sitting on the window ledge overlooking Mill Pond.
Content and curious too in her surroundings.*

*Visiting Monica in Colorado. Even though this was a whirlwind trip. It was
great just being with my daughter.*

Celebrating our daughter's fourteenth birthday in New York. We climbed to the tippy top of the Statute of Liberty. Ring the bell, ring the bell.

My son Duane will always gravitate to the piano. Like his mom he has a love of music and many other interests. Plus responsibilities that goes with.

I still have that tree that I decorate for the seasons. Christmas this time, then some
hearts for Valentine Day and Easter and Spring around the corner.
And, I've got my cowgirl boots.

*On the stone patio steps going down to the lower level and the Mill Pond.
I still have my cowgirl boots.*

Right after New Years this horse would come to our patio on Tally Ho Drive. The kids would give him or her apples. That was always a wonderful surprise and a great way to start the new year.

*Rick and I in Sanabel Island meeting friends Janice and Jim Destaso.
A rare but much needed break.*

*We took Monica to New York for her fourteenth birthday. A young man with a top
hat offered a ride on a horse drawn carriage. A stroll though Central Park. Rick
and I sitting in the back seat. Capturing a fleeting moment in time.*

CHAPTER 6

1981 – 82

*A*ND SO WE SETTLED IN. It was fall of 1981 and our oldest son Mark would be starting his senior year in the newly merged Edina High School. He was adapting in his own way, his music going by the wayside, only occasionally picking up the trumpet but not with the same intensity or interest. There would be a somber quality to his practicing, sometimes ending with a furor of frustration. I felt his loss and had no idea how to rekindle his passion for his love of music. I searched for private instructors, but it seemed no one could compare to his previous mentor, Mr. Lovin. Augsburg College had an excellent music program that I thought would appeal to Mark. But his interest was waning. I believe there was not enough time to fit it in at school and the social dynamics were overwhelming. Mark would end up completely immersed in his religious studies, seriously considering becoming a priest.

Mark would take on this quest with great ardor. It was a source of amazement to me. He never did anything gradually. It was full force for Mark, all or nothing. In that regard, he was like his father. He studied and read the entire Bible several times. He would search for answers to his questions, memorizing verse and scriptures in English and Latin. Many times the priests that he met with were not necessarily encouraging or receptive to his type of percipience. They wanted more of a quiet acceptance, to embrace the mystery, not to question or challenge.

Occasionally, during this time there would be visits to various synagogues and temples for comparative studies, questions, and search for deeper meaning and truths. This brought out an exciting new dimension in Mark's thinking and attitude. Finally, he found the province where he felt his senses heightened and once more the passion of learning and excelling, giving him new meaning. The Rabbis became his mentors, his confidants and trusted friends. But most of all they listened and took his questions seriously, encouraging him in his search, giving Mark an entirely new and exciting reason and purpose. Mark was my serious and intellectual child, born on his father's birthday. He could have very easily followed in his father's footsteps, but there was a rebellion within or maybe it was discernment.

Our youngest son Duane was totally opposite. Duane was very precocious. He had no fear of anything or anyone. He thrived on challenges. I don't believe there was anything that he couldn't do. He was another source of amazement to me. He seemed to have a combination of the most endearing qualities but at times also the most exasperating too. He was an enigma. For he could be very patient and tolerant but once his patience had been pushed to the limit—watch out! We both were night owls. I would usually be painting or writing in the wee hours. Sometimes I would check on the kids, everyone would be sleeping except Duane. Maybe he would be reading a history book, going through an encyclopedia or quietly working on a project, sometimes not so quietly. As he got older, it was tough, for I liked to have everyone in bed and sleeping before I went to bed myself.

Duane was an excellent student but many times would get bored with school. So it was not unusual for him to skip classes. (Something I never would even have considered doing!). I know he challenged his teachers throughout high school. Sometimes he would find errors in the textbooks and point out an error, which was not always appreciated. Duane was the most inquisitive child. He learned very quickly. It did not matter if it were an activity or any subject that interested him or seeing the necessity of learning and conquering the challenge. Duane would be very introspective at times and come up with ideas, solutions that surprised and sometimes intimidated those of us who were not as bold and daring. As bright and talented as my young son was, his attitude became more rebellious, needing a healthy outlet to release his pent-up energy in a constructive manner.

We had these two teenage sons asserting independence and individuality, way too smart and a young mother trying to figure the whole thing out, with not a whole lot of help or support. With our daughter it was much easier. I could relax, pamper her, and pamper myself. It was wonderful having a gentle feminine child. Teaching our daughter seemed more fun and more natural for me. Monica was my most independent child, perhaps because she was my third. I was more experienced. If she didn't eat her peas, I didn't panic. Actually she was my best eater. She would want to taste everything and anything. She even liked to help me fold laundry, especially when it came to her little socks, jimmies, or whatever. It is amazing how doing simple chores can turn into a game or teaching tool. But maybe that shouldn't be so amazing either. It is just how it is presented. I felt that even doing chores or work could be fun, like learning a new skill or new way or just plain work. And I chose to make most things enjoyable and worthwhile.

This move made it more obvious how quickly our children were growing up. This would be like a moment in time never to be recaptured, replaced, or duplicated. One big chance to do it right. Our children were depending on us. I remembered Rick's promise to make a more concerted effort for quality time with our family, especially our sons. I was determined to do my part and trusted him, never dreaming.

The beginning of the year of us moving to our house on Edgebrook Place symbolized many sudden changes. Our first son would be graduating from high school. It was also during this time that he made his decision to convert to Judaism. It seemed everyone was doing their own thing. This was not an ordinary experience. How does anyone address a situation like this? Our son was growing up, wanting approval, some guidance and reassurance and recognition of his own. Would this be a temporary phase testing our unconditional love or the limit of our patience and especially our acceptance? Between Rick and Mark, life was proving to be quite the complex challenge. Yet ultimately, there would turn out to be a big difference in the types of paths each of them chose. Mark's search was for a higher calling, searching for a direction in life that would be meaningful and revered. While his own father's ambition would culminate with a disturbing finale.

Meanwhile, our younger son would be expressing his teenage independence, along with a growing frustration that needed attention. This was an important time for Rick to step in and do his part, for there comes a time in any boy's life that is imperative for a father/male attention that they can relate to, along with their mother's.

This would also be a critical time for Rick and me to work together. Could Rick keep this promise to me and to his children or would he slip so readily back into the same pattern? I still felt that his intentions were genuine. That basically he was a good man, although extremely driven by his own needs to prove his worth. I have always felt that people were basically good, and wanted to do the right thing. But I would learn there are certain elements, experiences, and people that influence our actions, even our state of mind, as if a metamorphosis gone too far into the extreme.

My story is a difficult one to tell, so if you can bear with me as this all unfolds to enlighten for a complete understanding. Originally, I wanted to focus primarily on the endless court proceedings that would take precedent and take a strangling hold on my life for ten years and actually longer. For it is now the middle of 2005 and I am still trying to break free of the legal bonds put on me, keeping me tied and restricted to a man that sacrificed his family for money and position and now I am to be just another tax write-off, another form of business to him. He would be allowed to put restrictions in our divorce that would not allow me the freedom to grow in my own independence. I would not be allowed to work, for whatever money I might possibly make would be deducted from my alimony—or as the courts say now "maintenance"—leaving me always at status quo, not moving forward financially, nor giving me the incentive or the same opportunities as Rick himself was fortunate to have. I would not have the same freedoms and rights as others, all because he had the monetary means, the right connections along with the cunning lessons learned in his world of hostile takeovers. He would use these skills and more during and continuing long after our divorce.

It is not a crime to get a divorce. The courts should never be used to cause even more adversity. Divorce is difficult enough. I read once that the best gift a man can give his children is to love their mother. I added a thought in a Father's Day card, "And if you cannot love her, then at least treat her with the dignity and respect she is owed after twenty-eight years of marriage." Adding for the sake of the children, giving the names of each and dates of their births, representing the long history together. We were just divorced and Rick was eager to move into his million-dollar home on Lake Harriet with his girlfriend. She was a career woman, never married, never having children. She was the perfect woman at that time for my now ex-husband to finally bestow his wealth on. A woman that was so willing and encouraging for a price they determined. I sent this innocuous card and he would take me to court. He did not want to be reminded. It touched a response, a chord, a consciousness that he was taught not to feel and it angered him to be reminded of his flawed ego. How far would the courts accommodate this wealthy man? What is considered a frivolous lawsuit?

I should continue with going back in time. It's not where I want to go. I want to write of the injustice, the ultimate betrayal, the bittersweet memories and the disappointments, running too deep and painful, the loss of innocence and the vulnerability exposed for the world to see and maybe to exploit for their own advantage. Learning lessons, the hard lessons that keep coming as if testing my will and endurance, my fortitude, even my sincerity in my intentions. Is this "for myself alone or something deeper," or something innate that was experienced before me but never addressed? I never intended to be married so young. That was not my dream and definitely not my goal. Yet, once I realized I was to have a child, I never looked back. I took my role as a wife and mother seriously. I still liked to have fun. I still managed to be very creative and I never stopped learning. I would not let any outside influence take precedence over my husband and family. I felt that people who achieved their goals had high standards morally and ethically. I learned that was not always the case. My husband had the same values at one time, I know.

With each pregnancy I experienced, I will always remember that my husband made me feel loved and cared for. Always remarking how beautiful I looked with each pregnancy. In that respect, I was fortunate, for I know that not all women have been so well nurtured and pampered during this special time. Those times I can look back and know that was what gave Rick and me our greatest joy and pleasure, when we felt secure in our love, not needing or wanting any outside intrusions for we were content with out little family. This was my catalyst for my creativity and existence and I know we were the reason and incentive for Rick also. This was the time that would bring out the best qualities in both of us, for there has to be the best of times to get through the worst of times.

There has to be a solid base or foundation and that is what I relied upon. I knew there would be obstacles—and there were be obstacles. But I felt with each obstacle we overcame, it made us stronger. But what we did not know was there are some challenges that when too frequent and demanding can seep into the core affecting and influencing us all in some diverse way that we cannot express or explain, and we can't prevent. Wheels are set in motion and there is something of interest or fascination that compels us forward. The scenery is beautiful. A fleeting memory, but the pace is too great to savor or acknowledge or contemplate our separate journeys.

We all tried to make this transition, but I felt we were floundering, being pulled in too many different directions. We were asking and expecting too much from ourselves. For myself, I felt our sons' resentment, but also their resignation along with my own. I think that Rick felt that time would heal all wounds and the problems would disappear. Our sons were growing up and I really didn't think Rick was ready to acknowledge this fact. In many ways, I now believe that he held us all back. I think the wanted to be our hero, always capable and in charge. It took me a long time to realize that he wanted complete control, but we all were experiencing tremendous changes that needed encouragement and validation for our own personal growth. If Rick could or would have participated within the family, before this late stage, he would have recognized this. But it seemed easier for him to focus his energies and attention on his work.

Our family was complex. We all had our own wonderful intricate personalities that needed attending. Rick's life was a steady forward climb, not straying too far from his ever-attaining goals. In his mind, he was doing his part, but the reality was he needed to be more involved and I needed a break, some support, occasional help would have been nice. How about some recognition and a little pampering before I drop from sheer exhaustion? A retreat—is that asking too much? A spa would be so nice, but is that too indulgent? But more than anything would be working together, uniting our family, preparing our children for the world outside so they could be invigorated by life, not stifled and restricted. It was important for me to provide my children with the most loving and secure environment that I could possibly give them. It was not a profound revelation, nothing new, but what every loving parent desires and would strive for universally. We always want better for our children, our future generations. I knew that is what originally Rick believed too. But the 1980s would bring about an attitude in the business world that really did not regard families or marriages. It would not be the original purpose or design that Rick planned for his family. But he would become entrapped, enslaved, addicted, and compromised.

None of us would foresee the ramifications of the events that would unfold the cause and effect. I could feel and sense a certain foreboding but I had way too many distractions and not enough help or support for myself from the ongoing needs of my growing family to recognize the warning signs. Besides, we were too far removed from family and friends and that gave us a different kind of isolation and vulnerability. Meanwhile, Rick was surrounded by tremendous support. He would have his secretaries at his office to do his bidding and his receptionist to screen his calls. In his mind, seeing and knowing that all was well on the home front gave him the tremendous freedom to achieve his dreams. The stage was set and the sky was the limit. He had the incentive, reason, and purpose and now the rewards would be too great to look back or give up. But he still needed his family, for now . . .

CHAPTER 7

NEW YORK AND THE VIRUS

*A*GAIN THIS IS A DIFFICULT *time, especially to revive all those memories from the past that I would like to put to rest and move forward hopefully unscathed, if possible. Time has a way of softening some experiences and eventually there is healing and understanding. But there are some problems or experiences that are too serious to be ignored or forgotten for the consequences are too far-reaching. It is now Memorial Day 2005. I feel I am at the crossroads of my life and time is running out. Every decision and every move is mine alone, my own fate, my own destiny. What will be my legacy that I leave for my children, my family, and society?*

I think of these things as I write the story of my unusual life. Even as a young child, I felt like I was an observer of life. I knew there would be obstacles and difficulties, lessons to be learned even through the struggles of trying to comprehend particular acts that would confuse and sometimes frighten me. Trying to keep this perspective in mind, it seemed as if the struggles I was going through now served no purpose but to hurt and tear down. No one should live their whole life that way. Some do. They become beaten down, accepting their plight almost as a badge of honor. Some succumb to all the trials of life and become immune or indifferent and numb their feelings with excess, then becoming part of the problem itself—too afraid to learn from the reality of the consequences or too overwhelmed by life itself. It seems even now my life is on hold, in limbo, and I am living in uncertainty at the mercy of others, dictating the rules and putting restrictions on my life. Meanwhile giving my ex-husband the ability to rule over me and control my life. Even though we had a long history together, and our marriage brought tremendous financial success, in the end I would be the one that would be the pawn used to secure my husband's success. But when the love of money, power, and success became the main priority, focus, and reason, Rick would sacrifice everything that was good or kind in himself. He would forget his own family in the process, using all the techniques, connections, and skills he learned in his ruthless world of hostile takeovers in our divorce. That is a harsh word and eventually, the less abrasive term of mergers and acquisitions seemed softer on the palate. He was once a good man. I will always say that. It was and still is inconceivable that he would now become my tormentor.

I remember reading an article in the local paper when his ego was so inflated that he was a man who "worked hard and played even harder." I cringed, for he had no idea at the time of what he was so callously giving up. It was all about pretense, the big show to cover up for his real loss, his real feelings. It was all so insidious. I remember feeling the tremendous emptiness as our marriage was drawing to a close. Our last child, our beautiful daughter, would be going off to college. She wanted to go into fashion designing. During this time, we were also to move to New York, and Rick would be working in the area of banking for Ernst and Young. Rick at this time already had an apartment set up in Manhattan. We made the decision that we would not move until Monica graduated with her class. We decided no more moving in the middle of the school year. We had learned that lesson well when we moved our two sons to Edina in mid-semester just before Christmas when they were teenagers.

Our move to Minnesota proved to be one of our most challenging. I felt that this new move to New York would open wonderful new possibilities for my family. Monica would be able to pursue her interest in fashion designing. For me, I felt a new hope in restoring the delicate balance for our family away from the demands of the corporate world that wanted the mind, body and soul of my husband along with anything else he would be willing to part with. Here in Minneapolis he was considered the visionary in the world of high finance. He became bold and daring, and his successes were many. He also would be well compensated. But there was also a terrible price to be paid, for there was never enough money or power.

It is almost surreal to observe the gradual transformation that took place from a distance. But to be in the midst of these dramatic changes is life-altering, changing one's perception in many ways. Sometimes that is not a bad thing, but when the quest for more is never enough and the erosion of ethics and integrity is compromised, there becomes a moral decline and eventually breakdown. I did not like seeing and experiencing these changes in my husband. The corporate world took too much of him, leaving very little time for his family. He was becoming cold and indifferent, critical and demanding. Nothing was ever good enough. We were becoming strangers to each other. He was never home anymore, traveling to excess. He was on call night and day—intruding into our family life. Meanwhile I was super busy and vigilant in the needs of my family.

Ours sons now were out in the world testing their independence but were also estranged from their father, as he was always absent.

I felt like a single parent. I did not feel valued or cherished as a wife or a mother any longer. I would look at my husband; his face was like stone, emotionless, his eyes dark and empty, devoid of feelings, and his lips taut, almost cruel, and determined. On some level, I was aware that I was losing my husband, as I could not compete with his world of compensated glory. It was too ruthless, uncaring, shallow, and seductive. With each success, the greater the compensations, perks, special privileges and entitlements, the more his ego grew. He was discarding his true friends for his peers with similar prestige, position, and values.

I felt that our move to New York would be a positive distraction, away from all the elements that took from our family. His new best friends or buddies were ruthless men that did not value women—thinking of them as a commodity. And they certainly did not value family or family life, as they were on the fast track, running from their own misdeeds and broken marriages and relationships. I know in Minneapolis, Rick was like a big fish in the small pond, but in New York, I felt he would not always feel the pressure to stay on top, or feel the need to topple every bank and floundering business. In many ways, New York seemed appealing, offering so many different opportunities not only for Rick and Monica, but for myself as well. I had thoughts of taking wonderful art classes again, also getting back into my dances classes, ballet, and jazz. I would be creative again, for there is everything positive in the fine art of dance. But I also wanted to give back, by getting involved at one of the big hospitals taking care of the AIDS babies, holding and comforting them when needed.

The main thing was I felt it would reunite our family, a new start, new vitality and we would do it together. Our sons would eventually move with us, if they chose to. We had plans of having an apartment in Manhattan and a house in Connecticut, New Jersey or somewhere in Upstate New York. I felt that our sons would thrive with new opportunities available. I had tremendous hopes and expectations for all of us. Yet I sensed and felt that Rick was a bit apprehensive. I could not understand why. I knew he was emotionally and physically drained. There never seemed to be a relief for him. The corporate demands were so constant and relenting for so long that he did not know how to have a normal life anymore. Conversations would stray and fall flat until turned to the topic of his last professional accomplishment, and then his eyes would light up and he would be engaged. For that was becoming his total world that he could relate.

During this time, Rick would be in New York adjusting to being just another fish in a very big pond. I don't think he liked that feeling. He was riding high in Minneapolis with his peers and he had accomplished what he wanted. Yet, there was hesitancy, a holding back that I had never experienced before in him. I could not understand this strange attitude. I equated his darkened mood to exhaustion and just plain adjusting, but in our past moves Rick would be eager and we would plan our new life together. This time I felt his reluctance as if he was torn between two worlds and would have to choose.

I also knew that Rick was very concerned with some problem that First Bank was having. This was in 1990. I thought that part of his reluctance was the fact that his now good friend was in serious trouble and he had stressed his concerns to me. This person also happened to be the president of this bank, Dennis Evans. Without consulting anyone, he invested $500 million in junk bonds and lost it all. To me it was too incredible and irresponsible. I had met him before and there was a lackluster about him. But I contributed this demeanor to the fact that he was getting his third divorce. He was not taking that well and Rick expressed again his concerns. I resented the fact that this grown man with such prestige could warrant such sympathy and compassion from my husband when Rick was so out of touch with his own personal life. It got to the point that Rick would choose to meet with Dennis and he would ask me to attend a dinner at the club and he would meet me later . . . maybe. He would claim that Dennis felt too uncomfortable around married couples together. It hurt Dennis too much. At first I could understand, but then enough was enough. At this time in his life, it seemed "now" was a time for quiet contemplation, a time to feel and a time to heal . . . and that is a very difficult thing to do. In retrospect, what he was essentially telling me was that he was caretaking the feelings of this powerful grown man, who may feel vulnerable about his own failed relationships. Yet Rick somehow thought it was important to diminish the importance of his own family in order to maintain his good standing with this financially successful man who likely sacrificed his own family to acquire "success."

Throughout this time, I had some kind of virus that just would not go away. It started out with a high fever for several days, a burning sore throat that felt like razor blades when I swallowed. Eventually the high fever dropped but did not completely go away. The burning throat eased but was replaced by a croupy cough. I could barely talk. My voice would be very soft. Just talking would fatigue me. I lost my appetite and could only take small sips of water, juice or any kind of liquids. If I tried to take larger swallows, my throat felt like it was closing. I felt I could drown just by drinking a glass of water, and this lasted six months. It was a mystery virus that doctor after doctor could not diagnose.

The combination of the constant croupy cough, difficulty swallowing and low-grade fever for so long brought about an incredible fatigue, for even sleeping at night brought no rest. I went to several different doctors that were recommended, but they were stymied as I was. I even went to an allergist thinking maybe there was something I was allergic to, but that was not the case either. She did prescribe Seldane, a popular prescription for allergies, and a throat spray. I thought, Uh-oh, I hope this works. I rarely took medicines, so I was a bit apprehensive. I never had allergies before, but I was willing to try for relief.

I did not have to take that medicine very long for my cough worsened. Rick was home during this time. He was somewhat concerned but more annoyed. Meanwhile I tried to carry on as usual, thinking (which probably didn't help) that since I couldn't rest I might as well be semi-productive. I dreaded going to bed, as my cough would continue through the night. But this particular night the cough and sore throat was relentless. So as not to disturb Rick, I dragged myself out of bed, through the foyer and into the kitchen where I had put the throat spray on the shelf. I was coughing so hard I didn't know if I could reach the medicine. I sprayed my throat and immediately my throat went into some kind of spasm. I couldn't breathe. My throat felt so tight, with sharp burning pain. I thought, My God, I'm going to die right here in my kitchen. Rick will wake up and find me here on the floor and wonder what happened.

I was shaking from that experience and it made me feel weak, but I dared not go back to bed for fear that my cough would start up again. I looked at that medicine and thought no way will I take this again. This is not working. By this time Rick got up to go to the office, he liked to be the first one there. What a guy. I told him what had happened in the night. He didn't seem too concerned as I was still breathing, able to stand, plus I even made his breakfast of fresh coffee, orange juice and toast.

I called the doctor's office as soon as I could and they told me to come in immediately. It was obvious that I was having difficulty trying to talk between the croupy cough and the pain, so the doctor said, "That's okay. You don't have to talk, but let me look at your throat." When she peered down my throat, she was rather dramatic and told me to stop taking the throat spray immediately. I whispered, "I did." We eventually did all the scratch tests to find out what I was allergic to. The results were I was slightly allergic to dust and horses. So I had no allergies. Hurray. But I had a mysterious malady that I would either have to live with—yuk—or I could continue thinking good thoughts, living my healthy life and get better on my own. I could do that.

It would take six months. The strange thing is that after that horrible coughing seizure, I knew I had to get better because it certainly couldn't get worse. I realized I was much too dramatic a patient, so I couldn't get sick for every one's sake. Another unusual thing about this was the timing. This was the time that I should be strong and here I could hardly talk and everything exhausted me. Rick didn't have the time or the patience. I now understood that he could not relate for he had always been taken care of. All his needs were always met. Since I married so young, putting my life on hold for my husband and my children that responsibility was needed and necessary. I always thought and believed that was the most important role anyone, male or female, could ever undertake. When there are children in the picture, it requires both parents, mother and father.

This was another critical time in our marriage. Our last child was going into her senior year. Ours sons were both still trying their independence, future still uncertain, but they also were not getting real guidance or support from their father. Rick just was not there, and when he was, he was impatient and critical. He never took time to really listen to their problems, or know their needs or even encourage their interests. And he certainly never took time to teach his sons. Rick fulfilled his dreams, reached his goals, having tremendous support and encouragement the whole nine yards. Yet he could not take the time to acknowledge or appreciate his own family and sadly not even to really know them.

Having my mysterious virus awakened something in me. I knew that I would have an empty nest once our daughter left for college. I always thought that would finally be Rick's and my time to restore our marriage, to rekindle the magic. I had dreams that we would always be together, safe, secure and surrounded by our children and eventually grandchildren too. Isn't that the way it is supposed to happen? Now I began to really notice the hardened changes in my husband—the way he related to me and even our children. I did not want to believe that the man I married, the father of my children, could change to such an extreme. What was this all about anyway? Something was happening and it was beyond my control or ability to comprehend the magnitude of this transformation. I had no idea of the ramifications that would unfold through this metamorphosis. I was aware of an uneasiness that left me doubting and uncertain.

I knew I had to get healthy again for myself, for my children and if possible for our marriage. I felt at this point that I would concentrate on getting my health back. I would continue to do my normal activities, but also monitor myself, not pushing to exhaustion. I would try to get the proper rest, if my cough kept me up through the night, I would at least relax my body and quiet my mind if possible. I read good books that brought me comfort, while also learning. Music always had a way of healing. I would listen to my music that brought me to another place, helping to relax or help lift my spirits. Occasionally, I would catch up on my letter writing, but also do some journaling, thinking I could uncover the mysteries of life and all its complexities. This time of intentionality gave me the opportunity to slow down and survey my whole situation.

I knew I was basically healthy, for I always lived a healthy lifestyle, wanting to set a positive example for my children, but also for myself. I decided if the doctors were so bewildered with my croupy cough but would also give me medicines that would give me adverse side effects, I would just cure myself. If I got worse then I would set up some kind of complete physical. Gradually, through the months, my cough became less severe, which I think lessened my irritated throat. I still had a low-grade fever, not the best appetite but I would try and drink as much liquids as I could. At night, I started bringing a cup of water or tea, set it on the bedside table and if I started coughing, I would take small sips that would soothe my throat. I found myself gradually getting better, so a quiet victory.

It would have been wonderful to also find the magic formula that would transform my husband back to the man I once knew. That was when I felt loved and protected and our family was his priority. How could I ever compete with all the trappings of the corporate world? I did not like the negative influences that kept filtering and intruding into our home, affecting our own personal space, our home, our lives.

I felt as if I were living in a state of major uncertainty. We were making plans to move to New York, but I wondered if it really would materialize. Rick was already working in New York but I felt disconnected. I thought my vague illness could be a factor, for me—but I also felt an uneasiness in my husband's lack of concern regarding my health. What would our life together really be like once it would be just the two of us? It bothered me also that Rick and our two sons' relationship was so precarious, hardly ever talking but avoiding conversations of substance and necessity for fear of a confrontation. Rick had no patience and certainly no time. He could not relate beyond his corporate world. I found myself not liking this person he had become. I could not trust him any longer. He seemed so preoccupied, detached, cold, and uncaring.

I held onto a small thread of hope that this move would wipe away all the negative experience that had touched our lives. I hoped that by being in a new environment that Rick once again would realize how precious a gift we had as a family. I hoped that with this move he would realize to take time out to renew the broken bond of relationships with family and friends, and to mend all the hurts from years of impatience and neglect. We could forgive. For I knew my children and they loved their father. They needed their father's love, his approval and it wasn't too late to give guidance. I wanted also to feel loved and appreciated once more. So I could once again return that love also.

There would be times that I would fly to New York to meet my husband and we would look at apartments in Manhattan. I still had the lingering effects from the mysterious illness but I tried to ignore my symptoms, telling myself I was getting better. I found it intriguing and exciting flying by myself to meet my husband. I felt worldly and sophisticated, all five-foot-three-quarter inches of me. I would take a taxi to the hotel where we would be staying. Sometimes we would stay at the Leona Helmsly Palace Hotel, which was very lavish with plush furnishings, the finest silks, velvets, and brocades. Beautiful chandelier of cut crystals hung from the entry meant to impress. It was all grand and beautiful, but also crying of too much, too excessive. I could feel it, the pretense.

The puzzling thing when I had not seen Rick for a while would be his reaction to me. For a moment, his face would soften and his eyes would look at me intently and intensely, as if in amazement. He would then smile, sometimes beam as if he was so thankful that I was there and knew that he was a very lucky man and I would feel love, safe and secure. During these fast visits to Manhattan there would be discussions of where we would live. Should we get a small apartment close to Rick's office at Ernst and Young and eventually move into one of Trump's Towers. Hmm, that might be tempting and quite the experience, but I also wanted a place that would be warm and inviting and not too pretentious. This relocation would also require us to have a second home away from the city. This venture seemed to be the key to unlock the door to promising new possibilities for our children and family and for our marriage. For that, I rekindled my own hopes and dreams.

I envisioned this time to be the awakening of our commitment to each other, replacing the harmful experiences and memories that kept chipping away and intruding into our home and our family so cavalier and insidious. My first trip to Manhattan was of course the seduction. I could see through that. For me it wasn't about the glamour or the big money, for we had enough. I wanted this to reunite our family, opening fresh ideas and exciting possibilities. I was born out east in Neptune, New Jersey, on the seashore. I was naturally drawn with revived curiosity. Our oldest son Mark had also spent a year in Crown Heights, New Jersey, during his religious studies. Our youngest son was ambivalent but I felt he would embrace this new prospect, and our daughter would do wonders in one of the colleges in fashion design.

This would be a chance for all our family, not just my husband, but for all of us together. I remember how I felt Rick's exhaustion, but I could also feel his inner turmoil. I could not quite grasp the real reason, for it was unknown to me, maybe because my own hopes were so obvious, and he had this reluctance. I remembered the time that we went skiing. We would go occasionally to Vail, Colorado, with some dear friends of ours Norm Jones and his gracious wife, Unice. Norm happened to be the president of Metropolitan Bank in Fargo, North Dakota and was one of Rick's clients. We became friends exchanging invitations to golfing, tennis, dinners and banker's conventions in various exciting places. They were the ones who would reintroduce us to the world of skiing. We would take several ski trips together from Tahoe, Beaver Creek, and Vail.

We had planned another ski trip with the Jones. It would be in spring and I loved spring skiing. So I was looking forward to this with great anticipation. Unfortunately, the weather was warmer than usual, but the Jones were not to be deterred as they knew all the ropes. Our skills must have impressed them. As Norm in a manner of fact way said, "We'll just take the gondola to the highest mountain where there always is snow." That sounded good to me after all I was ready. I felt Rick's uneasiness. I knew he had rushed into getting his rental ski boots and they felt too tight, so immediately he was uncomfortable. But I do believe the higher we went up that mountain, the tighter those boots became. I knew he had a fear of heights, but once we were on the mountain and on the lift we would be fine.

It is difficult to enjoy the beauty of the moment if one is in an agitated state of mind, and you can sense the higher we went, Rick's fears surfaced. Norm and Unice were great in relaying how to go down this terrain. I listened intently and said "yes we can do this." I was thinking, "I'm just going of think of this as a series of little hills, gradually getting used to the feel of the curved plains of the mountain." It was breathtakingly beautiful on the highest part of the mountain. The sky was a beautiful shade of blue, the sun warm and inviting, the air crisp, so clean and clear. I could see forever and I felt free and exhilarated. Rick was saying he had a fear of heights. We all tried to encourage him, saying we would go slowly. Follow the mountain as a series of small hills. We will go down together. I started skiing and I felt my own fear lifting and I was so grateful to have this experience. Just, when I thought all was well, Rick took a terrific tumble.

He definitely was shaken by this fall and decided that he wanted off this mountain. I was so disappointed. I wanted to ski the whole mountain, and now I would be taking the gondola back to the bottom with my husband. Rick never skied again after that. When we returned home, I dreamed three nights in a roll that I had skied down that glorious mountain. Only in my dreams, in retrospect, I realize the symbolism in this.

The amazing thing is that we all have fears but we can also conquer those fears and not let the fears determine who we are. At any rate back, I will continue with New York. I could not understand Rick's attitude. I had a feeling that there was a big reluctance on his part, and I didn't know what exactly to contribute this attitude. It seemed we never really talked about feelings. I don't know if they even existed in Rick's world anymore. It was always about business. Being in New York with my husband, I felt as if I were out with a stranger. I felt an uneasy distance between us. When we would be having a dinner at the end of the day, he would seem distracted at times, as if he was on overload. I felt for him. I knew he needed a rest away from all the demands of the corporate world.

The last time Rick would come home from New York would be the weekend of October 13th. It would be on our youngest sons' 24th birthday. I would always make their favorite dinner. It was a pleasant sunny day and for once there was a certain harmonious ambiance that permeated our home that we hadn't had in so long. It felt good to have all my family together. Rick also seemed more relaxed than usual and seemed to actually relish this time with his family. Our son Duane decided he wanted his favorite spaghetti and meatballs and instead of a birthday cake, he wanted his favorite homemade chocolate oatmeal cookies. On Sundays, we would usually have an early dinner.

The phone rang. I never should have answered it. The call was for Rick. It was Peter Ankeny from First Bank, wanting Rick to meet him and Daryl Kenuteson at Edina Country Club. This was during the $500 million bank failure involving Dennis Evans. When Rick got off the phone he was upset, saying, "I can't even have dinner with my family!" They wanted Rick to meet them at the club, which was across the street from our house. He said that it would not be a long meeting and he would be back shortly. Once again, we were left waiting. Finally after about an hour, I decided that we would just go ahead and eat our dinner. We no sooner sat down to eat when Rick came home. He was pumped up, eager to tell us about this meeting. I was somewhat irritated for now it was not about Duane's birthday but about him. They wanted Rick to come and work for First Bank and try and save the bank from the $500 million fiasco. We ate our dinner, listening to Rick, knowing that nothing had changed. That evening Rick would fly back to New York. That Monday afternoon, he flew home. After twenty years with Ernst and Young, he finally quit without even a day to reflect upon his decision.

Now he would have the challenge of saving this bank, and possibly redeem what was lost. He was tired of doing all those mergers and acquisitions. He was paid highly but he was tired of always having to acquiesce to everyone's demands. Now his peers at Ernst and Young would look at him with the respect that he had for so long sought.

The stakes were high but there was also an even larger motivating factor. Shortly before we were to move to New York, Bob Kelly the partner in charge of the Ernst and Young office was transferred to New York. Rick felt that he would be made the head partner, for he was the partner that changed things around dramatically for now Ernst and Young, making millions for his firm. It was a known fact that no one worked harder, longer hours and gave so much of himself for this company. Rick became known as the banking expert. That was his area of expertise. He felt naturally this would be his big payoff. Not that he wanted more money, for he had enough. We had enough. But he was tired of the burden of all those successes. What good is all that money when there is never enough time to enjoy the benefits? When there is not even time for your friends, and your family is growing up without you, and you forget how to return love or appreciate the simplicity of life. For now it is about bigger and grander, being in the fast lane nonstop. Not your body or your mind. It is too high a price.

I remember Rick coming home after his meeting with Bob Kelly. Rick would not be made the head partner. He was too valuable, too needed in his area of acquisitions. But even though he would not be the big partner with the title, he would actually be making more money. Rick could give a damn about the money. He wanted out. He wanted his life back. When Bob told Rick who the new head partner would be, he was in disbelief. The new partner in charge would be Ed Finn. He was laidback, tall, dark, and relatively good-looking. He also had a law background and had been educated out east with an impressive resume. Bob said that Ed was more approachable. Rick could be pretty intense, but after all those years of mergers and acquisitions that would change anybody. Rick was so angry and I was angry for him too. Ed Finn was the total contrast from my husband. Ed was tall; Rick was not tall at all. Ed was relatively good looking, but was rather bland in personality, while Rick was a combination Woody Allen and Danny DeVito in personality and appearance. On a good day, he could be cute, funny, charming, and fun to be with.

There also was a big contrast in their work habits. Rick was driven, determined to succeed and hardworking. Ed was very laidback, rarely coming in earlier than necessary, and rarely worked overtime. Ed took all his holidays and vacations, while Rick many times worked through them and rarely taking a real vacation without interruption. Urgent business required him—*needed* him to be available immediately! Right now, and on a time clock too! I could feel his resentment of this intrusion, but it would be momentary.

I was reminded of the time when we first moved to Minneapolis and Rick was the only one to make partner. There was much resentment and little recognition of his accomplishments. It was from that experience that my husband would set out to prove his worth. His successes were many from corporations to banking doing the auditing and eventually the notoriety of the mergers and acquisitions. Ernst and Young would grow and many would profit from the agony of Rick's obsession to prove he "was deserving."

Rick would be compensated well. That is not what he wanted or needed. He needed a change, a reprieve, some honorable recognition. Ed had an impressive background, relatively good looks that some people felt signified success. Is that what it is all about, looks and credentials, but not necessarily performance?

I could understand why Rick would want to leave Ernst and Young, but I did not feel this was the way to do it. I knew he needed a rest, some time to think about all the changes, not only in his corporate world, but also within himself and especially our family. But that would not be allowed to happen, for it was imperative that the reputation of First Bank be restored for the patrons and shareholders. The fact that Rick's friend Dennis Evans was responsible for this $500 million loss was also another deciding factor. Rick would have less than two weeks to achieve this.

Between this possible transition to New York, the First Bank fiasco, and in the deepest most remote part of his thoughts would how this all would impact his own family. It was a whirlwind of mental and physical energy that he pulled it off. He set up a war room. He also brought in a few of the most knowledgeable and trusted staff that he could gather. I know two were from the Chicago office. The first few days, Rick would work through the night nonstop. It would be a success. Whatever they did, it worked. There was a solution. Eventually, First

Bank again was solvent. Rick was weary, a bittersweet success. There would now be a hardened arrogance and impatience that permeated his persona. All the hopes and dreams that I had for our marriage and our family now seemed an impossibility, and to make matters worse—it was as if he transferred all his rage to me. It seemed in Rick's mind I and his children would be an extension of his business. Meanwhile, Ernst and Young would now cater to the new CEO of First Bank. In that respect, Rick once more accomplished his mission.

This all happened so fast. Just before we were to be transferred to New York, Ed Finn and all the partners and their wives would be giving Rick and me a recognition and going away dinner at the Interlachen Country Club. It would be one of those memories I would like to forget. I remember being in physical pain. My virus left me weakened and vulnerable. It was exhausting to speak, and I could only speak softly. Rick was oblivious to my pain, my condition. It was as if I was an annoyance to him that he had to tolerate.

I remember the clubhouse being unusually quiet, not a lot of activity. It all seemed surreal to me. I was not on any kind of medication, but maybe it was from the virus and the pain. I felt alone in the vastness. There were not enough people to fill this large space. Although the wives and partners were there, I somehow felt removed. There was an edge to Rick's words, a bitter sarcasm. I wondered if anyone else noticed. I felt too exhausted to address this to Rick. There was not a time or a place or the energy.

This did not seem like a celebration of any kind. We were all to be seated in the dining room. Our table was long with nondescript white on white linen tablecloths and white china and crystal wine and water glasses. Again the room seemed too large to fill with this sparse group of people. After we ate our meal Ed rose from his chair to say a few words of acknowledgement and presented Rick with a new driving wedge with words of inscription etched on the club face. I was given a silver tray and pitcher from one of the wives.

One of the traits Rick learned so well was how to detach so easily, how to cut and humiliate. No one was exempt. The reason would be unknown. Rick was seated at my right side but I felt he was purposely avoiding me, almost like ostracizing. That was another trait he learned so well. When he was asked to read the inscription he said he could not read it. Instead of turning to me, he turned to the woman on the right of him and asked her to read the inscription. I was puzzled by his behavior. After the reading, Rick stood up and said his little speech, addressing all the partners. He would start out with relating experiences with certain partners, but there would be a smoldering anger to his tone at times and an edge of condescension in his attitude. I watched the people's faces in disbelief. Their eyes would be wide with a bemused expression, speechless, hoping for the grand uplifting finale.

I kept thinking Rick would turn this around, saying something like, "In the end, I learned to admire the character of this partner." But he never did. He just left everyone hanging, their mouths agape, not knowing what to think or to say. After all, he did make millions for their firm and that impressed them. They would overlook his rudeness. I left the table, unnoticed. I sat down on one of the overstuffed chairs in the vestibule, waiting for this travesty to be over. I was in deep thought when one of the partners from Chicago came and sat across from me. At one time, he had worked in Minneapolis, but had moved back to Chicago to be close to his family. He was a very kind man, somewhat tall, not heavy but not thin either. He had reddish hair. I was always impressed with his gentle demeanor. He would also be one of the men that Rick would call on to help him when he set up the war room for First Bank. He had an unusual first name, Arnie, and I can't remember his last name right now, but he was a gentle comfort amidst this surreal experience.

I tried to be composed and not appear stressed. Because I was in pain and could only speak softly, Arnie wanted to know if I was okay. He was a sensitive man. I told him I was fine, except for my overuse injury, I had acquired in a tennis tournament and the difficulty with my throat. I could only speak softly. He expressed his concern. Finally, Rick was ready to leave. It had been a long evening and now he was in such a hurry. It was if I didn't exist. I am sure Arnie felt as awkward as I and since Rick had left, Arnie offered to walk me to the car. At this time, for the hour was late, the valet parking was closed. As we were walking down this dark inclined driveway, Arnie took my arm as a polite gesture. As we approached the car, Rick was putting the gifts in the trunk. He was cool and abrupt, even to Arnie. I felt embarrassed and confused by this situation. Arnie gave me a gentle hug. I don't know if it was out of concern or reassurance and understanding.

When I got into the car, Rick turned on me and wanted to know what was going on, for he was a possessive man. Amazing that he could not allow himself to see the ugly side of his eminence. It saddened me, making me feel isolated, alone in my marriage. I gathered whatever reserve left to me and quietly told him, "Arnie was just doing what he should have done." I could not believe that I felt so powerless and so physically and emotionally drained. I could hardly speak. I certainly did not feel loved or cherished any longer. I think at this time

Rick looked at me as a possession, his property and a business. But what I did not realize at this time is that he was distancing himself, putting up walls and barriers, for that is how he survived his world of all the hostile takeovers. He would be rewarded and his wife and family would be forgotten.

It is too bad that we did not have hindsight. Fro then we all would have been spared this experience. For within a matter of weeks of that dinner, Rick would accept the challenge of saving First Bank and if it proved a success he would be greatly compensated and then Ernst and Young would now acquiesce to him. Money, position, and power—" that is what Rick craved and he would use it all to his own advantage, building his confidence with each success while also testing his limitations.

We would not be moving to New York. It all happened so quickly. It felt as if I was dreaming and now so rudely awakened. Was this to be my karma? Was I to learn unlimited patience, the utmost in loyalty and total selflessness? I could understand if my husband was a good and loving man with sensitivity, kindness, and compassion. But those attributes seemed long removed. Now he seemed incapable and unapproachable. How could I possibly continue in this marriage? We were married a lifetime. Our last child, our beautiful daughter Monica, would be going off to college. We would have an empty nest. I did not want to be in a marriage that was in name only, a pretense. I could not live my life this way. I did not want to waste my life on this man, even if he was my husband, for he could not appreciate what he had before him. He was the father of my children, but I might as well have been a single parent with all the neglect that he bestowed his own family.

I remember Rick coming home from another combination golf and business trip.

He was in an unusually buoyant mood. That would have been great, except I was in the midst of my virus with not a whole lot of support or understanding. He made this comment out of the blue for whatever reason: that "beautiful women were a dime a dozen." I asked him why he would even make such a chauvinistic statement. He said, "Because it's true." I realized that sometimes people will compromise their values and integrity, especially in desperate situations. But for my husband to make that statement when just returning from an important, but extravagant, business venture did make me wonder—at all these important and necessary combination business and golf trips that excluded the wives to save expenses, what went on behind the scenes?

CHAPTER 8

LAKE POINT AND MONICA'S WEDDING
(SEPTEMBER 4, 2005)

*I*WOKE UP THIS SUNDAY morning to the sound of cracking thunder. Throughout the night, the rains had woken me. Usually, these sounds would not disturb me, for I enjoy the gentle rains and the occasional storm that brings thunder and lightning that streak across the sky. Right now, I am living at Lake Point on the twentieth floor. The views are spectacular, overlooking Lake Calhoun while in the distance, and through the trees, I can also see Lake Harriet from my balcony, which I have filled with a wonderful assortment of colorful flowers in pots and flower boxes.

I marvel at the flowers cascading down the railings. To me it is a beautiful and wonderful challenge and delight to discover what I can grow in my little space. I have a wonderful frog, molded from concrete, tucked in the southeast corner of my balcony filled with decorative tall grass. Every year, the frog gets a different look, from flowers to thin grasses that spike, to the majestic bluegrass. Right now thick grass has draped the frog's back for he is proud and pretends to be fierce, but it is all bluff. He is just doing his job—protecting his domain.

This building was built around an enclosed space, to surround, and to take advantage of the spectacular views, so the winds will twist and swirl around the corners. So it can be pretty windy, especially if there is a storm. That is what was happening this morning. I was not expecting the rains to continue through the night, for I was to meet my friend Arman at his parents' house and from there we would walk to the Minnesota State Fair. But the storm continued looking more daunting than promising, for a day of such festivities. I wanted to check on the baby booster chair that I had washed and set on the black iron chair to dry. It was so windy that I had a vision of this little chair flying in the air. I was happy to see it still securely nestled between the heavy, mosaic-tiled, table. I get to watch baby Lucia this week, my new precious granddaughter. My daughter

Monica, is to meet her husband Phil in Denver, Colorado, for a few days. A business trip, but because it will also fall on their fifth anniversary, they will end business with celebration.

I remember when I discovered Lake Point. I had never contemplated living in a condominium. I had just started doing volunteer work, as a *guardian ad litem*, a speaker for children in family and juvenile courts. It was time to settle in a home, but I realized that I needed a place safe and secure, yet warm and inviting.

The year was 1999, and though I had looked at many different homes I felt very vulnerable. Monica would be getting married in September and she suggested the idea of renting a place in Minneapolis. The closer I came to making the decision, the more I liked the idea of this new experience.

I rented a two-bedroom on the main level at the Calhoun Beach apartments, facing the reflecting pool that seemed though it had an infinite edge, where the water would cascade to the lower level pool area. It was very serene even amidst the hustle and bustle of the city, well, almost of the city. It actually was on the city's outskirts, with lots of walking and biking trails, wonderful lakes - that were perfect to walk, jog, bike, or skate on roller-blades. There would be always be some sort of activity around the lakes, or on the lakes, in all seasons. And everything was within walking or biking distance from little boutiques, grocery stores, restaurants, theaters, and more. Everything at your fingertips, I was impressed and I discovered I loved being in the city. I loved the vibrancy, but I also noticed a regard and respect that the city people seemed to share. I felt safe, which probably sounds unusual but I liked to be surrounded by good people. I could feel the positive energy.

There were tennis courts across from the reflecting pool and I would often invite friends to play tennis. The ambiance was great. It would be fun to play and occasionally look up at the balconies that enclosed the courts and see people watching our match, critiquing or acknowledging a well-played shot. With a very good imagination, you could almost feel that we were at a fabulous tennis open and we were in the grand slam finals. So we would take our tennis seriously, grinning ear to ear. Many times I would start the day or end the day looking over the cascading falls across the street to Lake Calhoun, looking so inviting to walk once more around this wonderful lake. I felt fortunate during this time— almost like a child again, playful. and free-spirited, embracing the moment and so grateful for this little reprieve. I wanted to give back.

Monica was engaged to a wonderful young man and the wedding date would be September 2000. I was so excited to be able to focus on supporting her in this important time of her life. I had also begun to work as a speaker for the children in the courts as a *Guardian ad Litem*. I would live here for almost a year and then would start my search for a house in the city. Since I was now single, looking at family homes seemed overwhelming and I would get waves of sadness along with uncertainty. Don Rasmussen, my agent, sensed my apprehension and told me about Lake Point across from Dean Parkway and the Calhoun Beach Apartments. I could not imagine myself living in a condo, at least not yet. But I would at least explore my options. I looked at unit 2004.

I was impressed. I loved the balcony and the wonderful light pouring through the large windows that were in every room. There was not one straight wall or ceiling as this building was built in the round to accommodate the dramatic and pleasing views. The terracotta tiled floor in the foyer leading into the den and bedrooms on one side and opening into the airy living room was warm and inviting. The ceilings had coved moldings and unique beams, adding a special quality. The detail was thought out with care. I could live here, make this my home. This would be my creative space. My healing place.

I looked at this place four different times before returning to my decision on Christmas Eve. It was my present to myself. Then I signed the papers on my birthday, February 1, 2000. Happy birthday to me. Because of all the windows and not one straight wall, most of my furniture from my large house would not work. For almost a year, I lived with not a lot of furniture. I liked it this way, for I liked looking at the almost bare rooms and envisioning the window treatments, which would be minimal to not obscure the views. From my living room looking out was Lake Calhoun. From the kitchen and breakfast room, den and bedrooms, I could look out at Cedar Lake and part of Lake of the Isles. From these rooms when I looked out, I almost felt I was in Europe, for I would look down at Dean Parkway, the tree-lined boulevard leading to the lakes. The surroundings were amazing because of all the trees and houses nestled among them, lending grace and beauty. I wanted to savor the simplicity of my almost empty house, so I could contemplate the beauty that each season brought. Then I would decide a unique décor for this almost perfect place.

The only furniture in the living room was part of my sectional sofa from my house in Edina, which I had recovered and now sported a two-tone cream color floral brocade. I also had a side table with three drawers, which would serve its purpose, for storage space is a necessity in a condo. I felt that a piece of furniture should complement the theme or ambiance but be functional also. Off to the side of the large corner windows stood my black lacquer baby grand piano. It would be one of the last cherished gifts from Rick—a Christmas gift. I kept my oriental round glass table and it looked elegant in front of the curved brocade sofa. I also had facing the corner windows a leafless dried birch tree that I would hang a few ornamental treasures that inspired good thoughts and feelings. Sometimes I would add a touch of whimsy. People would love it. I liked the idea of bringing nature into my condo home.

The first year at the condo I decided to paint a few murals throughout the walls in some of the rooms and I would start with the kitchen. If it was a success, I would move on from there to whatever my spirit led me. From the kitchen, I would look past the eating area and ponder what type of table and chair would be appropriate for this special space, as the windows were large and low. I felt the table should be higher than an ordinary standard table. I wanted the dining set to enhance the views. From my kitchen, I would look past the table, through the large corner windows looking down at Cedar Lake. I had a blank wall within my kitchen area. I decided to incorporate the beautiful terracotta tiled floor that also led into my kitchen as a winding path leading to a mystical lake of its own, but somewhat duplicating Cedar Lake.

The idea intrigued me and I was talking to a young artist who had heard about my paintings from a mutual friend. Since my condo was so unique, I set up a meeting at my place to meet me and see some of my works. She was very soft-spoken and gracious. At this time, she had long wavy or curly blonde hair, depending on the humidity, with expressive pale blue eyes. She was very striking as an artist, but also unaffected. She was tall and slender, almost fragile but did great pieces of art that also required a lot of strength. Her love of her work fueled her stamina. I could understand the artistic quirks, the artistic mind, the importance of being surrounded by beauty and creating something grand and beautiful, and the need along with the ability to create the right mood, transforming the ordinary into the extraordinary.

When I first met Susan, I felt the vulnerability of an artist. I listened to her and could feel her strong sense of pride, the passion, and determination. All the hard work, sometimes accompanied with blood, sweat, and tears, producing tremendous works of art through a labor or love. The heart and soul of an artist is a gift to many, but too many times can be appreciated, but not understood, and many times not valued, at all. Often such a wondrous spirit is used as a prize to conquer and sometimes, without even understanding its nature, stifle it for the creative spirit needs nurturing and space to grow and be.

I understood Susan. I felt a bond, a kindred spirit of sorts through our creative talents. She was an artist. I was now a single woman, divorced, a homemaker, and mother of too many years who painted on borrowed time. When Susan saw my paintings, she exclaimed that I should still be painting. I told her it was difficult to paint through the pain and I did not want to express my hurts on canvas for the world to see or feel. I just wanted my work to portray something of beauty, conveying positive energy. I liked looking at works of art that inspired me. That is what I wanted in my home, nothing dark or foreboding. She understood. She was an artist capable of many dimensions, but her works also could stretch beyond the refined boundaries that only a true artist can bring to light, what is needed to see and feel.

When I told Susan my idea for the mural in my kitchen, she suggested we work on it together. Through this endeavor we became good friends and confidants. We would have great conversations about life, our faith, our beliefs, and of course we could not escape this problematic political time that could not help but play an effect in all our lives taking its toll in many different ways.

Sometimes we would talk about our love life, the lack, or uncertainty of. We would cover any controversial topic, trying to understand humanity—flaws and all. If we could only solve the world's problems with our passionate desire for a better place for all, our prayers would definitely be answered. But we are in the time of complacency and fear brought by dysfunctional or misdirected leaders that cause corruption in high places. They do not want to see or hear and would rather not feel, nor do they have to.

The mural in my kitchen took months. We started with repainting the kitchen cabinets. That gave my kitchen a European appeal. The results were better than I expected. Each added touch brought even more creative ideas. Many times Susan and I would paint together, but occasionally, I would paint late in the evenings. One very cold winter night, I was deeply engrossed in painting my mural, oblivious to the lateness of the hour, or anything else, when the phone rang. It brought me out of my bliss. It was from my friend Pat, who knew I would probably be up and about. She apologized for calling so late, but I had actually no concept of time at all. I assured her that it was perfectly fine and that I was busy "planting flowers." It was the middle of a very cold winter and almost midnight. She thought it was strange that I could be planting flowers at this time, and so did I. I laughed and said, "I meant painting flowers." I was so into painting flowers that I felt as if I were planting them. We both laughed and decided it was as good as a tropical vacation.

I explained I was painting flowers along the winding path, incorporating the terracotta tiles from my kitchen. It would look as if you could walk into a mystical garden. It was rather unique. Susan painted a stone archway framing the garden walk. This archway wrapped around one corner, ending at a large wall, where the scene actually began. We added a few touches of vines, with shadows from the stone giving depth. Susan painted small houses of various styles, tucked among the thick trees in the distance. In the background was the magical, mystical, Cedar Lake surrounded by trees, with a misty sky, which represented a new dawning or beginning of a beautiful romantic evening. I wanted the path to lead to a fountain, which it did. Our creative minds were working.

Susan wanted to work on the fountain. I was out doing errands or volunteer work. I came home to find the fountain with a statue of a woman in a toga, holding a staff with a symbolic circle. Wow, it wasn't quite what I'd pictured, but the interesting thing was that the statue looked so much like Susan. She explained the woman holding the staff was a symbol of wisdom and strength. I liked that. Then when I told her I liked the fact that the statue resembled her, she was horrified. "Oh, no," she exclaimed. "We can't have that." I said, "That's perfectly fine. This way you'll always be part of my kitchen." In an attempt to disguise herself, she would work on the nose, then the cheeks, and the lips, , but for me to no avail. The statue would always look like the majestic Susan.

Many artists, who draw or paint people or portraiture, bring their own likeness into the work, somehow, somewhere: maybe in the shape of the face, a line or shape of the nose or mouth, the intensity of the eyes. It is a very interesting phenomenon. I noticed it in my drawing and painting classes. We would paint or draw the same model, but we all put something of ourselves in the body's shape, even the hands, and many times the face. Even when I taught CCD (or Catholic religious education) at Our Lady of Grace, I noticed how, when asked to draw a self-portrait, it was startling and amazing what my young student drew. I would know just by looking at their portrait—that the child was. You do not have to be an artist; it just happens, so fascinating and fun.

The mural in my kitchen was the beginning of a healing process for me. Susan and I would maintain a deep respect and friendship, along with our other creative endeavors. We would paint falling leaves in the main bathroom. As a gift to me, she painted a border of intricate cornucopias, intertwined with vines and leaves, swirling around, with dusty pink roses sitting atop. That turned out to be much more involved, but so much fun, with lots of laughter trying to make this intricate gift so perfect.

Originally, when I first saw the cornucopias for some reason they looked phallic. I had to tell her because it was rather incongruous, for between the sink on the wall, Susan had inscribed one of my favorite sayings: "What you are is God's gift to you. What you make of yourself is your gift to God."

I knew Susan had worked hard, but I felt it needed some subtle changes. When she stepped back and surveyed the cornucopias, she agreed and proceeded to feverishly restyle the cornucopias in a more dignified and elegant state to complement my favorite adage. That turned out to be not such an easy task, for some reason the more changes she made, the phallic resemblance would still be there. Whenever she would ask me in earnest to check on the changes, and I would, but when we would look at each other, we could not help but break into laughter. Well, you know, even God has a sense of humor. He had to. We all have to.

I had an idea for my little powder room. Since I lived in a condo, I wanted to bring a little nature inside. I told Susan my idea of painting tall grasses and sky, just something simple in the powder room. She offered to do it, since now I was busy with the wedding plans for Monica, and still very involved as a speaker for children in the courts.

She painted beautiful tall golden grasses of various shades, and a beautiful, vibrant blue, sky with wispy, white clouds. She wanted to reflect the golden fields that I had painted on canvas during the time when my life was good and filled with inspiration. I had painted a flurry of clouds against a stormy dark sky, but the sky was also clearing. There is a simple church or an austere house in the distant background, whatever one chooses, with a smattering of trees.

It was one of my favorite paintings. Susan decided to use this painting as an idea for the grasses in this little powder room. It is amazing how painting a room in a different color or being a little bold and daring can transform one's mood or temperament and can be quite the conversation piece too.

* * * * *

It did not take long for me to enjoy the luxury of time. I would find myself once again being on overload, being pulled in different directions. I was finding life as a single woman more complex, than I ever thought possible. Monica would be getting married in September. I was still trying to comprehend and heal from my last court experience in July 1999, which had left me practically reeling in disbelief. My belief in the judicial system was shattered, for my experiences had left me feeling victimized and discounted by the courts. All because of my ex-husband's misdirected wrath, from which the shackles had been removed. He was a man of money, position, and connection, and I was just a wife, mother, and homemaker. These aspects made it easy for him.

In my volunteer work as a *guardian ad litem* I was shocked and disappointed to learn how the system worked. And didn't. I would talk to different social workers They would tell me that because I was a volunteer I could speak out, whereas if they did they might lose their jobs or be forced to resign. Ever since I can remember, I have had a strong sense of justice and fair play. I thought the majority of people felt the same way. But now I was beginning to feel I was a minority and a novelty in my passionate beliefs. I wanted to help children and families. I wanted to help them regain their dignity. I wanted to teach them to believe in themselves, about being healthy in mind, body, and spirit. I wanted the oppressed to rise above their situation. I wanted the addicted to stop their harmful habits that would destroy their minds and weaken their bodies. I wanted them to find the will within themselves for the love of their children and for their own person.

I learned so much. I could see the parallels between my own experiences in the courtroom and the mother and two young daughters that I represented. It seemed as if it was a game on display, pomp, and circumstance to impress or intimidate. There would be rules, a lot of rules, tons of mind-boggling red tape. I would be given information that was erroneous or exaggerated. I could now understand the expression of when people are allowed to slip through the cracks. I thought that was more fallacy than a reality. But I would learn that success was a rare thing for a person caught up in the system that would hold them tight, for the more people in the system, the more government funding. So there would be no big hurry. I was in almost staggering disbelief, but I was resolved and determined to help at least one family. If I could see that there was even a remote possibility that I could save them that would be enough. I could not turn my back without attempting.

On the last day of the course, we would receive the names of children/family that we would be representing. The last day was also when they told us of all the known and hidden dangers that were possible. Anytime there is dysfunction or addiction, be it drugs, alcohol, or sometimes even aberrant behavior, be cautious, vigilant, and alert. I was suddenly frightened at this very serious responsibility. I was a woman alone, myself. I wanted to help the children and families as in a classroom situation. Tell them the philosophy of life in a way that would open their eyes with renewed wonder and excitement in life. It would take a while, but with each session they would be inspired to live a different life that was healthy and invigorating, giving and being the best they could be and the proud moment when they could achieve their goals and reunite their family in a wholesome atmosphere and loving environment.

I was dreaming and now rudely awakened to the reality of my awesome responsibility. I reminded myself, one step at a time. Tread softly and gently. Stay mindful of the fact that there is always hope for when treated with respect, the importance of seeing the complete picture and gaining their trust and confidence. I could do that. I could at least try.

I would be given the family of Marie Miller, a single mother with two children, Tiffany, ten years old, and Andrea, nine. I was disheartened to learn that the mother was incarcerated. I would meet Charlene, the foster mother bearing a gift of a terracotta chicken that could be a planter or hold fruit, eggs, or whatever she would choose. I felt strange coming to her home to basically survey the situation, inspect, and report. That did not appeal to me. I was surprised to see that she was a somewhat elderly black woman. She was like a sweet grandma. In fact, that is what the girls called her. That was endearing. I met the girls. They came into the living room, hanging their heads in a shy manner, but would peek up at me out of curiosity. Tiffany was a pretty girl of mixed-ethnicity, slender and graceful and her younger sister Andrea had pale skin, with soft pink cheeks and clear blue eyes that she would lower in a very shy way, her long blond hair hanging loosely at her shoulders.

As we talked, I could sense the reserve of the foster mom lifting. She gave me some of the background on the children, the mother and also of herself. Shortly, as we were talking, the phone rang and it was the mom calling from Shakopee prison. I sat there, my eyes wide, thinking, "My God, has my life ever changed!" I have never been in a situation like this before. She talked briefly, and then let the girls talk to their mother. The girls sat close to each other, eagerly waiting their turn to talk to mom. I told Charlene I would like to talk to Marie also. The girls seemed to cling to their mother's words, and cried when they had to give up the phone. I was touched and saddened. When I got on the phone to speak to Marie, she seemed somewhat upset and offended. I could understand her reaction. She seemed to be in shock and needed reassurance, for all this had recently happened. I reassured her that her girls were in good care with Charlene. She told me that the social worker would be bringing the girls to see her in the following weeks. I told her that I was new in this field and this might be a good time for me to meet her. Thinking this would give me an opportunity to talk to the social worker more in-depth and I could see the situation firsthand. I could not believe I would be going to a prison to meet the mother of these two beautiful girls. At this time I truly felt irritated that a woman and mother could let her life take such a perilous turn that would produce such dire consequence to herself and her children. I could not understand it. I knew I would have to get to the core of Marie's background, to understand the downward spiral in her life, especially if this family could or should be saved.

That was an awesome responsibility. I had no idea what to expect. To me it was hard not to prejudge this mother, for already she was in prison. For what I had no idea. So of course I expected to see and find the worst. From the very beginning of this case, it was fraught with complications. I was expecting a call from the social worker, Karen D. But I never talked directly to her. I left numerous messages. For some unknown reason she never returned my calls. I was getting nervous, as we would be attending our first court hearing right after Thanksgiving, November 29, 1999. I was surprised that the seriousness of this situation was not given immediate attention or at least an acknowledgement that the professionals themselves were on top of things and would be there for guidance and support. I thought we all would be working together for the children and family's best interest, to me that meant communication and availability.

I remember going to the courthouse, myriads of people scurrying about, some talking in the quietest corner amidst a hub of activity. There would be men, women and children sitting on benches waiting their turn—for information maybe, with looks of despair, uncertainty, defiance. It was too much. It was hard to believe that this many people depended on a court system to give their life direction. I looked around to see if I could find Karen D., the social worker. I made myself as obvious as possible, even stopping the most professional-looking persons to see if they were or knew Karen D. I would stay fairly close to the door numbered where we were to meet. I noticed a woman sitting quietly. She seemed to be troubled, certainly not impressive, or approachable.

I learned that this was Karen D. I walked up to her and introduced myself. I had the feeling she was burned out, overwhelmed. So far I was not impressed with what I was walking into. Where was the order amidst the chaos, or faces of determination along with compassion? How could there be so many troubled and dysfunctional people, overworked, left with so little hope or help? I would learn that this first hearing would be cancelled. I breathed a sigh of relief for this would give me time to learn more about the Miller family. I would use this opportunity to spend some time with Tiffany and Andrea, occasionally taking them for a small dinner or shopping for Christmas gifts for their mother or each other. I wanted to give them new positive experiences but not overwhelm them either.

This would be during the holiday season. They would come and pass. During this time the social worker continued to be elusive. It was now the middle of January 2000. Charlene called to tell me the girls were given a new social worker, Joe M. Joe M. called me to tell me I should get in touch with a Mary B., that she could give me the background of this family. He did not seem to be actively involved. I thought it strange that someone from the *guardian ad litem* staff didn't inform me. When we finally connected, I thought, "Finally, a person I can talk to who seems to really care about this family." She seemed to know much more about Marie's background. She told me some positive things that gave me hope, along with the many trials that had brought her down. She also told me her fears of this family slipping through the cracks and her hopes that this would not happen. We would work together. Joe M. would be in the background not actively participating. It would be several months before I actually met him and when I did, his presence was intimidating, almost unnerving.

Fortunately, I did not have to interact with him that much, as he seemed to prefer to work from a distance. He seemed to have other priorities, but he did give me some good information, as least that is what I thought at the time.

The most important contact was Mary B., as she would take time from her busy schedule, to advise or direct me, even though her precious spare moments were few and far between. I could sense and feel her deep concern for this family. To me, this was like a gigantic puzzle, trying to find the right pieces. But strangely this entire event seemed to add an air of mystery to the whole process.

Finally, there would be some progress made, for Mary B. had set up a visit to have the girls see their mother and I would finally meet Marie and Mary B. I would then hopefully get a clearer picture, better understanding and making some progress. On the trip to Shakopee, Mary B. gave more background that would be helpful. The girls seemed quiet on the ride up but occasionally their anticipation could not be contained at seeing their mother. At times, Andrea would break into tears, her sister would try to console her, while Mary and I would reassure the girls.

We all signed in. I remember walking through the long stark white corridors, cold and devoid of any kind of loveliness. I could not help but wonder how one could even work at such a place without being affected in some way. We reached the large room, filled with long generic tables and metal chairs. There would be security guards standing here and there, always surveying the scene and scrutinizing the visitors. I told Mary I wanted to stand back and observe from a distance. I wanted to give the girls this short time with their mother that they so desperately needed. I watched as Tiffany and Andrea rushed to their mother's arms. Marie and her daughters once again reunited in tearful embrace. The girls stroked their mother's long auburn hair, wanting to see their mother looking pretty again. They would caress her face as Marie held her daughters close.

I gave them their time. I slowly approached Marie and her daughters. The closer I came, Marie would look up at me beseechingly. What was my purpose? Her eyes were brimmed with tears. Her daughters clung to her broken fragile body. She held onto her last shred of dignity for her children's sake as well as her own. She seemed to search my face for a sign of hope and understanding. This would be my first introduction to Marie and this memory will be forever imprinted in my mind, as I introduced myself. She spoke with a hoarse, whispery voice that even sounded painful. I thought of my painful virus that had affected my own voice for so many months. She told me that she had some surgery on her larynx that affected her voice. Eventually her voice would return but would always be a bit raspy. Before Mary and I were to leave, we gave Marie and her daughters a few more minutes for their tearful goodbyes.

On the way back home, we were all immersed in our own deep thoughts and emotions. Andreas sobbed most of the way home, while Tiffany took on her role as the brave and loving older sister. I would not get home until nine-thirty that evening. Too emotionally exhausted to sleep. My thoughts were with Marie and her daughters being torn apart. What happened here and how could this family ever be whole again? I could not imagine a young child seeing her mother in prison. After bringing the girls back to the foster mom's house, Mary B had a better history of this family and I got a strong sense that she felt this family could be saved. She told me of her frustrations, and that because she was in a paid position, but I was a volunteer, there were things that I saw or experienced that I could express without any serious repercussions. I hoped that would be a rare and minor occurrence. She told me again of her fears of the possibility that Marie and her daughters could slip through the cracks. To hear her say those words made me more determined than ever not to ever let that happen.

* * * * *

It is amazing how quickly life can take a turn from pretty comfortable, almost idyllic, to a very serious nature where the demands are constant and many times critical. Now I would go home to my ivory tower haven, savor briefly the unique surroundings, but always in the back of my mind were the urgent responsibilities that were ahead of me. My daughter Monica would be getting married September 2000. Fortunately, she was very organized and her father was very willing and able to finance the extravaganza. The wedding would be held at the Basilica of St. Mary, the reception at the Minikahda Country Club where my former husband now had his membership. I was uncomfortable with these arrangements, as Rick had continued to make life as difficult for me as humanly possible, the very act of one final court proceeding in July 1999. The emotional wound was still so raw and painful.

I think most of the time, after the divorce, all the appeals for so many years ongoing left me in a somewhat traumatized state, never really able to recover from the previous assault. I find it amazing that I could make any type of good decision. Yet every decision made was mine alone to make now. There would be so many that would profit off my vulnerability and inexperience. I had no one really to turn to, whom I felt I could truly trust or was knowledgeable of my now complex situation. After all I was born to be a singer, dancer, artist, and missionary and now I would have to master the skills of the business books. I understood the dynamics of business for I did have to take a couple of business courses reluctantly. Even though it was pretty meager, I'm glad that at least I had a rudimentary knowledge that could be expanded. I would see how the real financial experts knew how to use others' inexperience or financial crisis to their advantage. I saw it and more times than not would be at the mercy of an opportunist in every shape and sizes that would insidiously take unfair advantage. Well, I had a lot to learn. And I did and I always will for that is a fact of life. Actually, that can be one of the most interesting and challenging aspects of life also, as we rise above the unexpected and persevere.

I was given probably the most complex case at that time, because of Marie's long history in the system. She was also a woman of high intelligence but put her trust in the wrong people. She did not have family here for both her parents were deceased. Shortly after her last daughter was born, she inherited her brother's house. It was his way to insure some kind of safety net for his sister, as they were always close. After his untimely death, Marie was in shock, grief-stricken, with two babies. This would be a time when she needed some trusted guidance, loving support, and positive direction. Instead she would be misled in her emotional state of mind to sign papers that would give a distant relative this property. He would quickly sell this property, taking the money and running back to California with his profit. Like many women or victims, they are embarrassed or in too much shock to respond properly. Many times they do not know who or where to turn for help. The worst scenario is when they cannot afford the help that would have prevented this in the first place. So the downward spiral beings. What I have seen and experienced is that more times than not, the criminal or the criminal mind has more rights and protection than their victims.

I would be going to court numerous times for Marie. Many times, the hearings would be cancelled for some reason. It would be an incredible waste of emotional energy and time to be prepared and not be told of the cancellation. But it would be worse for Marie, as she would have to depend on the bus. It would not matter that she might be sick with a cold or flu, she would have to wait for that bus in some of the worst weather—cold, pouring rain, to freezing sub-zero temperatures. It would be crucial that the person in the system report to their programs on time. Sometimes they might even have to leave one of the programs designed to help them to report on time, to a program on how to budget their money or do their laundry. Time was of the essence. Tardiness meant going backwards. It seemed an impossible situation, for the rules were for rules' sake to be enforced on the weakest.

I realize that there has to be some form of punishment and restitution, but I feel that there are limitations also. I believe in the importance of awareness, communication to have a voice and be heard for understanding. I believe that education is the utmost importance for every child everywhere. No exceptions. When we can afford to spend millions and more for athletes, movie stars, throwing money to politicians that live in gated communities oblivious to the needs of the common people and could care less for they are so well taken café of for life. They huddle in the security of their peers, knowing that money buys power and gives them special exemptions and entitlements unknown to the average man and woman, for the average person is too exhausted just trying to keep their homes and pay their bills and taxes.

I remember when attorneys were paid not by the hour but by the result of their case. Now we have more attorneys creating the most dramatic and sensational situations to prolong and convolute so unnecessarily to their own or their wealthy clients' advantage. No one stops them because it has become a normal way of life. The dysfunction that has crept in and is now the accepted corruptive normal way of conducting business, legal and government. It goes on and on because it is so pervasive and people are too tired, too numb, too burned out, too drugged out, or over-medicated. Too confused to know where to turn or know what to do. This should not be happening. It is the middle of 2005 and it seems we are all going backwards morally, intellectually, spiritually and it makes me feel sad for our future generations. What kind of future or values have we given our children when it seems families can be expendable, replaced and sometimes erased?

I hope that they can be wise, more loving, and compassionate and learn from the too many errors of our generation. I hope and pray that they can find the courage and strength to stand up to their oppressors and wisdom in their thoughts and words, depicted in their actions. I wonder and worry about the neglect—when raising a family is not considered important or valued any longer. When daycare or the nanny replaces the parent I worry about the overworked parent trapped in careers not of their choice but of need. I am concerned about the excess and extravagant monetary packages, perks that is never enough for the greed that has become the elixir for the corporate climber that will sacrifice anyone and everything for his love of money. It is time that we look at the cause and effect of our actions. Have we helped society or have we been a part of the problem? Have we stood up for our belief and honor or did we look away and pretend we did not see or understand? Do we have the courage to admit a mistake, or to admit a wrong and right that wrong, especially when we know if we don't there will be adverse effects for many years to come.

Will we be known as the victim or the victimizer? Or will we be the revered teacher and healer or the oppressor of truth and knowledge? Will we be the courageous leader or the glorified opportunist cloaked in his pretense awaiting that opportunity? Okay I've said enough. Aren't you glad I'm not your mother, sister or lover? I think I can get too serious. A dear friend of mine, Pat Duffey, would often remind me I should be painting. And, oh, how I wanted to free my mind to paint wonderful works of art. But I would always be expounding on some issue or philosophy, wanting to understand or fix the world's problems. It seemed so easy, but egos are frail and personalities are complex and unique and it takes time to really understand all sides and most of us are too impatient. Here I go again. I guess that is part of my nature, but now I realized my experiences were too vast to be ignored. Pat finally said, "Patti, I always felt you should be painting, but now I realize you are a crusader." I said, "Well, maybe I am but I still want to paint and sing and dance." We both laughed. But I had to admit when she said that I immediately thought of Joan of Arc and I know what happened to her. I am not that brave.

At any rate, I needed a safe place. My creative and healing space and I am here for now. I will continue with my experience as *guardian ad litem*. I worked with Marie and her daughters for about two years. It seemed much longer, for it took such an emotional and physical toll. Eventually, the judge that knew this family thought that it would be good for this family if I became their mentor. That appealed to me, for I at least wanted to help one family become independent of the system. I would speak to different people in the programs, telling them of my observations that disturbed me. I would tell them of the lack of communication and the distortion of facts. I felt like I had to be a detective in my search for information because everyone was so evasive in there privileged information. I decided that would be my one and only case.

I know because of my own experience, I would detect omissions that most new or even experienced *Guardian ad Litems* would overlook or not understand the significance. To me they would be as if a red flag, warning of serious neglect and problems ahead. That would bother me for I felt a responsibility in knowing. My mind would be in a state of turmoil and I had to make a decision on how to approach and to whom. My first concern would be for the girls and for their mother. I knew that she really was not in a position physically or financially to have her children at the moment. But, given time, with the right help and support, I could see it happen.

My daughter would be getting married soon, and that was important and should have been my solitary focus. We would shop and finally select her perfect wedding gown, the tiara that would secure her beautiful long veil, along with all the accessories. We would work together deciding the right style and color for all the bridesmaids. I was so proud of my beautiful daughter, not just because of her appearance, but for her sweet nature and her graceful demeanor. It was bittersweet for I know she wanted to compensate for her father's lack of consideration.

Having my daughter's wedding amidst a tenuous situation when Marie would be getting released from her transitional housing was not an easy or gentle place. It put tremendous distress on me to bring the girls there to visit their mother. I was eager for the girls to be reunited in their own place. As the date of the wedding kept getting close, life became a whirlwind. I still had to find my gown. It was so difficult to do. I could not understand why I had waited so long. I finally found a beautiful bronze two-piece silk that seemed stately and elegant. There would have to be some alterations to the skirt, which made me nervous for time was running out. The top was fitted, cut lower than I normally wear, with small, capped sleeves. There would be trim of beads around the edge and touches of beadwork throughout the fabric. This probably was not what I would have chosen, for I envisioned something more understated but elegant. This seemed as if I were pretending to be queen. Maybe subconsciously I wanted to make some kind of statement. Who knows? I just know I was stretched to the max and it was starting to take its toll. I would get waves of sheer exhaustion but would dismiss the signs, for there was way too much to do.

Marie had finished her seven months at Shakopee Prison. From there she would be in a temporary transitional housing or group home, attending various introductory programs. We would keep in touch and I would bring her daughters to visit weekly. When I would pick up the girls at the foster mom's they would eagerly be waiting. Charlene would have them all dressed up, their hair done. Sometimes Andrea would have her hair up in along ponytail or some kind of knot, which was rather sophisticated for this nine-year-old. Tiffanie was so pretty that it did not matter what her hair looked like. Occasionally they would both have their hair done in cornrows. Angela standing almost prim and proper with her hands folded in eager anticipation of seeing her mother. Stephanie would be more talkative and animated telling me about their day and how much they missed their mother and could not wait to see her again. They would fantasize that one day they would have a house with a big yard so their mom could have her flower gardens and they would have a dog. That would be my dream for this family also.

Within the system, it takes time, a long process of many procedures that must be followed to the letter. Eventually, Marie was allowed to have her own place. She was able to get temporary housing near a very pretty neighborhood, schools with small classroom sizes, with lots of big windows and skylights in the long hallway. It was the first progressive designed school built in Minnesota. It was like a gift. The one thing that Marie wanted for her daughters was an education that offered the best academically in a most pleasing and inspiring environment. The apartment, though, turned out to be a temporary arrangement and one day would be condemned and torn down. It was actually uninhabitable. Marie would be given this place, attending her programs here and there and everywhere by bus. She also worked part-time for a pittance. The first time I saw the place, I felt outrage and despair for this family. How could these girls attend any kind of school coming from such surroundings?

There were unopened boxes stacked along the walls with opened boxes where clothes were spilling out for there were no drawers. The hardwood floors were many times varnished, scuffed, and worn. They seemed to slant to the end of the tired living room. It was impossible to organize for even the rods in the closets were broken. There was not a place to sit, for there were no chairs, not even a table or desk. How could anyone place a family in a place like this? How could anyone flourish in these deplorable conditions? The bare ugly ceiling lights just added to the austerity (desperation) of the rooms. I felt for Marie already so emotionally burdened and physically exhausted. The system once more let her and her children down, yet she still was able to cling to some hope and the joy, just being with her daughters finally. That was not acceptable to me. My thoughts would go back to this family, needing a real home. These conditions did not offer any kind of comfort or any sense of dignity or refuge.

I reported the conditions to the appropriate people. They stated that Marie would be given a check to buy some furnishings. Their check was slow in coming and after the third week, I decided to check out estate sales. I was able to get a bed, sofa that also would suffice as another bed, couple of chest of drawers, table and chairs dining set, pots and pans. They needed kitchen utensils for they were using plastic. I gave them a start. A very nice woman was curious about all this furniture and supplies. It was obvious I was on some kind of mission. I told her about the family, what they had been through and the lack of furnishings. She listened, concerned, but then her face brightened. She asked me the ages of the girls. I told her nine and ten. But in October and November, they would be having birthdays. She then exclaimed with such enthusiasm that she had bikes, rollerblades, all kinds of games and did they like music? For she had all these old rock 'n' roll records. She would like this family to have them.

Wow, I love music. Music can brighten any austere room, change a bad mood or just bring some life away from the doldrums. I wanted to give this kindhearted woman a big hug, but I think my gratitude showed on my face and she was spared. I called Marie and told her of my fortunate find and about this wonderful woman. Now all I had to do was find someone with a big truck of some kind and maybe more muscle than what I had. A dear friend that I knew from tennis said he could help. We would pick up all the furniture and stuff the next day, after his work. Of course, it turned out to be a very hot day and sweltering evening. We worked hard, packing everything in his big truck. He would make two trips.

I called Marie from my cell phone to tell her we were on our way. At this point it was starting to get dark. The girls were waiting for us in front of the building and were eagerly waiting to help. That was a good thing, because I was feeling pretty rundown at this point. The girls and I brought several smaller pieces in, Marie and Gary did the larger pieces of furniture. At this point, it was quickly getting dark. Thank goodness for the few streetlights that were on. When lo and behold, all the surrounding lights went out. I thought surely this is a temporary blackout. I looked up at the old redbrick apartment, not a single solitary glimmer. Suddenly, this place seemed to be pretty spooky, not a place where I wanted to be. We all gathered around the truck, waiting for the lights to return but to no avail. Gary had a flashlight, but I was still concerned about making our way up those long wooden three flights of stairs. I told Marie if she could scrounge up some candles for some lighting to prepare to bring the last few pieces of furniture up, for it did not look like the electricity would be returned for a while.

This was disheartening. I felt bad for Gary, as I knew he had to get up at some ungodly hour the next morning. But I also was so disappointed that we could not now help place the furniture together. I wanted to see their faces as they sank into their sofa to finally relax and feel the beginning of hope return. I was hoping that this would not be some kind of omen predicting the difficulties that might lie ahead for this family, even for myself.

It was getting late. We said our goodbyes in the midst of our bewilderment and uncertainty, intermingled with an exhausted determination. As Gary and I descended the darkened stairway, I felt the immense gratitude for this help and tremendous support in this arduous venture, which proved to be more complex and demanding then either of us imagined. Neither of us had any kind of dinner. Gary had already put in a full day at his work and was already pretty skinny, so we decided to get something to eat before heading home. We ate in a daze. It wasn't just the physical labor that affected us, but the emotional aspect that was so draining.

Shortly after I helped with the furnishings of Marie's apartment, she finally received the check. I told her she could use it for other household items but to let Joe M. know. He was the person she had to report to. He was upset that I took it upon myself to buy the furniture. I knew I had to stay within the budget and that I did. But I was shocked at the attitude of the hierarchy. They let a family live in deplorable conditions, letting them wait when they should have been helped immediately. I felt by taking the initiative and helping this family, and helping them, they would appreciate. Instead, it just made them look like they were not doing their job.

Amidst all this Monica needed help with her move from her apartment off Gerard Avenue. She loved her apartment. It was a redbrick four-story building with beautiful ivy climbing the walls. She was very organized and had finished most of the packing. I helped with the cleaning but the big thing was the oven. She had never cleaned an oven before. That has never been my favorite job but since I was the one with the experience, I volunteered. Spraying the oven seemed toxic. The timing could not have been worse. The combination of Marie's big move and Monica's move within days was taking its toll on me physically. There was still so much to do and the wedding was so near. I didn't have time to even begin to think of the lack of sleep or even any kind of relaxation. I was simply on overload. Nonstop. I was physically and emotionally exhausted, making me feel numb.

We had the rehearsal dinner. I cannot even remember where—some trendy restaurant near the Basilica. My dear friend Red would be my escort. The family came from out of the state. But, I was just going through the motions. Nothing seemed real. Rick with his new wife. The room was dimly lit, lending an air of sadness, instead of festivity. We had, what everyone said was, a wonderful dinner. I tried to eat, but it was an effort. I pushed my food around, taking a few bites for nourishment. Was I exhausted from all these moves? Or was I emotionally drained? I could not discern the difference. I was just trying to get through the night. There were slides of Monica as a baby, a toddler, Monica with her friends and family, at dance recitals, and my beautiful daughter going to proms.

The years kept flashing by. It was surreal. There was wonderful footage of Monica and Phil young and so in love. Occasionally, I could hear someone say, "Monica looks so much like her mom." Hearing that made me feel sad, but honored too. I wondered what Rick was feeling for his new wife.

Rick got up to speak. I thought it would be a few words, but he spoke on and on. It reminded me of all the speeches he would practice over and over again, until he had prepared himself perfectly like a robot. Nothing he said seemed to ring true. However, vague words, full of self-importance, kept spilling from his mouth . When he spoke of his daughter, he tried to sound like a loving father, for he truly did. But even those words were hollow and meaningless. It was strange. He never once said anything about me. I was watching the whole scene. I felt a weariness. It was as if I had never existed—that Monica had just happened, cultivated from an embryo on a plate. I was just a whisper in the wind, a thought, a feeling, a distant memory not to be acknowledged for then he would have to remember. I wondered if everyone else felt as uncomfortable as I. I was grateful that I had not come alone.

* * * * *

The next day was September 9, 2000. It would be a hot and blustery day for the wedding. I spent the morning getting my hair done with Monica and all the bridesmaids. I loved her friends and for me to be a part of this was special. But I was so exhausted. I just did not feel right. I probably should have taken the time to have a breakfast, but there was so much to do. It slipped my mind. I was berating myself for not being more attentive to my own needs. Maybe it would have been better if I had quietly done my own hair and nails at my leisure in my own comfortable surroundings. I had no idea I would be feeling so drained. I would look at my daughter so happy, surrounded by all her dear friends and me, all of us getting our hair and makeup done together. Everyone looked beautiful, although I wondered about myself, as I never wore face powder and now I did. They accented my eyes with heavy color and liner. I could feel the heaviness of the makeup. My lips were painted on a deep rich color, outlined to their perfection. I looked in the mirror. I was starting to feel like the queen waiting to be summoned on command.

By the time I got home, I had to get myself ready for the wedding. During this time, I was dating a wonderful man named Red Gallagher. I had met Red two years before on Halloween. He was and still is a musician. He was performing at a lounge where my friend Barb wanted to go. She was dressed as a black cat with ears and tail and painted-on black whiskers. She looked cute. I was coming down with a sore throat, so I reluctantly went, dressed in my fitted leopard pants, black long top and cowgirl boots. This gave me an opportunity to wear my cowgirl boots, which I would wear anyway sometimes. During a break, Red who was dressed as a convincing pirate asked if he could join Barb and me at our table. I noticed he was rather cute with a mustache, probably too tall for me but too tall for my friend too. Barb sipped her wine, while I sipped my cranberry juice, hoping I could ward off this cold. Red had a friendly, down-to-earth manner, very much at ease with himself. I found myself very comfortable talking to him and felt very relaxed. We talked about Ireland. I had just returned and he would be going for a family wedding and to do a few gigs. We set up a time and place to meet for dinner. Our friendship blossomed.

Red was my escort at the rehearsal dinner and now would pick me up for the wedding. He was the perfect escort, for he was very outgoing and understood that my attentions would be all over the place. Susan Lynn was also at the house. She offered to help me with my dress and give me moral support. After I was dressed and ready, I could do no more. This was it. Susan said I looked beautiful, even though I felt I looked like a pretend queen, standing out in all her glory. All I needed was my own tiara.

Red picked me up, looking handsome and debonair in his favorite tweed jacket. Seeing him made me smile. I was beginning to feel more relaxed. Red exuded a warmth and friendliness that would bring a wonderful energy to any room. For me at that moment, Red became a comforting presence that helped renew my spirit. Now we would be on our way to the Basilica of St. Mary, meandering our way through the picturesque streets around Lake of the Isles. I just wanted to savor this one relaxing moment before we approached the influential and impressive cathedral. As we walked up the long steps, I could not help by feel somewhat shaken. This was the same church where Rick had just remarried. It wasn't the fact that he'd remarried. It was how it was done that was so disturbing. I tried to dismiss the memories from my mind.

The wedding was a formal affair. There was not given much leeway for creativity but the old traditional pomp and circumstance. I wondered if this was Rick's influence and Monica wanting to please him went along. Weddings can bring out so many emotions and longings. I could not help but remember my own wedding. I was so young, a reluctant bride. At least my daughter went to college and graduated. She traveled abroad, so much more worldly and sophisticated about life. She had a career for a few years in the world of fashion, setting up fashion shows, working with models and doing everything that was needed. It was all very exciting but the consistency was not there for they were cutting back. She needed a more dependable income. Monica eventually would work for her father as his receptionist and doing whatever else needed to be done. She would work for him until she and her husband had their baby.

Monica would be married in an extravaganza, for Rick would spare no expense. It was surreal. I was the mother of his children, yet now so discounted and replaced by the private secretary wife who stood at his side. The years of endless court proceedings that would erode my financial security, while he flaunted his wealth to further humiliate. He never had to be accountable or responsible; therefore, he had no idea of the pain he caused. I wanted to rejoice in the happiness of Monica's wedding, but the memories of betrayal, still so painfully raw, surfaced. I wanted to sink into oblivion, start all over somehow, somewhere. I wanted to forget, but when someone has been traumatized for years, it is impossible but not to be affected adversely, for I was surrounded daily by memories and the results of the injustice that would permeate every aspect of my life. The inequities would plague my life, even seeping into the joyous memories, intermixing the sorrow with the joy.

The beauty of the wedding and all the heart-touching sentiments felt were marred by the memories. I was annoyed at myself for feeling so deeply. Why couldn't I just be dutifully compliant? But I remembered my own gentle mother and knew that masking or overmedicating feelings or denying our experiences was not the solution, but extended the problems. What are the lessons we learn that will help create a more caring and promising future? This was another important passage of life not to be ignored.

The wedding party, family and friends would all gather on the steps of the Basilica for group pictures. It was a bright sunny day with the balmy winds whipping at the skirts and hair, while everyone was trying to stay composed and unruffled and beautiful. To me it added energy to the day, blowing all the cares and sorrows away. The photographer took beautiful pictures of Monica and Phil under the shade of the aged magnificent trees, the winds playfully whirling about them. My daughter would reach in graceful ballet moves to contain her veil, while her husband added to this wonderful happy scene. The street in front of the Basilica was lined with vintage cars awaiting to take the bride and groom and the wedding party on a picturesque drive around the surrounding lakes and then to Minikahda Country Club for the reception. I wistfully looked on as they happily scrambled in their cars.

Eventually we would all arrive at the impressive clubhouse with the beautiful grounds overlooking a splendidly challenging golf course on one side and Lake Calhoun on the other side. The gardens were rich with vibrant color and a wonderful assortment of flowers lining the paths and walkways leading to the patio. Minikahda had clay tennis courts, with also platform tennis, a smaller version of tennis on a raised platform. The platform itself is heated enough to melt a falling snow. We played with a short racquet and a smaller squishy ball. It was a fast game, needing concentration and agility. This was a game that was played year out even in zero-degree weather. The funny thing is we would dress in layers, hats, gloves, sometimes scarves around our necks, vests over or under our coats. Eventually getting so hot that we would take layer upon layer off. It was a hot game that got your body temperature rising. I only played it a couple times, but I will always remember the great fun and laughter we all shared. Overlooking Lake Calhoun was a beautifully groomed croquet court. The grass was cut low as a carpet. The players would wear all white, looking very proper and dignified. The real croquet players took this game seriously. I played as a child and I played here a few times. But for me as much as I like games, tennis took enough of my time and golf was not becoming a rarity.

It seemed strange to be here for my daughter's wedding reception, having experienced the country club life, but now I was a guest. This was Rick's club now with his new wife. The club was something that I would lose with his appeals. Actually, I was so busy trying to regroup that it was an insignificant loss for me. But it still did not seem right or fair, but another added twist to the insult and vulnerability of a wife, mother, and homemaker. We would gather outside the clubhouse as the winds were winding down and now a gentle breeze. There was a peaceful quality to the air. I felt almost dreamlike, one foot in front of the other. So tired. At moments, feeling like a spectacle myself, on display, Rick with his new wife. There was a natural curiosity factor.

We would adjourn for dinner inside the clubhouse, using two large rooms to accommodate the guests. The rooms were stately elegant with beautiful views of the shimmering lake and the palatial grounds. It was good to finally sit down. I would be seated with my friend Red alongside of us were my youngest son and his wife and my grandsons Michael and Joseph, and my dear friend Stacy and her husband. There were a few tables around me with my closest friends. Rick would be seated with his new wife and new mother-in-law and his proverbial imposing cronies in the world of high finance. It was all rather bizarre as if also announcing the extreme shift in family order was now complete.

I did not feel physically right, almost like being in a haze. I could look at the long table in front of me where the bridal party sat. Monica and Phil got up to thank and again greet all their friends and guests. Others would say a few words of acknowledgement and best wishes. Then Rick got up and sauntered to the center of the room with a microphone. The room hushed, waiting for many reasons to hear what this man, husband and father would have to say. I sat listening as Rick recapitulated the same speech he had prepared the night before at the rehearsal dinner. To me it was the epitome of arrogance and denial. I was ashamed for him. He was beyond understanding the pain and humiliation caused by his own self-importance. For now he was simply oblivious.

I don't think people knew how to respond. Red looked at me with understanding and grasped my hand. Then my oldest son, born on his father's birthday, strode up to the microphone, his head held high. He introduced himself and started speaking unrehearsed with bold determination. He told the story of when his baby sister just came home from the hospital. How his father was busy at the table, so absorbed with his work that he did not want to be distracted and sent Mark and Duane out to play. I noticed everyone was now taking notice. I had no idea what Rick would say. But I do remember that day so well; Mark and Duane devised a running game using planks of wood and their father's car. They placed the planks of wood slanting from the driveway to the car, then proceeded to run from the back and up to the top of the car, down the hood and then down the front of the car. Well, Mark told his story with such dramatic flair that everyone was captivated. He described how—with each run up and down the car, the boys getting bolder and making this incredible rumbling sound, Rick finally shot up straight from his work and bolted out the door enraged. I could hear him yelling. "What are you boys doing?!" with numerous expletives. He was angry and frustrated while our sons were restless and needed some attention.

As Mark was telling this story, it came back that I had not been feeling well, for I had just had my baby and it was a difficult birth. Monica was under the lights for six days for treatment of yellow jaundice. And I was delirious with fevers that would spike and then return once I came home from the hospital. Rick brought the boys back into the house, verbally reprimanding them, especially Mark, for he was the oldest. I remember feeling already weak and this just compounded the misery. What a homecoming for a new baby and for a mother who just gave birth! I remember Mark's little face so serious and his eyes brimmed with tears streaming down his face. I had never seen my little boy looking so sad and dejected.

This was not the way a homecoming should ever be for a woman who had just given birth. There had to be some consideration not just for me but for our sons. They had a new baby sister and they were excited. I could not understand Rick's own behavior, and I told him that our sons needed attention at this time. I was surprised that he could not realize that himself. I wanted this to be a joyful time for our sons to remember. I put my arms around my son and looked into his face, streaked with tears. I told him, "Mark, you have a beautiful baby sister. And I know you are going to make the best big brother." Then I asked him if he would like to see his sister in the bassinet. He shook his head yes. I took his hand and we walked together to my bedroom, where the bassinet stood by my side of the bed. He looked down at his sleeping sister and touched her cheek. Mark would stand by the bassinet for over and hour just watching Monica in awe.

All the guests were captivated as Mark told his story to acknowledge his mother in a way that said it all. He ended this recollection on an upbeat note, making an impression that people still remember. That was the true story that my son told all the guests that evening.

*　*　*　*　*

My thoughts traveled back to that time so many years before. This was my role I would take on at a very early age. Rick would climb the corporate ladder that would lead to success beyond his own imagination, but now he wanted to forget his original motivation and purpose. His work would come between his family and he would be rewarded for doing so.

There was more to Mark's story, for he went on to explain how Rick would go out of town the next day. He would leave, while my temperature kept climbing. I knew he felt a financial responsibility for his growing family, but his drive to succeed and the thrill of the challenge kept him entrenched, taking him away too often from his family. Seeing that he was not much help at home, it was just as well that he be where he wanted to be, at work. There would be many times that he would still go to work even if he were ill himself. But being sick with a cold or flue was ordinary, while having a baby is a time that should be celebrated. A shared experience that one cannot recapture if other priorities are allowed to take precedent.

My younger sister, Ginny, was staying with us at this time. It was as if my sweet little baby knew I was not feeling well, as she slept when I did. When I would wake Monica for her feeding or to change her diaper, she seemed to tune into her new surroundings, absorbing all the new sensations. With that she was content and would soon fall back asleep. I would rest when my baby would sleep, she in her bassinet and I in my bed—so aware of her sweet presence. Sometimes her brothers would quietly come into the room to see their sister and check on me. I was thankful to be surrounded by my beautiful family. My sister would be there for my boys. She was sixteen years old at the time. The days and nights were blended together. I slept almost as much as my baby. I felt I was drugged, chilled, shaking, too weak to eat, and could manage only a few sips of water or juice. What was wrong with me? Monica would sleep when I did. Did my little baby know somehow that her mother needed her rest too?

Ginny was concerned because my temperature kept rising. I would be too weak to do anything but hang on to my existence for my children. One evening,

I felt in such a haze as if I were walking in a thick mist. I thought that washing my face in cool water and brushing my teeth would be the cure. I leaned against the cool sink for support, my hand weak and shaky, as I tried to grasp the washcloth to press against my burning face. It took so much effort to squeeze the toothpaste onto my toothbrush. Not feeling well at all, everything was such an effort. I had to get better for my baby, my boys, and my family.

I barely made it to bed. I checked on Monica, who was sleeping. I had to get better. Although my body was shaking with fever, I fell into a fretful sleep that deepened into a heavy serene state. I felt my body rising. I could see my room that I had painted pink and felt that it was sweet that my husband was okay with that. I could see myself sleeping in the bed. I looked so peaceful, as my long dark hair fell around me. This was a unique experience. I could see Monica, quietly sleeping. I was rising higher. I thought of my boys and I started to cry. I remember saying, "I can't leave my baby. I can't leave my sons. No one will love or take care of them as much as I can. My children need their mother." I could see a light through the tunnel, but I did not want to leave my children. I was sobbing, crying out in my delirium.

The next thing I knew, I was back in my body. I was awakened by Ginny, looking worried, telling me that my cries had woken her. She was going to call my doctor, for my fever was so high. Since she did not drive at this time, Dorothy, my next-door neighbor, took me to the hospital. There they gave me a big shot of penicillin, which was the cure. *But* they also gave me penicillin tablets to take home. However, these pills would give me a tremendous rash from the top of my head to the bottom of my feet. The rash, which would last for three weeks, was so dense that I looked like I had a terrific sunburn. I itched like crazy, but at least I was finally on the road to recovery. I would never forget my experience and often wonder what it meant. Now looking back, I know that it changed my life profoundly, as it made me realize even more the importance of a loving and nurturing family. I had not planned on being a wife or a mother, for I did have my talents and abilities of my own that I wanted to pursue and experience. But this experience was an awakening and a revelation also, for I never knew the depth of my feelings would be so strong, giving me a greater meaning to life.

* * * * *

Fast forward now to my precious baby girl's wedding. Here we were, our last child just married, but still lingered unfinished business and unspoken truths that would resurface. Rick would use his business prowess that would empower him. His world of entitlements would stand guard, shielding him from his conscience. He learned those attributes well, never daring to hear or see the consequences of his actions. He would turn a blind eye and a deaf ear to avoid knowing the truths. Without wanting to, it seemed I'd absorbed physically the emotional and mental traumas that he so skillfully acquired. But, I also think that I was an enigma to him for my determination, my need for wanting me to go away, vanish in the mist. I was a reminder to him of his dark side when he went too far. Now he himself wanted to forget. He learned the rules of the corporate game, but he used his family has pawns.

He sat at the table with his private secretary wife and his corporate guests surrounding him, disregarding the original wife. At one time, I was needed, necessary, valued, until he bought into the hype, when he reached the pinnacle of his career. Now he did not have to answer to anyone because his ruthless world of entitlement offered no consequences to his overt actions or accountability. He was of the select few, where his wealth compensated for his lack of humanness or compassion. He would surround himself with people of his kind that were easily impressed and swayed by the allure of big money. It would not matter how he gained it or who was harmed in the process. They could make their designer rules to protect their assets and assure their financial security at the expense of others' trust and vulnerability.

I was so painfully aware that I gave too much of myself in our marriage. Rick took as much and more than he deserved. The big difference was he would be able to dictate the rules and the outcome using his banking expertise, along with his influential connections. Why does the inequity and injustice come back to haunt me, marring what should be a lovely event——even the happiest of times?

The memories intruding into my thoughts in unexpected and unwanted moments, not wanting to let go of the past until acknowledged and understood. A friend once told me that I was too selfless. I didn't quite know what that meant. I knew I cared too much and would do too much. Many times I would go beyond what I had to do. I thought I knew my own strength and endurance, until it took its final toll. I am too patient at times, too forgiving and definitely too trusting. Where is the protection for the innocent? Why is there no accountability or restitution from the transgressor?

CHAPTER 9

PHYSICAL AND EMOTIONAL EXHAUSTION
(PNEUMONIA AND MARIE)

I *LOST FIFTEEN PAGES OF* work. I didn't want to write about it, think about it or relive that experience. I think of Monica's wedding and being so involved in the *guardian ad litem* family that took a critical turn during the same time as the wedding. I was stretched to the max, physically, mentally and emotionally. After the wedding, when I went to bed, I drifted into an exhausted state of sleep. My last thoughts were of my children and how our family was so irreparably broken in such shattered splinters that I could still feel the pain. When I awoke the next morning, my heart felt heaviness and an ache when I breathed. Was my heart broken? I sipped on orange juice and made some hot herbal tea, sipping slowly. It hurt to talk. I felt unusually tired. I laid down on the sofa, and would drift in and out of sleep. Friends would call and when they realized that I could hardly talk, they said they would call later. I could not eat; sleep was my cure, a few sips of tea or juice, more sleep. Surely I would get better.

After a few days of this, Red insisted on taking me to the doctor. When the doctor saw my deteriorated condition, he was concerned. After checking a few vital signs, my doctor said I would have to go to the hospital. I was too weak to protest. The X-rays showed that I was severely dehydrated and had pneumonia. I would be in the hospital for six days. I would have medication and some kind of fluid going in the veins of my arms and wrists. Now when I think of all the needles I cringe. Lots of rest and lots of fluids. They said I had a classic case of pneumonia and could some of the medical students listen to the crackly sound made by my lungs so they could hear what that type of pneumonia sounded like. Even in the hospital I was of some purpose. After six days, I finally went home.

Red picked me up from the hospital. He was sweet and gentle telling me interesting and humorous tidbits of the past week. On the way home, we stopped at the pharmacy to pick up some kind of medicine, which to me seemed quite the ordeal for it made me so weary. For some reason, it seemed I hardly ate at the hospital. The last day, I could finally have a real breakfast, so I ordered pancakes and orange juice. But I never did get to have my breakfast of my dreams as they had to take one last test, right at the time they delivered my pancakes. Surely they would save it for me. But no that was not to happen. I wondered who ate my breakfast. Since breakfast was already over for the day, I hadn't eaten. They ordered me whatever they had left over. I was so disappointed as they gave me two cups of coffee, and I do not even drink coffee, two large glasses of orange juice and apple juice, and two hardboiled eggs. I looked at my breakfast in dismay. I don't like hardboiled eggs either.

That was the story of my life. I hardly ever sit down, except to write. I hardly ever get to eat a warm piece of toast, for the phone rings. Sometimes just the simple pleasures in life are allusive to me. But not that day. Red thought of everything, and since he had a hearty appetite he could tell by looking at me I needed sustenance. Food would be an elixir vitae. He would take me out to lunch at a small cozy restaurant off Hennepin Avenue. We parked across the street and he took hold of my arm protectively. The gentle warmth of the sun welcomed us, and I felt a sense of peace and was grateful for his comforting presence. I remember that day but I can't remember what we ate. For me it was soup, which I didn't finish because it took a while for my appetite to return.

My strength returned faster than expected. It was such a relief. As the days passed and I had not heard from the *guardian ad litem* family, I wanted to believe they were all busy with their progressive activities. I had tried calling them at times, but I knew with all the demands on Marie that would not be unusual. One day I received a call from Susan S. at the *guardian ad litem* office. She would tell me that Marie lost her housing and would be going to the correctional facility for women in Plymouth. I was stunned and so disappointed. I asked her what happened. She said Marie had broken some of the rules, but was vague, giving me very little information. Later I would hear from Joe M., asking me if I could gather some of the girls' clothing, for they were staying with a new foster family in New Hope. He did not know where Marie was staying at the time, so I would have to try and locate her. I thought this was strange.

Since I had been working on this case for a little over a year now, I had acquired a list of people who might help me find her. After several phone calls, I was able to get a phone number. It was someone from her past that had sheltered her before, a very nice black woman with several children of her own. We talked.

She told me that Marie was in a traumatic state, and was very concerned about her daughters. When Marie came to the phone, she sounded shaken and would break out in heart-wrenching sobs. I told her the girls needed clothes, and that I would pick them up to give to her girls. She started sobbing, telling me that everything happened so fast, out of the blue, so unexpected. She was distressed for the girls saw her taken away, crying hysterically. This would be just before their birthdays. Suddenly, I was being jerked back into an element of fear and uncertainty. Was I ready for this?

I told Marie I would call her back after I talked to Joe M. and then I could pick up the clothes and a few other items such as books and toothbrushes and other personal items. When I called him, he told me not to give Marie the address or phone number of the new foster mother. I had enough on my mind just locating Marie and now dropping off clothing for the girls in another unfamiliar area, as long as the girls were safe. I didn't think it was my place to divulge that information anyway.

Then I had to contact the new foster mother. She gave me directions to her house, telling me that the girls had been going to school there temporarily. But they did not have any change of clothing and it was hard washing clothes every night. I could not believe that what had transpired was so drastic that the children were torn from their mother without any form of sensitivity or dignity. Just taken away with the clothes on their backs. She then said that she had never experienced a situation cloaked in such an undercurrent of intrigue. Why was I not surprised?

The next day I saw Marie. I wanted to see for myself what her face and her eyes would convey. I had my cell phone with me and as I finally located the street, I called to tell her I was almost there. She tearfully greeted me at the door. She told me that she felt humiliated and degraded not only for herself but also for her daughters. Seeing their mother so harshly taken in the police car. She pleaded to gather up some clothes for herself and her children, but that was not to happen. At one point when she talked to Joe M. he told her she could just put the clothes in those big plastic trash bags.

She was insulted by his rude attitude, and knew her daughters deserved more dignity than that. She told me about the stray dog the girls had befriended and would occasionally let in the apartment. She told me about needing more coins for the launderette. It was a hot day. She and the girls walking back to the apartment and the girls wanting to stay home at that point. She relented and ran back to put the coins in and returned, probably less than ten minutes. One of the staff saw her running down the street without the girls and immediately called the authorities. The girls were nine and ten, almost ten and eleven. This, apparently, was the transgression that prompted the heartache and indignity they would endure.

Before I left she asked me if I would give her girls a small note and to be sure to tell them she was okay, that she loved and missed them. She knew I would have to read the note. Another invasion of privacy and rights denied. I felt awkward and angry that I had to be part of this. We embraced in compassion for that moment. I would go home and have to set up an appointment with the new foster mother.

I called the new foster mother. She sounded concerned for the girls and was pleasant. I asked her since it was around the girls' birthdays would it be okay if I baked a birthday cake and brought it with a few small gifts. She thought that would lift the girls' spirits. I would make my devil's food cake with two layers using white fluffy frosting and adding colorful birthday candles. I did not want the girls' birthdays to go unnoticed.

I managed to find the house relatively easily, which is not always the case. The houses had nice big yards with newly established lawns, shrubbery, and trees. My car was laden with clothes and books and book bags, birthday cake and the few gifts. The foster mother greeted me at the door and helped me with the suitcases filled with the girls' clothes. I did not know what to expect when I saw the girls for it seemed so long. Yet it was only a matter of weeks. The last time was when my friend Gary and I brought all the furnishings to their apartment and then the unexpected blackout. Then I had my daughter's wedding and becoming so ill afterwards. How could life take such a traumatic turn in such a short period of time? We all need that loving support and occasional time out. When life becomes overwhelming and constant and needs and even our basic needs are not attended or met, it takes a toll. The consequences will surface. Unfortunately, we are not always aware of these warnings or listen to our body or our instincts.

The girls and I would end up taking a walk in the neighborhood for there was a pretty lake up the street and to the right. There were a couple of twists and turns but we found it, with a small beach and a park for children looking very inviting, especially on this very hot day. Andrea asked if she could put her feet in the water. Since it was so hot, it was nice to see a playfulness emerge through all the seriousness. Tiffanie would break out in tears, missing her mom. That was unusual for Tiffanie was usually the one who would comfort her little sister. As we watched Andrea wading in the shallow waters, I wished that Tiffanie could seize the moment and be a child again, to forget even for a few moments the heavy burdens that rested on her young shoulders. For Tiffanie, the experience was still too raw. She could not forget. I tried to comfort her with encouraging words and reassurance not to give up hope.

Andrea would kick her feet, sometimes reaching down with her arms, gently spraying the water around her. Finally knowing that her big sister's sorrow was too great to be distracted, she emerged from her reverie to comfort her sister. We sat at a bench and talked for a while. I did not want to stay so late that the foster mom would begin to worry. I felt every minute, every second, was to be savored. We walked back to the house. The girls told me about the dog they had brought into the house, to play, pretending it was their dog. An ordinary life. They told me of their mother running to put the coins in the launderette, leaving the girls for such a short while. How the police came and took their mother away, crying and protesting, wanting to be heard, but the ears were deaf.

I still hadn't heard anything that would provoke such extreme reaction that Marie would now be going back to confinement. I was starting to see a pattern and I felt a chill even though the sun's rays were beating strong on our backs. Surely, they did not want Marie and her daughters to fall through the cracks. I hadn't seen or experienced any indication of real help or support or compassion from these people that were to be the lifeline for families such as this.

The girls told me about the lack of privacy in the apartment. Sometimes in the middle of the night security or staff would come with a flashlight going through each room and closets, checking for who knows what. They would waken from their sleep. It would be very disturbing. I was shocked. But then Andrea said, "One time, they even walked in while our mother was changing her clothes." Her young disbelief was evident, and I felt an outrage for this family and saddened by the futility of it all. Where do I begin to try and make a difference and where does one turn to for refuge when all the resources have failed?

We walked back to their new temporary foster mother's house. The girls seemed to be feeling better having some of their own personal possessions with them. I gave the girls their gifts and left the heart-shaped cake for the girls and the foster family to share after their dinner. Before I left the foster mother said she had never had an experience that was filled with such secrecy. The girls could not call or receive calls from their mother and the mother wound not be able to get in touch with her daughters. She did not question but it was a bit disconcerting.

I would return to my almost perfect place with thoughts of Marie and her precious daughters. I knew I would have to call the *ad litem* office with my inquiries that they might not be so willing to give or acknowledge. The people I talked to were not helpful but evasive and resented my questions. Marie had a few days of reprieve before going to the correctional facility in Plymouth. She would be there for four months, October to January. She missed both her daughters' birthdays and all the holidays. She would not be allowed to go outside even when the days were beautiful. It was all so harsh. I had decided that I would not continue as a *guardian ad litem*. I would try and mentor this family if wanted, for that is what Judge Leung had suggested.

I still had some loose ends to take care of. Later I learned that all my questions were being brought to the attention of too many people and they did not like it. I would receive a letter from the programs office suggesting I resign. It was obvious this was not working out for them or for me. My expectations were too high. That was true. For some reason I was almost relieved instead of offended, although I could not just turn my back on this family. One day I received a call from the foster mother, Charlene. She was like a grandma to Tiffanie and Andrea. She said she had heard that the girls might be adopted out and maybe even separated. She was distressed for she had grown to love those girls. She told me she was willing to be their permanent foster parent, for she did not want the girls to be separated. She also realized that the girls' mother was important to them, and she would keep the girls until Marie was able to give them proper care and stability.

That would be a step toward progress.

The girls would be given a new *guardian ad litem*—a "professional"—who was quick to tell me that she had been a guardian for over seventy children and now she was working on seven cases—alone. I looked at her. She was a large foreboding presence. Her black hair was pulled tightly in a knot accentuating her widow's peak. She had streaks of white hair pulled severely at her temples. Her face was pale with heavy black eyebrows and lips that were thick with bright red lipstick. Oooh, I hoped there was still some compassion and sensitivity hidden beneath all the hard layers of experience. She told me it would not be necessary for me to attend the next court hearing for the girls. I told her I would consider it.

I would learn that the girls not only had a new *guardian ad litem* working for them, they would also be given a new attorney and a new judge. Unbelievable. Their files were already so convoluted and complex because of all the erroneous and distorted facts, that more often than not was embellished and exaggerated, either purposely or because of sheer carelessness or some other reason that would not be questioned. I had talked to Marie and told her I could be there for support. She said now that Tiffanie was twelve she could be in the courtroom and that bothered her. She seemed drained emotionally, just accepting their fate.

I did go to the hearing. I felt it was important as I would be the only one who really knew or cared about Marie and her daughters. I knew the love that never wavered between the girls and their mother. To me that was significant. As we were walking down the long hallway, the new *guardian ad litem* walked up to me, brushed against my arm to make sure I had her attention and told me to "get a life." I was shocked at her blatant rudeness. For what reason I will never know. But I can suspect. She was not worth my energy.

I was surprised to find that Andrea would be in the courtroom also, especially because of her young age. They decided to make an exception in this case. There would be Marie and her daughters surrounding her. The *guardian ad litem* and new attorneys assigned to the case and a new judge. I could feel the energy in the room that was unnerving. The appropriate people were introduced. I told the judge that I was the former guardian, but now I was their mentor. The new guardian uttered some comment under her breath. I ignored her.

When the proceedings began, the new guardian held nothing back, painting the worst possible picture of Marie in front of her children. It certainly did not sound like the Marie I knew. Marie looked so defenseless and broken, while her daughters listened in confused disbelief. This was their mother. Who was to protect her? I could feel my heart beating and an anger that I could not contain any longer that I stood up to protest the mockery of this so-called hearing. I could see Marie's look of surprise on her face and a hint of gratitude. I had caused a bit of an uproar at this point. I walked out of the courtroom. My head held high. My heart was pounding, and my body was shaking. Was it from anger or fear? It didn't matter. I just wanted to be far away from the horrendous scene. That brought back too many memories.

I was both disheartened and relieved to be free of the heavy burden that was presented to me at every turn taken. I needed some time to regroup and process these last few months. The first thing would be to respond to the letter I had received regarding my resignation. I felt that for now I would wait until I heard from the foster mother or Marie before getting further involved, for maybe my letter would be a helpful influence in the outcome for this family and the family court system also.

October 29, 2000

Attention: Susan S. and Lynn B.

I am writing this letter in response to your letter dated October 27, 2000. I am really surprised that you could decide my termination with the McGill family without even calling to hear my side. This is what I have experienced throughout this case, inaccurate information, speculations, evasiveness, exaggeration and avoidance. I thought our role was to help families, not make their lives more difficult and painful, to keep them forever in an emotional debt that lingers and holds back their progress.

I NEVER gave Marie Miller the telephone number, address, or anything regarding the shelter family's whereabouts. INCREDIBLE THAT Joe M. CAN OPENLY LIES ABOUT THIS—and that YOU can so readily accept his words without further investigation really surprises me.

I have worked hard on this case. I could see this family torn apart, subjected to incredible mental and emotional abuse, made by the system. Unbelievable scrutiny that would make anyone feel degraded. You never gave me the opportunity to speak out or to hear my or the Miller family's experience.

If there were an inkling that this family should be separated and punished further—torn apart—if it would have been the best interest for the children, believe me, I would have stated that.

But I got to know the girls, their love for their mother. They are incredible bright loving sisters, young girls growing up trying to understand their experiences. Through it all, they have a deep love for their mother. They see her strength, her determination, know her love, but they also have seen what she has been subjected to, through the bureaucratic system that are supposed to help, not hurt.

I also came to know the mother Marie Miller. I was very skeptical at first, after all she was in prison. It was very scary for me to go there for the first time. But things got worse. The transition home was very frightening in itself, where the children would go visit, see their mother in this hardened environment.

Marie came out despite and under incredible odds and bizarre setbacks and has still managed to continue going to school, determined to do well for her children. I have talked to her probation officer, who vacillated from being open to also being insinuating. Two different sides. But yet not telling me even though I was the guardian for these children. I have to know both sides: the good, the bad, the here and not just the past. Otherwise, it is playing games with other people's lives.

I was not impressed with Marie's first social worker. She seemed terribly burned out. She was difficult to talk to or to reach. Mary B was helpful and concerned, but Marie was then given Joe M. He is very argumentative, on the defensive and he has a history which either you are not aware of or choose to ignore. He saw Marie's strength and intelligence but was determined to squelch her. I have no idea why. I do know that people like having a sense of power over others and are many times threatened by others' intelligence or success. I want to see people overcome obstacles, not punish them forever.

We have to work together. It is not about numbers, but lives that can be productive and children can be children.

Call me,
Patti Zona

Well, I wrote that letter in the heat of the moment, while emotions were still strong and the experience still freshly engrained. Maybe that would be my last meager attempt to convey this message to the people and for the people, for we are all the same. Our dignity, rights and freedom to be heard not ignored or oppressed, to be given that opportunity and encouragement to succeed in order to do and be the best that we can be. Then we can be valued and appreciated for not only our own self-worth but be a contributing influence for our children and society itself. Everyone has the ability. It is only a matter of the contributing factor and what is prized and rewarded. Do we honor those with ill-gotten money, power and position that impressed but wreaked havoc in the process and compromised the mind, body and soul or the future of our children? I hope we can do and be better than that. I hope our children have more wisdom and compassion in the process that inspires true greatness.

I would occasionally hear from Marie and the girls. The girls were growing up fast in the city. That would be the concern of Charlene, the foster mother, but also a major concern for Marie who was also still vulnerable, for the pull of the past would tug hard and fast. The temptations to go back seemed easier to embrace than the long road ahead with glimpses of something brighter, but still somewhat obscure. I wanted Marie and the girls to hold onto their hopes and dreams, not give up. I wanted them to show the world of their courage, their plight, and fight for dignity and respect—finally gained, conquering their past.

The following two years, I periodically heard from this family and it was hopeful and encouraging. We would play telephone tag as all our lives overfilled the brim. I returned Marie's call one day. She sounded bright and cheery, saying, "Patti, I was just talking about you to my counselor." She giggled. She sounded so happy, telling me about how proud I would be of her daughters. I told her to call me back or I would call her. But we had to definitely connect. And we did. That was early summer.

That evening she called sounding so happy. She said she told her counselor all about me and how I had helped her. She then said, "Patti, I could not have gotten through this without you. You encouraged and believed in me. You were the only one." I told her that I was only the catalyst, that she had the will and determination herself. The credit was hers. Then she laughed and said, "hat is exactly what my counselor told me." I told her to believe that and that I was so proud of her.

We would connect via telephone, but finally get everyone together toward the end of August. We made our plans. Maybe we would walk around Lake

Calhoun, have lunch at m house—the Ivory Tower—and just talk, catch up on everything. She then told me again how proud she was of her daughters and she couldn't wait for met o see all the changes. Then she giggled in a shy way that would occasionally surface and said, "Patti, I have changed too." I listened and said something profound like, "Change is good." She then laughed and said, "I put on some weight. I've gained thirty pounds." The doctor said, and then she giggled some more, "that it's my menopause." I then told Marie, "I bet you look great now. You were way too skinny," which brought out a laugh in both of us.

Finally, after way too long, Marie and the girls arrived at my place. The girls had grown tall, much taller than my five-foot-three-quarter inches. Marie looked great with the added weight that happened to fall in the right places giving her a healthy appearance, looking pretty for her age. The girls seemed shy, but not for long. For as soon as we all hugged and chatted, the ice broke. The girls looked out the windows at the lakes, oohing and aahing. We looked at the big bulletin board filled with pictures of all that is near and dear, with Marie and the girls in their prominent spot.

The girls were doing well in school. Tiffanie would be taking her driver's training for she would be sixteen soon. We eventually settled in the living room. Andrea looking pretty and poised gravitated toward the black lacquer baby grand piano. She sat down at the bench. Her mom said, "Patti, you should hear Andrea sing. She's got a beautiful voice." I was so pleased to hear that for music is such a gift, bringing healing and joy. Tiffanie sighed as she sat down on the leopard chair of deep bronze and black striping. That chair suited her today. Marie and I sat on the royal blue small sofa. The back gently curved. I always liked the gold piping that softly accented the richness of the royal blue. From this location we could look out onto the balcony filled with colorful flowers overlooking Lake Calhoun. It was a flurry of activity outside with the joggers and walkers taking advantage of this beautiful day along with the small sailboats sailing in the gentle breeze.

I knew this was a moment in time that could not be recaptured. Tiffanie wistfully exclaimed, "I want to be rich. I can't wait to be rich. I hope I can make lots of money quickly." I softly spoke, "Tiffanie, money cannot buy your happiness. And if anyone has made a lot of money too quickly, one has to be suspect of how that money was gained." Then I told her and Andrea that they were fortunate in that they were so young and had the whole world ahead of them. I couldn't stop there, so here I go again. Children always open the door to wonderful opportunities for discussions of myriad of topics. We just have to be aware and available to seize the moment before it disappears.

I told the girls the importance of learning that we never stop learning. The importance of education that opens the doors to all kinds of possibilities and opportunities. I told them about the love of books and the importance of having good hobbies and interests, for many times they can be incorporated in your career and would always enhance their lives. I told them again as I had told them times before the importance of surrounding yourself with good people and the importance of living a healthy life in mind, body and spirit. For your body is a gift. They listened closely.

As we sat, Marie looked at me intently and said in such earnestness, "Patti, what was it you saw in me that made you believe in me? You were the only one that ever believed in me, the only one that treated me with respect and dignity." The girls sat quietly, listening. Marie was so serious that I almost felt overwhelmed by this request. How could I explain but what I saw and what I felt? So I told her the first time I talked to her and heard her deep concern for her daughters. I could also detect the vulnerability and need to trust from her voice. But it wasn't until I brought the girls to visit her when she was in Shakopee and saw from a distance the love of her children for their mother, how they clung to her, stroking her hair, her arms. I told her how she lovingly comforted her daughters. I'll never forget those pleading eyes as I approached for the time was near. I could not help but believe in her.

She was in deep thought. Probably thinking back to that other time and place. I then asked the girls what their goals were. Andrea brightened and said she wanted to have her own beauty salon. Tiffanie was quiet. I told them the importance of having a goal in mind, for without a goal or goals, there is no direction in life and you are floundering here and there. Suddenly, Marie spoke up, telling her daughters, "Listen to her, Tiffanie and Andrea. That is what happened to me. That was what happened to me." Then she slid to the floor in her revelation, which was quietly dramatic and then she continued. "That was my problem. I never had any goals. I was smart enough. I always got good grades but I didn't have any direction in life, and when my mother and father died and then my dear brother, I just foundered. I would just go along with the crowd, doing whatever they did. I didn't think for myself or give any thought for what I wanted to do with my life. That is what got me in so much trouble. I didn't have any goals."

After that, we all had a lot to think about. I was proud of Marie and the girls. My heart was overflowing with gratitude for this time we shared. I then asked Tiffanie if she was still writing for that was one of her passions, reading and writing. She quietly said she was. I told her how one night I could not sleep and I had these thoughts and words in my head that had to be expressed. So I got up in the middle of the night and started writing feverishly. I was surprised what I wrote and thought I might as well use this in my book somehow, somewhere, someday. I told her I was so inspired that I wrote until the sun came up. I could tell her creative mind was attentive.

Since that day was so beautiful, we decided to walk on the trail to the new restaurant called Punch and then to the bookstore. We ate outside under the canopy of large colorful umbrellas. We ate pizza, chatting away and savoring the moment more than the pizza. After our lunch, we walked a few doors down to Barnes and Noble bookstore. Our spirits were high as the girls picked out their prized books with such joy and care, their mother beaming at her young girls. Marie's gratitude was overflowing at these simple gifts, while I felt so thankful to be part of this important passage in both our lives. Again as they left for home bearing their gifts of books, hopefully keeping the magic of this day alive in their thoughts and hearts that will help to fulfill their hopes and dreams.

CHAPTER 10

THE DANCE OF LIFE

Time passes, sometimes smooth and tranquil
Almost like a graceful dance.
Even the intricate steps add to the drama and excitement,
But always well-prepared and planned.
No errors or slip-ups,
For what is at stake is too precious,
Too valuable to risk a fall.
A fall hurts or breaks or the worst—
A fall to disgrace.
Eventually, one grows weary with the dance,
Forgetting to rest the body, the mind.
Too much that it hurts,
What we once loved becoming our torment,
Causing cracks and flaws.
We stumble and fall,
But the love the dance still persists
And pulls at us to regain our rhythm,
Moving in unison once again.
We feel invincible, riding high on the success
And luxuriating in the revelry of our gifts.
We can't stop the music.
We are taught to dance,
Not enough time,
No intrusions blocking everything and everyone out
For we are in the spotlight.
Alone.
Numb from excess.
Will we ever get this right?

There would be a flurry of activity, preparations, invitations, and expectations as the holidays approached. This year, 2005, seemed even more pronounced. I would notice it, especially in my circle of friends that had a loss, divorce, a death, or some kind of trauma in their lives. It did not matter that it might have been years, way too long. For the feelings would relentlessly resurface. There would be no escape. Some would try and immerse themselves in work, or drink more than ever, to drown the memories of the past. There would be constant activity, looking forward to the next party, the invitation. Doing, and being everywhere and anywhere, with anyone-just not to be alone. It seemed the majority of people were living in uncertainty or fear, but not really addressing the causes or issues, just keeping their blinders on, not wanting to know or see.

I have heard that every seven years we change physically, mentally, emotionally, and spiritually. It just naturally happens the cause and effects of our experiences that shape and affect us. I have heard that we also come full circle and this is supposed to be a significant factor. Is it more significant when the full circle occurs before and after the New Year?

I am curious about those full circles. Is there one big circle, or do some people have several smaller circles intertwining with the large circle? Is the one large circle representing a more placid life, while do several circles mark a series of meaningful events, that have had a major impact on their lives? And does the large circle mean that one is already smart enough, wise enough, or can only take so much?

It seems I have been through so much ever since I can remember, even as a small child, observing, watching, taking everything in. To myself I always questioned certain actions, but not being bold or big enough or brave enough. I was just too young and now through all these years, and all these circles, I am still not big enough, but I've seen enough, experienced enough, that I don't want to take it anymore. Maybe this is my lesson and my purpose to share my journey and insights and not keep my lessons I've learned to myself. I'm tired of all those circles. How many adventures can I take? How many lessons until I really learn?

Toward the end of summer 2005, I learned several significant matters that astounded me and would culminate to a certain degree in 2006. Some just completed the circle or maybe not quite. I always have hope. Because of my divorce, the way it was done and all the years of frivolous appeals that my ex-husband was so boldly allowed would affect me in ways never imagined or expected. In the divorce decree, I could never remarry or I would lose my alimony/maintenance, after all the appeals. Rick eroded all my financial security, leaving me dependent on my maintenance. If I were to work or if I inherited any kind of money it would be deducted from my maintenance leaving me at status quo.

One of the most surprising twists was how unresponsive and complaisant people of position were, and how they disregarded dishonesty or criminality—especially if it were of their own. My first experience outside of my divorce happened when I sold my house in Edina. The agent, also my next-door neighbor on Edgebrook, talked me into selling my house. She brought in a husband and wife who were both attorneys. At this time, I was divorced. Rick was heavy in doing the appeals and would also reinforce his misdirected rage at me in the form of annulling our twenty-eight-year marriage. That was the ultimate assault and insult that he could ever do to me. I never thought he would actually do it, that he was just on a mission of testing his limitations—seeing how much he could get away with and for how long.

I was in stunned disbelief and intensely heartsick. He was the father of our children. Why didn't he tell me this years ago or before we even married? But I knew this was the way he could really hurt me and absolve his own guilt. If the church could grant him an annulment, that would mean he was justified. His sins were absolved. Isn't that the way some minds work? It was during this time that I would begin my writing, trying to comprehend the absurdity of the fragile and the super-inflated ego. I also needed to validate my own existence. Could this mean the past could be erased, obliterated at the sign of a pen, so innocuous, presumed, if the price is high enough?

All I could think of was getting away from here, away from Rick, away from Minnesota where it all began. There was a mass of questions that would never be answered, but ignored as if unimportant. I would put my house on the market. I never knew that my next-door neighbor had been fired from a large real estate company for creating havoc too many times. Because there was and is a clause that cannot be disclosed, I learned the defamation factor that would protect her and allow her to continue working in another company, faults and wrongdoings never disclosed. She was my neighbor and would bring a couple that also lived in Country Club. They were professional, both attorneys. I had no reason to doubt or question their interest at the time. They belonged to the Edina Country Club. They had two young children about the same age as my next-door neighbor's children.

They were eager to buy my house and I felt it was now time for me to put all this behind me and start anew. I was numb emotionally from the trauma of the divorce and now the annulment. I felt I was hanging onto my existence by a thread. So isolated, no one to turn to that understood the full impact and ramification of these actions. Who could ever understand the pain and humiliation of being divorced, appealed, and annulled, when there is the power of silence that protects the intent, never addressing honestly or honorably. They say when in mourning or recovery, from any kind of major trauma or event, one should take time to grieve, process, and heal before making any important and meaningful decision. It seemed as if, I was surrounded by opportunists, eagerly lying in wait all for the prized pickings.

While visiting a tennis friend in Las Vegas, my next-door neighbor and real estate agent called to tell me I had a buyer for my house. They lived in the neighborhood and that I even knew them or they knew me. I remembered seeing the woman at the pool a few times. She was very thin, almost too thin. I sensed the presentation for her was very important. She was sugary sweet, but was the sincerity real? There was also a couple from California that was interested in my house, which eased my mind when I left for my trip. So I was surprised when she informed me of this new development. I questioned her about this and she gave me a quick answer, which left me rather vague, but her enthusiasm overrode any further dialogue. Nothing was set in stone at this point anyway and nothing could be done until I returned.

This was my first trip by myself. I would be visiting B. J. Richards, a tennis friend I had met when I was helping with score keeping for the thirty-five and over national tournament. I also would occasionally house a player or two if needed. Actually, I could have played in these tournaments myself, but I was still recuperating from an overuse injury that I had acquired during my long virus. So when I was invited to help with scorekeeping, I thought it would be interesting and fun meeting players from all over the states.

To do scorekeeping, it is important to know the game, have a calming presence, and have good concentration. I guess I had all those qualities for I was asked if I would like to be trained to score the big tournaments out of state also. I was pleasantly surprised at this invitation. I wished my life at that time was not so tumultuous, but more settled. I liked to have important things in order, complete, before moving on to other areas. My first match that I had was B. J. Richards from Las Vegas and her doubles tennis partner Shelby Torrance from Texas. They made a striking team, with lots of flair, and personality. I am sure they were one of the favorites. Shelby was tall, probably six-feet tall or close to it, with short reddish hair, which had a will of its own, not to be contained or adorned. She definitely looked like she was from Texas. Her manner and speech were warm and friendly, with a playful manner. She was practically invincible at the net and with her long legs and long arms could reach the most impossible shots.

Now BJ had a striking style of her own. BJ would walk on the court, her hair perfectly done "afro" style, looking regal and confident. She was very fit. She loved clothes and enjoyed the attention she could draw, but was never affected. We became friends, for we both had a natural interest in philosophy and the spiritual side of life. She moved like a dancer, very flamboyant. She would leap for her shots with such grace and agility that inspired and definitely entertained everyone. I cannot remember the other team, but I'm pretty sure BJ and Shelby won.

After one of the matches, BJ asked if I would like to meet some of the other players and friends and get a bite to eat. For the first time in several years, I felt that my life was going to take a positive change. I felt a connection and a friendship walking down the halls. The tennis players would acknowledge BJ, even myself. As we were approaching a group of players, BJ tells me, "Patti, I want you to meet Vicki. She's very interesting. She's a psychic and can read auras." Wow, this indeed was a most unique experience. The closer we approached, I'm studying the faces of the group of women coming toward us, trying to decide who this unique person was. BJ introduced me, but meanwhile this woman, with brown curly hair slightly past her shoulders and a big smile, was looking at me as if studying me, around me. Then she says, "You have the most beautiful aura." Oooh, I didn't know what to say. I wanted to ask her what the colors were. What did it mean?

BJ and Shelby would be some of the first tennis players to stay at my house. After their long matches, they would come back to the house. The house would come alive with stories of their matches. They would unwind. Shelby would read the paper at the kitchen table, as I would be preparing a meal. If there were something particularly catching, she would read aloud to us with her Texan accent. I loved that memory. Since I lived on Mill Pond at that time, BJ would get a magazine or book and sit on the swing that overlooked the pond. For her it was a real treat for she lived on the desert in Las Vegas. Sometimes she would walk or sprint around the neighborhood. She loved music and so do I. She would listen to my CDs. This was around 1994 and remarked at my collection of music and could she make copies for herself. She would be in the den for hours, taping away. We all felt comfortable just being ourselves. We would sing, we would dance, we would read, and be read to. Life can still be good amidst pain.

The love of the game, the game of tennis, is pretty amazing. You do forget your aches and pains as you play. I sent my beloved mother- and father-in-law an article on how important keeping active was even for senior citizens. Even if you take up tennis at an older age, the concentration of what you are doing, moving to the ball, gripping the racquet, learning a new skill, keeps your mind and body active, and for some reason energized and ready for that next lesson and eventually match play. It is important to start gradually, build your skills, and enjoy the process. It helps keeping your body, your legs, hands, and shoulders in movement even if it is ever so slightly.

We would not get the change to have that enlightening discourse with Vicki for there was not time or the place. For me it is a message and the sincerity of the context—what I want to hold onto, will it be beneficial or adverse? Years later, after I moved to Lake Point, my friend Deb asked me if I would like to attend a meeting where this woman could see angels. Of course I would never miss such an opportunity. I was coming down with another dreaded cold, which always goes to my throat. I kept drinking my hot water, lemon, and honey and I pretended to get better. We went. We had our discussions about my wonderful angels. Then she asked us to quiet our thoughts and open our hearts. There was probably a dozen or so of us. She would stop in front of each person and tell them if there was an angel or angels. When she came to me, she stopped and I could feel my throat. I did not want to breathe for I didn't want her to get sick. She told me I had several angels surrounding me and I knew that.

At any rate, this is how I came to be in Las Vegas, visiting BJ. Now I was on the flight back to Minneapolis and my house in Edina that I was to sell. I had never sold a house all by myself before. Rick was always the pontificator of transactions such as this. Sure, I knew how to prepare the house, make sure everything was in working order. I knew taxes had to be paid and on time too. Everything was taken care of on my end. We had never had any complications before and I didn't expect anything different—selling a house always seemed pretty straightforward. A person either loved a house or didn't and could afford that house or couldn't.

I would no sooner get home when my neighbor and agent called to ask me if this attorney couple could show their young children the home. They were eager to get their reaction. I reluctantly said okay, but whatever I felt on the flight was obviously not getting any better. We set a time for late afternoon, after her children came home from school. It was toward the end of the school year. I unpacked and went to do some errands. I ran into a tennis friend and she asked me about my trip. I told her it was great, but now I felt I was coming down with something. She told me there was a bad strain of flu going around, but if I bought some Theraflu that would really help. I told her I didn't react well to most medicines. She said maybe try the Theraflu for daytime instead of the nighttime, which would have been stronger. The way I was feeling with each passing minute, I decided it was worth a try.

I had taken the dosage of the daytime, and was starting to feel the medicinal effects, a little foggy or was that the effect of a fever starting to simmer? When the family came, I pretty much let them go through the house. The kids were excited. I don't think they stayed long, just enough to renew their interest or not. The way I was feeling, I didn't care one way or the other. After they left, I laid down chilled and feverish. Later that evening the husband called and asked if it would be okay if he stopped by for me to look at some documents. I told him that I really was not feeling well. He was persistent and said he would not stay long, just drop off the papers.

Mr. Attorney must have come over between eight and nine that evening. He was very charming, telling me that his wife loved the house, that it was perfect for them and their children. Then he started spouting off dates and figures, which was meaningless to me. I came out of my fog temporarily when he stated he would like to rent my house for two years, with the money going toward the sale of the house. Even in my foggy state that didn't sound right. That is not what I ever would consider. He was still trying to get me to reconsider when the phone rang. It was my oldest son Mark. I told him that this neighbor wanted to buy the house, that I wasn't feeling well. He told me, "Mom, throw the man out. No one does business at eleven o'clock at night."

After the encouraging pep talk from Mark, I walked back in the living room and told Mr. Attorney that I could not make any decision at that time. He asked me why. I told him the figures didn't seem right and I never wanted to rent my house for two years. I would have considered a year, but his contract-that he had written himself-had too many troubling questions. I would have to think about it, but at this time I had to say no.

Well, Mr. Attorney was persistent. "What about the numbers?" I didn't want to tell him that either he was not very bright or he was not being honest. I could not believe that he was not embarrassed for himself. He was an attorney. Aren't they supposed to be rather bright, upstanding, and have scruples? At least, once upon a time, they did.

With that encounter, it was amazing that I could sleep. But the combination of my warm fever and the daytime Theraflu induced me into a heavy lethargy, making me both asleep and awake. I was sick for several days and being by myself I just drank hot water, honey, and lemon and geared myself up to eat a cracker. That was enough. Through this weird illness, Mr. Attorney kept calling. I would tell him I was too sick to talk. I had to be my own secretary and receptionist, even in my illness.

One day, mid-morning, the phone rang. It was Mrs. Attorney. She told me that she had heard that I was really sick. She sounded concerned, actually overly-concerned. I told her I would get better. Then she dramatically exclaimed how awful it must be to be alone and sick. Well it was. But I felt so miserable that I didn't think much about it. In fact, I probably was used to it. Rick was hardly ever home with work and his travels. But hearing her say it, I was starting to feel somewhat saddened and dejected. I have to admit, with good reason.

The amazing thing was she kept talking even though I was sick. The other amazing thing was that I listened! I waited for her to mention the house, but she never did. To me that was a good sign. Maybe she truly was concerned. Before we ended the conversation, she told me that she would like to bring over some soup, juice, a few groceries to have in the house. I told her it wasn't necessary. She insisted. What a nice gesture. I was surprised at this unexpected turn of events. Had I misjudged?

Well, Mrs. Attorney came to the door, arms laden with grocery bags. I invited her in, but did not expect her to stay. I did not want her to get sick, but she had no fear. She proceeded to empty the bag of groceries, almost everything I liked. She brought Jell-O and orange juice. She had stopped at the Convention Grill and picked up some of their famous chicken soup, with carrots, and big chunks of chicken, and big noodles. I didn't know if I could really eat quite yet.

She then proceeded to set two places at my small table in the kitchen. I had a galley kitchen, but it was really quite pretty. I had new appliances put in, new white tiled floor, with pretty blue and off-white backsplash behind the stove, and kitchen sink. The kitchen was bright and airy, with nice windows over the sink, and the small table in the eating area. I had made some sheer white curtains, which framed the sides, with valances that adorned the top in graceful elegance. I had carefully chosen a beautiful soft blue and various shades of the softest pinks and lilac, with touches of green on a background of creamy white, for my wallpaper. It looked like a Monet painting, a painting done with pointillism. I loved the effect, making my galley kitchen a work of art.

In the eating area, I had a border of flowers on the top of the walls, which coordinated with the Monet motif. I even did my large pantry, but it was with trellises of the same floral design. Believe me, I know it sounds odd for a kitchen, but it was beautifully subtle.

I am sure Mrs. Attorney just wanted to have the experience of eating in this unique space. She brought companionship and nourishment. As Mrs. Attorney sat down, I hoped I could eat. I took small tastes of the soup. I was surprised that I could eat, that I was actually hungry. Was I getting better or did I just need a caring friend? I thanked my new friend for her concern. We continued to talk, but I was getting weary. I rose from the table and told her I felt stronger. That was probably just what I needed. I proceeded to clear the table.

Oddly enough, Mrs. Attorney lingered. It seemed she was in no hurry to leave. She still did not mention the house. I thought she just accepted my decision and she was fine with it. We walked from the kitchen into the inviting large foyer. It really wasn't that large but occasionally if I had a party with music, a couple or two might mosey over to the foyer and have the dance floor. I had been known to do that myself.

As we were standing in the foyer, I mentioned that I was getting rather tired and that I was sure she had things to do. I also knew that she had two young children who would be coming home soon. She asked if she could look at the views from the windows in the living room.

The spacious living room was impressive, with a black marble fireplace, and a large oval sofa, with oriental key design fabric, in a shade of blue on a light beige background. A beautiful round oriental glass table was placed in front of the inviting sofa. At the end of the room, there were curved steps leading up to the bedrooms. To the right of the stairs large corner windows overlooked the Mill Pond. In front of the large windows, stood my black lacquer baby grand piano that Rick had bought me for Christmas. On one side of the piano and off to the side of the fireplace was my Queen Anne chair with pretty red poppy fabric. My eyes wandered to my chaise lounge, where everyone would be drawn. Memories flooded my senses as I looked at my chaise lounge. I wished to be alone, to be still, quiet, and rest on the worn chaise lounge.

We would sit. I thought this would be brief. But that was not to be. Mrs. Attorney looked at me and said, "Patti, what is it about the offer that you don't like?" She had been so kind that I didn't quite know how to tell her that

I questioned her husband's ethics. I told her I did not want to rent my house for two years. I felt it was risky, too many variables. She understood. I also told her the money did not add up to cover my expenses. She said, "Wait a minute. Let me call my husband. I want you to have what you need and I won't accept anything less." I told her that it was getting late and that her kids would be coming home soon. She insisted on calling her husband right then and there.

I think I was more concerned about her children coming home to an empty house than she was. She made the call to her husband. Mrs. Attorney was telling her husband in no uncertain terms that he was to be fair. In fact, more than fair. Then she proceeded to change the numbers on the papers her husband wrote up himself days before. When she finally hung up, she seemed irritated with her husband. She told me the changes were made and that all I had to do was to initial where she made the changes. Gosh, I wished someone were here to help me. Where was Mrs. Agent? Shouldn't she be in on this transaction? I did put my initials in the proper places. I felt drained.

As I saw a school bus go by, I told her, "Shouldn't you be home with your children now?" She left, I'm sure, quite pleased with herself.

I immediately called my neighbor, Mrs. Agent. She was not home. I left her a message telling her what had transpired and I said, "Tara, where have you been? Mrs. Attorney just left and I signed these papers. I think you should look at them." I then called Rich Passault, also my neighbor and a friend who did my taxes. He said he was going out of town, but that he would stop over and look at the papers.

Thank God. I was suddenly very alert. Rich came over, looked at my papers and shook his head. "Patti," he said. "This is a great thing for Eichorn-Hicks but terrible for you. They will make a hundred thousand off you and you will lose a hundred thousand." I was physically getting better, but now this was worse. I felt sickened. Rich told me to call an attorney, and that the papers probably were not legal anyway.

When Rich left my house to leave for his trip, I immediately called an attorney, whom I had met and he directed me to a real estate attorney. It was a coincidence, because the last name was familiar. It turned out his father was one of my art instructors at the college I was attending in South Bend, Harold Zissla. What a small world. I met with Paul Zissla. He looked at the papers and assured me that it would not be a problem for several reasons that were obvious. I also knew that there is a grace period, in which one can change their mind, usually three or four days-depending. Mine was just a matter of a few hours. I breathed a sigh of relief.

When I returned home, the phone was ringing. It was my neighbor. Mrs. Agent. She was frantic. "Patti, I hate it that the Eichorn-Hicks keep calling you. They can't afford your house. They didn't sell their house. They lost it. They were not making their payments. They overextended themselves." It was unbelievable. How could that be? They were both attorneys. They had two children. They belonged to the Country Club.

That explained their persistence and desperation. But I could not understand why they would resort to such measures. Isn't it against the law, unethical, and immoral, to use knowledge and credentials to deceive, cheat, and misrepresent? I could go on. There is a term for that: fraud and extortion. I felt that when they received the letter from Mr. Zissla, they would be mortified and I would never see or hear from them again. I felt sad for their children. What kind of example were they teaching them?

I felt this was all so surreal. I still could not understand Mrs. Agent's part. Shouldn't she have known the background? I would learn later that they were known to do their own business negotiating and always in their favor. Mr. Attorney had approached other people who lived in the neighborhood, but they were experienced and savvy enough to know how to dismiss them in no uncertain terms. But I was surprised that nothing was ever done about this. That it was never acknowledged, so people could be aware. I still could not understand why Mrs. Agent suddenly was so absent and how did she know that they kept calling me relentlessly?

It was not long after that I received a call from Mr. Attorney telling me that he was going to legally tie me up in court if I did not follow through with those papers. I told him that he and his wife had harassed and deceived me. I also told him that I learned he could not afford my house—that I didn't trust him. I also told him he could be in a lot of trouble. He did not like hearing that. I could see his face in my mind turning even more red with rage. I hung up the phone wanting him to go away.

I called my attorney and he wrote a letter to Mr. Attorney saying that he did not have a case but that he was not to deter Mr. Attorney. I thought for sure he was bluffing. Weeks later, we would go to court. Since I thought this whole thing was so ridiculous and I really could not afford to spend any more money on court proceedings, I would tell the judge myself. I remember meeting with the judge. He was an older man with a kind, gentle manner. He listened intently and would look at Mr. Attorney in disapproval. He looked at the papers. He listened and told Mr. Attorney, "What are you doing? These papers are not legal. Leave this woman alone. This is dismissed."

I was so thankful that this was over. I looked at Mr. Attorney, trying to discern his reaction. It seemed he was indifferent, oblivious. He showed no sign of emotion. I walked away. He stopped me outside the door. I thought he was going to apologize, but instead he said, "I will continue taking you to court and keep you from selling your house for years, and it won't cost me anything because I'm an attorney. But it will cost you years and thousands of dollars. I will drop this whole thing if you give me thirty thousand dollars."

I looked up at this big man, with the red face, and told him, "I'll give you nothing. Not even a dime. You can go to jail for this."

Mr. and Mrs. Attorney would continue to legally harass me. But it was uneventful for them. Now he was just doing it for fun in his spare time, when he was depressed or when he drank too much. He could wield his power using his legal position and so-called legal expertise. I don't know if Mrs. Attorney encouraged him or not, but they would tie up the sale of my house for two years. Meanwhile, Rick would find new ways to take me to court. Since my divorce, my life had totally changed overnight. Now I was at the mercy of every predator around, my ex-husband among them.

Was I having a breakdown? I was the only person I knew who was married for so long, and been punished and sacrificed to the wolves, with no defense. My last child was off at college and I would not even be able to mourn this change in my life. I could not be just divorced with dignity, but as a business to be destroyed. I would be subjected to years of appeals and my marriage annulled amidst the destruction. Even that was not enough for the Eichorn-Hicks and Tara, the real estate agent, intruding into my life, as vultures circling their prey.

I could not understand how this could happen. Why was it allowed? I suddenly felt so frightened, discouraged and defenseless. I would have to go over my horrid experience again. It seemed so incomprehensible that this nightmare was allowed to continue. I broke down, sobbing. I could not stop. I felt my strength drain from my body. My heart ached and my throat was so tight I could not speak.

People in the neighborhood would try and help me. In fact, several of my neighbors offered to help, but to no avail. I remember one particularly kind neighbor, who was an attorney, who genuinely wanted to help me and offered to meet with me at his office. I felt so overwhelmed and discouraged, I literally broke down when I met with him. My heart-wrenching sobs racked my body. I was beyond caring even though Kelly wanted to console me. Kelly's intent came from a good place for he was an honorable man with sensitivity and compassion. But I felt that this was even beyond him.

There seemed to be a special barrier that could not be broken by ordinary reason, common courtesy or rationale. Once the wheels of legality were set in motion, there would be no stopping, right or wrong, just moving forward mindlessly. The designer laws and rules made by man behind closed doors to protect its own but warped and corrupt.

I longed to feel the same security that I had in my marriage not so long ago. "How can I help you? What can I do? Is there someone I can contact?" Kelly implored. I shook my head, for speech would not come. How could he help me?

Show me your rage for the blatant and reprehensible actions, and your passion for the innocent who are wrong, and your strength to go up against the vile and corrupt. Could he do that or would it rock his secure world to another dimension? He was a kind, gentle man. His intentions were good and honorable, but was it his time? His eyes were so sad.

A faint flicker of hope. "Rick. If Rick knew, he would help me," I said through my tears. "Do you really think he would help?" Kelly asked. I think he was hopeful as I was and felt it would be worth a try. Deep inside me I felt if Rick only knew of the atrocities I had been up against he would want to help. It would also be a solution and a way to right the many wrongs. Now I look back and realize how unrealistic and naïve I truly was. But I wanted to believe that he was a good man that he still cared enough if not for me at least for his children, even for himself.

Kelly placed the call to Rick. He explained the situation and his concern. Evidently, his call made an impact for Rick asked to talk to me. Rick's voice sounded genuinely attentive and reassuring. He told me that he would make some calls and would call me later at home. I felt a weariness as if I had been through a mighty battle, left wounded and exhausted. Now I could finally breathe a sigh of relief, knowing help was coming. I felt the gentle warmth surround me.

Shortly after I returned home, Rick did call. But his voice was guarded. He now was indifferent, very businesslike. Not like someone who could or would rescue anyone. This was not a hero, not even a fallen hero who would awaken from disgrace to desperately try and redeem himself. Nothing had changed. Here was a man who had the best attorneys at his beck and call, had banks and businesses crumbling around him in his takeovers, while people were impressed and intimidated with his prowess in the world of high finance. Did he privately gloat at my misfortune for being at the mercy of all these opportunists?

I did not know what to believe, when he told me there was nothing he could do. I felt that either he was protecting himself or someone. I could have cried but I had my fill. I also could have pleaded, but he was too detached. I could have become enraged, but he would only hang up and take me to court, for he did not have to know anything for then he would have to acknowledge.

I knew then I could not count on him for anything. But could I ever? For some reason, this experience only validated the strength of my own convictions and made me more determined than ever to stand my ground. I was not going to be a victim. If I was going through all these experiences and was still standing, and still rather sensible, I might as well add pretty fearless too. There must be a reason. If I were to have all these horrid experiences and adventures, I was going to do something about it, not just keep it to myself. For then, how do we learn or change?

GALLERY II

Ingrid Welty was the captain of this team. A gathering of players through the years. Love the competition experience and the whole scene.

Ingrid Welty's tennis Team waiting to play our match. Two teams playing doubles and two players to play singles. Ingrid is to the far left. Love of tennis. I will look for the guardian ad litem family. For this is tennis.

Baby Lucia checking to see for any new teeth. Something is happening. Babies are much more perspective than we ever realize. Precious forever.

My sister and I flew together to Texas to meet our family for a solemn affair. Yet, we got to the airport we learned to our surprise that our nephew Dale would pick us up. Lots of hugs. I am peeking through my sister Marybelle, and my nephew Dale. The loving energy we all share.

My good friend and confidant, strong sense of humor, loved fashion, decorating, traveling too. With her leopard coat and hat, she was destined to gravitate toward my leopard chair.

Visiting my cousin Judy in Tucson. This is her back yard. Surrounded by mountain views.

From lake Point to little cottage house. It was the gardens that drew me in. From twenty stories up with a balcony to gardens that keep growing and changes every year. We can make and keep every place we live beautiful, unique and ours to keep in our hearts.

Coming from my condo at Lake Point, it was the gardens that helped my decision in buying this little cottage house. Now I have my gardens.

Carol and her daughters Stephani and Angela. All slept in the bed built for two, apart for too long so all three so happy to be together finally. The best sleep in way too long.

One night sleep over at my place.

*This was taken at a restaurant at Calhoun Square with sisters,
Stephanie and Angela, my guardian ad litem family.*

*My friend Jill and granddaughter Genevieve wanting to check out the whole
scene including the cabinetry we painted to go with the tile. Definitely a
European appeal. Everyone liked that.*

The mural in the kitchen finished. I set my small table and chair in front as a suggestion of possibilities. This was a very unique project that drew people in--or wanting to go into the gardens.

I believe I already wrote about this picture of me standing in front of the mural at lake point. All dressed up etc.

Betsy and Genevieve my godchild looking pretty in front of the mural, where everyone wanted to linger and be.

I took pictures of my daughter Monica and her grandma in front of the mural. So beautiful in more ways than one.

My mother in law Diva came for a short visit I had just returned from singing to be greeted by my daughter and Diva A gift to me for us all.

Flying with Pete in his airplane. We had so many adventures on land, air or sea. Thank you.

*We flew many times, even letting me take control when conditions were just right.
Now that takes a very trusting and adventurous person / teacher.*

We flew over the grand Canyon to Sadona Arizona. Breathtakingly beautiful.

Pete and I hiked up the mountains and made a special stop to the Chapel on the Hill. Sadona is a spiritual vortex. The closer I came to this beautiful chapel, the more awe inspired I became. There is a reason and purpose.

My cousin Judy and I had taken a road trip to Sedona.
She's standing off to the side and below the Chapel on the Hill.
I loved that trip.

I got to close the hangar door, a trusted responsibility And, then we are on our way to Colorado, to see my daughter, my cousin Judy in Tucson and to Sedona. My cowgirl boots are getting a lot of wear.

Friends Debbie, myself and Chris in the living room. My first guests in my little cottage house offering a wonderful housewarming.

My friend Pat Duffey and I took a road trip from Minnesota to visit my daughter in Colorado,. We read self help tapes the whole way to be prepared to present the best of ourselves. It was great being with my daughter. She thrives where ever she lives or what ever she does.

Was someone's birthday celebrating with my guardian ad litem family. I wanted them to experience another side of life carefree with joy to keep. My friends Red and Jill at the piano, ready to entertain helped accomplish this with Stephany and Angela and Mom Carol.

I had a little jute box that actually work. Michael and little brother Joe came to visit Mome`. Michael showing his strength lifting Joey to get a better look. Intrigued with the jute box, and the giraffe displayed. Always fun.

Just before the concert begins we gather in the big room to go over our music, our thoughts and our composure too. All for the love of music, the blend of voices, learning new pieces, friendships and challenge of it all. Always working together.

I'm surrounded by very special people during a break. Next to me is Tamie, our very gifted accompanist Tim Strand, Deb Wyrobek and her dear father in law.

Friends Tyra, Lee, Marty. Monica and more just after graduation .

CHAPTER 11

Going Back, and I Don't Want to

I LOOK IN THE LARGE empty room with the sun pouring from the large corner windows. My eyes are drawn to the inviting oriental key designed chaise, at one time a lovely shade of blue but now well worn and used.

I walk over to the windows to see one last time the view. It is peaceful and serene, a beautiful sunny afternoon. The sunlight filters from the giant trees and plays with the rippling pond below. I know this is a very special place, once filled with lots of laughter and good times where family and friends would congregate and enjoy the wonderful home with a view.

I feel a weariness. The chaise is so inviting in the warmth of the afternoon sun. It inspires me to sit for a while and rest. Maybe reflect a bit and maybe, if I feel inclined, have a replenishing nap. Sitting back.

I look at the landscape, the neighbors' beautiful flower gardens, which slope down to grasslands and gentle pond. I am mesmerized by the grandeur. My mind skips to another time and place, as if in reverie. The chaise is so comfortable. The place where I am drawn as others before me to ease into a moment of luxury before I begin my journey into the unknown.

Arghhh!!! How in the world can I possibly write when I have all these interruptions from every possible source created? Why does this computer lose my writing when I am finally into the flow and things are starting to come together? When I try and locate my writing, a little screen pops up out of nowhere, for who knows what reason saying I have too many files open. That my Microsoft Word is not working properly. But does not really tell me anything. I do save my writing files that say SAVE under desktop, which is what I am supposed to do. Then that silly twirly bird or whirling pinwheel goes twirling all over the place and I lose my writing. I am so mad, frustrated with the Apple computer. I think it is defective. Now why doesn't that little screen pop up out of nowhere, announcing I have too many files and Word is not working properly? I bet I won't lose this even if I tried. I am going to give you Mr. Computer that is supposed to be so smart, knows everything but can't find anything. I will give you one more chance. Where is my writing that I started this evening April 18, 2006? Otherwise, you are done. De nada. Finished. You have had your chance and you blew it the little voice in my head chastises . . .

* * * * *

Just do it. Like the popular Nike ad that catches everyone's attention for action that pushes us not to give up or give in. Just get through the hard stuff. Surely, I will feel better for the release, but it is so difficult to go back there. I don't want to, but it must be necessary because it is always there, pulling me to address what hurts and disturbs me so. It is my past and all my experiences that have made me different. I feel it and others see it, but they can't understand the mystique that had always surrounded me. That is a good thing in a way. . .

* * * * *

My memories were not to be spoken, but almost forgotten. Eventually, my dearest friends would notice my silence and want to draw me out. Growing up, while my friends would talk about their homes that were filled with love and laughter, I could not talk about mine. I would try to remember something pleasant, nothing too shocking, maybe something at least funny. That would appease for the moment. When I grew to trust, I eventually would open up to my dearest friends. The miraculous thing occurred. I really wasn't quite alone in my journey of life. But I do know and this: I have learned that there needs to be understanding and dignity restored to move on to forgiveness.

I learned through hearing bits and pieces, here and there, that gave me even as a small child a certain amount of understanding of the dynamics of my parents. Children are much more observant than many times we realize. They also can be very perceptive, learning what is right or wrong. Discerning what is truth and what is not.

I learned that my father lost his mother early in life. His father in his grief, or maybe in his self-condemnation, shipped my father to live with a cold and distant relative. It was not the best environment for a young boy, who had just lost his mother. They showed obvious favoritism to their own son, having my father do most of the chores at the expense of his studies. He eventually ran away and lied about his age and joined the Army. And I know it was never about the chores, but something much deeper, more meaningful—a longing perhaps of a loving home, a sense of belonging. Security to the freedom to be a child who is loved and nurtured, not to be exploited or to live in fear.

My mother lost her father at the age of fourteen. She had had a very close family. She always spoke lovingly of her dear mother and her departed father. Her life was full and was surrounded with family who were creative and musically inclined. My mother was a lovely, but frail, young girl when my father met her, and fell in love. How could he not? She was beautiful and innocent with long brown hair and pretty blue eyes that seemed a little forlorn still feeling the loss of her father. There was a gentle sweetness to her demeanor that stemmed from a sincere protectiveness that surrounded her all her life. My mother had bad asthma. The weather, overexertion or even what she ate could trigger an attack. So she was pretty sheltered. When my father met my mother, he fell in love immediately. I believe my mother must have been a little nervous about this, for he was twelve years older than she. But he was handsome and debonair, with dark wavy hair and a thin mustache that looked appealing, but maybe too sexy.

Now as I have written this small segment, I went through my closets to search for one of the few portraits I have of my parents. I found the picture that I wanted to examine once again to try to find a clue or some indication of some foible weakness that would foretell an uncertain future. The picture is shades of black and white. The young couple is seated on a high-backed leafy, floral brocade sofa, nicely done. I imagine the color as burgundy shades of red or could be greens with touches of rust and burgundy. I notice the white open-toed shoes with straps at the ankle. I like them. I like straps at the ankle myself, as they secure my shoes on my feet. The man that would one day be my father with black and white dress shoes must have been popular and stylish for that time, rested on the broad leaf designed carpet. I liked the effect.

This would be my mother, nestled against the arms of my father. He's holding her so tenderly, as a fragile doll. He has his right arm around her shoulders and his hand resting delicately on her arm, in a warm gentle embrace. She is drawn to him because of that embrace. My mother's arm crosses her lap, as my father clasps her hand as a definition of requisition or claim. My father's head is bending toward my mother's, tenderly. My mother's dark hair falls past her shoulders. She's wearing a pretty dress with sleeves that gather at the top and taper toward the elbows. I'm trying to imagine the color. It is deeper than my father's white dress shirt. Maybe it is a deep rusty rose and as I look closer with thin stripes going perpendicular, very nicely done. The waist is fitted and comes up under the bodice with a flared skirt that touches just below the knees, very feminine. Young and in love, they are a striking couple.

I look at the picture and I do see that my parents were in love. There is also a yearning and a hint of uncertainty in my mother's young face. My father has a look of sophistication and worldliness about him, but now he found his real treasure and he will not relinquish. Love can bring incredible joy and happiness. That is a gift. Love can also heal, giving us determination to go beyond ourselves, for then we have a reason, incentive and purpose. Love can also hurt when becoming obsessive or possessive or used as a bartering tool, to give or to hold back with strings attached. Love also changes, many times growing deeper almost as one heart, lovers, best of friends and soul mates. More times than not, the change is not what we want or ever expected, like an erosion unnoticed, so subtle and insidious, until the cracks appear, sometimes cannot be repaired.

I really do not know when the problems arose for my parents. I just know that as the years went by the problems escalated. I'm sure my father's background contributed greatly to his frustrations that led to dysfunction. For he did not know how to love only how to control the situation. Complete control. That's probably related to what he intuitively saw in my mother, her vulnerability. I know he also joined the army to escape a homeless situation. To him the army was the solution even if he lied about his age. He never talked that much about his experiences in the army, expect I knew he was in Africa and almost died from malaria. I know he had some deep-rooted issues that he never addressed, but back then that was not uncommon. When he fell in love with my mother, he loved her the only way he knew how—possessively. Maybe he thought that her gentle love would cure his demons within. But fragility needs to be handled with loving care. Anything else is shocking to the mind, body and soul seeking an escape.

* * * * *

I woke up this morning with tears streaming down my face. It is hard going back wanting to repair the damage. I try to understand the wrongs that were done either unknowingly and done intentionally. Where is the safe haven? When will we learn from the mistakes or even acknowledge them, at least for understanding? Instead we put on a face of stoic pride trying to pretend that all is right with the world. The past is what we have experienced and is carried with us. How we address and acknowledge those issues reflects in our demeanor. We want to do and be better than that. Don't we?

When I was writing last night I called my sister. I needed some verification and maybe some encouragement too. She was not home so I left her a message. She called me back a few hours later. "Patti, I got your message." I was happy to hear her voice. "Before we begin, have you set a date yet?" "Oh Patti, I broke off our engagement. I couldn't go through with it. I would have these flashbacks of Dad, all these memories that I can't forget." I could hear her fighting back the tears as she said those words. Now maybe was not the time to talk about the past. Although that was something that many times my sister could not contain. She would bring things up in the most unexpected places that would sometimes surprise or mortify my siblings and me. How do we heal the hurts that we don't understand and try to avoid, but follows us everywhere? I wanted to comfort and reassure my dear, sweet, courageous sister. She deserved better. She deserved to have the happiness and to share her happiness, not have the past experiences come to haunt her, interjecting fear and stumbling blocks of uncertainty.

I was angry for my sister. I wanted to help her get through this. "Maybe this isn't the time. I wanted to talk about what you knew from our father's army experience." This was interesting, for it was difficult for me to even say my or our father. I wanted to detach myself as I had believed as a small child that the hospital made a mistake and I was given to the wrong family. My father and mother are both gone now and I want to forgive. I won't forget. But I know my mother was weak, too beaten down in her fragility. My father never was taught or shown real love or given proper guidance or the nurturing we all need to strive and build. He wasn't taught. It was only in his dreams and his dreams were eschewed from his experiences. He didn't know how. In his frustrations and determination, his attempts to love and hold onto his family only instilled fear. It was a cycle of futility, spinning his wheels. Love isn't demanding or possessive. If it becomes that then it is confusing and distorted.

I asked my sister if I could read a few paragraphs to her, for I thought it was important that she knew I understood her pain. I then told her that I was writing for our family, a legacy of sorts, and validation of our experience through our experiences growing up. "Patti, thank you. I do want to hear," she said in her wonderment. I then said, "Originally, I just wanted to write about my court experiences during and after my divorce." "Oh, Patti, you're going to write about that?"

"Well, yes, I have for I am compelled to write, for it is too important to ignore or not address. Unfortunately, that means I have to delve into the past."

"Sounds like you're going to have a very big book. How many pages have you written already?" she exclaimed incredulously, my sister making me laugh again.

"I really don't know. I have an idea, but it is not so much about pages, but the content. Hopefully, it won't be that long. I want it to be read, savored. I want it to make a difference."

I read her the few paragraphs. She's my sister. What is she going to say but how proud she was of me.

"Patti, you always were the one that stood your ground, taking action. I want to buy your first book."

I laughed and said, "Mary Belle, no, no. I will give you my book."

"But I want you to sell lots of copies."

Again, I laughed. "I hope it does also. If it is meant to be then it will happen. If only the right words could heal the mind, body and soul, when absorbed fully, contemplated and truly understood."

Sometimes I felt like the big sister and that was okay. We all need our moments in the sun, a little bit of glory and then we carry on.

So there is a bit of background about my parents, little that I knew or know. I don't know anything about the wedding. If it was an extravagant affair or being swooped off in a small chapel somewhere. I was the third child, having an older brother and sister, until my youngest brother Billy was born, then my younger sister Sandy and my baby sister Ginny, who was ten years younger than I was. I remember feeling like an observer in my family, wondering when my real parents were going to come and get me. But that was not to happen. I continued observing quietly, most of the time keeping a distance, or busy with my little drawings or dolls. I loved my dolls and I treated them as if they were real, covering them up at night to sleep and if I was going for the day, would tuck them in a place that was protected and pleasant.

I'm sure my father must have been a loving husband and parent at one time. But by the time I came along he must have been burned out, overwhelmed by his responsibilities, for I could not understand his dark moods, when my mother was so gentle, fragile and soft spoken. When we were really young, my mother would comfort us, telling us little stories or maybe engaging us in songs. We were drawn to her gentleness, surrounding her with all the love that we could give, wanting to comfort and protect our mother. I remember lying in my bed at night, for I was very young, maybe three or two and a half. I would hear my father's strong temper. I could not understand it and it scared me. I could not understand what caused the anger that would inflict such fear that I trembled, praying that my real mom and dad would come and get me, to take me home.

I remember a time when we went to visit our grandfather in Canada. This would have been our father's dad. He had a big old white farmhouse with big trees. It was pleasant. He had a couple horses, and he would set my big brother on top. I would watch in awe, wanting to have the same experience. My sister Mary Belle was not too excited about this prospect. I remember when he swooped me up in his arms and set me astride this big white horse. I was probably three years old, but I remember feeling so grand on this lofty creature. I wanted to stay there. He would walk me around, while my big brother sauntered around the corral like a young horseman.

There was a grandmother too, now. She loved having two little girls come visit and to us she was Grandma. She made her own bread, and would cut a slice, spread some butter atop and sprinkle brown sugar on top of that. She would have this big smile, watching my sister and me, standing there on the old yellow linoleum floor, eating our very special treat. Our grandma found my sister and I an old baby doll, the body made of cloth, but the arms and legs and the face and neck made of flesh-colored rubber. The hair was painted on, and the eyes opened and closed. I remember touching the eyes gently to see how they closed. My sister and I were delighted with that doll that was almost as big as we were. We would each take a hand of the doll and walk her around outside the grounds. I remember that wonderful feeling. I wanted to have my grandparents always around. That to me seemed what we needed.

My parents must have been going to some kind of event while we were visiting our grandparents. For my mother was upstairs getting dressed for this special occasion, my father sitting in an overstuffed chair waiting. I don't know if he was in the best of moods. My mother started to descend the stairs. I had never seen her so dressed up, so beautiful. She was wearing a pretty yellow suit that accented her dark hair. The sleeves were long, the jacket fitted at the waist with a slight flair. The jacket was closed with white buttons encircled with gold. The skirt was fitted with a slight flare past the knees, tea length. This was my mother looking so beautiful. I looked at my father's reaction. My mother walked into the living room expectantly and instead of compliments to high heaven, he demanded my mother change her dress. Saying things that were not true. She looked beautiful. How could he say words that were not honest or true? I felt bad for my mother and worse for my father, for I saw and would learn the effects of jealousy and possessiveness. It is amazing that I would even remember that for I was so young, maybe almost three.

That memory has always stayed with me. I think because it was a realization to me for what it implicated. That episode, I believe, would set the pattern of acceptance instead of intolerance. I was surprised that no one disputed my father's actions. Before we left, Grandpa had words with my father and it didn't take much for my father to get angry. I think that was one of the last times we would return. I learned later that my mother left my father several times. Always going back home. He would eventually go after her and beg her to come back and she would.

Not too long after that trip, my mother would have my little brother Billy, although he is not so little now. He grew to six feet, and so did my big brother. I don't know what happened to us girls. But with each girl that my mother had, one would be a little taller than the last. The girls had light blond hair, and I took after my brothers will dark hair—and I wasn't six foot. Not fair. But I always thought I was taller than I looked.

My brother Billy was the most precocious child that I ever saw. Not that I saw that many, but he was a handful for my poor mother. A few years after Billy was born, my sister Sandy would be the next added addition. I don't think Billy was too happy about that as he would steal her bottle and then he would hide. One time we found him under the bed with her bottle. He was so inquisitive about everything and anything. His taste buds held not barriers. One time he ate sour berries from a neighbor's bush and had to have his stomach pumped for they were poisonous. Another time, he grabbed hold of an electrical something outside, and he could not let go. It was an awful sight to behold. Billy was holding on with both hands and his arms and body were shaking as if with an uncontrollable seizure. The children around him were screaming. I know we all wanted to help extricate him, but some older people were saying, "Don't touch him. The electricity has to be shut off first." I was so thankful when one of the neighbors finally was able to shut the current off. It seemed like forever. I remember my little brother being comforted in the arms of a stranger—to me. For the rest of the day, my little brother would be much more subdued, and he let my sister and I pamper him. Actually, when he wasn't getting himself into predicaments, he was an adorable little boy.

The best part of our family was each other, having brothers and sisters. I was in the middle, the youngest of three or the oldest of four. With each that was born, the dynamics of our family would change. For we all had our own unique personality. When Sandy was born, the strain of our expanding family was starting to show. I think especially for our mother, physically. I remember her getting so sick that the ambulance would have to take her to the hospital. I remember another time, our father was crying as our mother was whisked off in an ambulance. I was still too young to comprehend the magnitude of the situation. My sister Mary Belle and I would try and help our mother with the household chores, surprise her. One time we tried to wash the floor. We had so much water on the floor that when our father came home he was definitely not too happy.

But another time, I was going to make my own bubbles. My little friends and I found an empty jar from the laundry room. Standing on a bench to read the faucet, I put in the laundry soap and filled the jar with water. We mixed it up with lots of soapy suds rising above the top. We were so proud and excited to start making bubbles. I picked up the slippery jar and it slipped from my hands onto the floor, shattering in giant pieces. There was sudsy water everywhere. I knew the water would dry but I had to pick up the evidence. While picking up the broken pieces, a large sharp piece of glass stuck in my left hand. I still have that scar as a reminder. My father happened to be home. It was a warm sunny day. He took my hand and ran cold water over it and took the glass out, scrubbing lightly for broken shards. When all the glass was out, he gently wrapped my hand in gauze. It's funny but that was one of the better memories. I knew the glass had to come out. I was thankful that he wasn't mad at me for breaking the jar in the first place, for all the water on the floor.

My mother loved her children. When my sister and I were little, she would fix our hair and dress my sister and me as if we were her dolls. Sometimes she would braid our hair and put ribbons at the end of the braids. My hair tended to have some curl and more so when I drank my milk—for I would twist my finger around the strand of hair that fell by the side of my face. My mother would say that side of my hair grew faster and curlier. I believed it did. When my mother was well, life would be good. It is always easier to focus on the good times, wanting to feel that life was ordinary. It is interesting because as loving as our mother was, she didn't teach us. It would be our father who taught us how to brush our teeth and why it was important. He also taught us about washing our faces with warm water but rinsing with cool or cold. I remember when I knew I would be attending school for the first time. I was so excited. I could hardly sleep. At that time, I had no idea of my ABC's or my one-two-three's, but I was really good at coloring and singing and I was eager to meet my teacher, new friends and curious to discover what it was all about.

I remember my first paper that I ever brought home. When my teacher handed me my paper, she kindly said, "Patty, make sure you give this to your parents." I couldn't wait. I knew they would be so proud. There were some circles and some mysterious writing on top, but that must be a good thing. I happily skipped home with my sister Mary Belle and some new friends. When I showed my parents my paper, my father went ballistic. He would sit down with me almost every night after dinner and teach me my numbers and letters and wouldn't give up until I got them all right. At first I would be in tears, for it all seemed so overwhelming until I got a glimmer of the meaning of it all. My big brother Rammy—that's what I called him—eventually took mercy on me and would help me himself. It would not take long to master those skills. Now I looked to see if I had stars on my paper, striving for A pluses or 100s. They were the best.

I loved school that is where I was the happiest. I was fortunate that I had good teachers especially in those early years. I remember when my younger sister Sandy went to school for the first time. There was one teacher that I would observe that would actually yell at her little students, sometimes bringing them to tears. I was in disbelief that my little sister would have this teacher as her first experience of school. She had a difficult time, and never really wanted to go back. Sandy was the most sensitive child, quiet, not really interested in learning to roller skate or care to learn to ride her bike. I don't know why. She was different. She loved "her" mother. If our mother became sick, she would worry and cling to her. If our father was angry, especially to our mother, which was more times than not, she would rebel in a way that would hurt herself. I always knew that Sandy needed extra loving care. I know then she would have blossomed, but instead she retreated into herself. She could not find happiness amidst the storms. She would brood, worry about our mother, about herself, and then when she got older would beg our mother to leave our father.

Sandy was born on our father's birthday. That did not make her happy at all, not even from the beginning. Even when she was really young, I could see the anger and frustration in her little face when she would look at our father. The strange thing was, it seemed like it was mutual. I think she saw my father always as he was at the moment of his dark moods and rages, and to her were not to be forgiven or forgotten. It was as if she put our mother on a pedestal as if a saint, and our father not worthy. I would feel badly for my little sister for being around my father brought out the worst in each of them.

I wasn't too happy myself, and I thought if my real parents could not find me, I would try and find them. I felt even an orphanage would be better. I asked Sandy if she wanted to run away with me. She never hesitated. We packed a lunch. She rode her little tricycle and I walked alongside her. I was probably about six and a half and my sister about three on this hot summer day. We had never ventured by ourselves outside the neighborhood. We were on a serious mission. But the farther we walked, we started getting nervous. We had already eaten our meager lunch. What would we do when it became dark? Were would we sleep? We had already walked a long way, so it seemed and what seemed like the solution now seemed impossible. Then I thought we had better return home, for we could be in serious trouble once our parents found us missing. We reluctantly turned around and headed home. I had visions of a search party and everyone so happy and thankful to see my sister and me that our father would change his ways, like a fairytale with a happy ending. We would even be home for dinner. It was as if we were never missed. We tried and failed and no one even knew, for we dared not say anything about our runaway plans.

In some ways, I think I was fortunate because I did have a coping mechanism that naturally would kick in when I was frightened, stressed or fearful. I was aware. I knew when to be quiet and when to avoid. I also stood my ground if I had to. I would learn from my siblings, for being in the middle also offered me a certain protection that being the oldest or youngest did not have, a buffering of sorts. I was a child that was full of wonder and curiosity, yet also quietly observant while exploring within my reach and capabilities. I was not a demanding child needing an abundance of attention, but gentle and reflective. But I learned to stand my ground if I had to, for the consequences of not doing so I could see would be so much worse. A child should be allowed to be a child, to have memories of a happy childhood, for that time can never be recaptured.

What difference does it matter when subjected to abuse of any kind? The damage can be as severe to even witness—by feeling too helpless to intervene, especially for small children. If it becomes a normal part of the pattern in daily life, it is only a matter of time before the abuse will escalate beyond and out of control. To be a witness or a victim will leave an indelible mark, affecting how we live our lives or how we trust in others. Sometimes we are our own best advocate, and sometimes our only. I believe in rising above any situation, not to repeat bad habits or behavior. Never compromise your mind, body or soul. Avoid situations, people or places that want or expect you to compromise your values, your dignity and respect for a price that comes back to haunt you at the expense of others and in the end yourself.

I avoided my father as much as any child could. I wanted my mother to protect but she was too fearful, in her fear became too sick, too weak and eventually beaten down. My father grew to have no boundaries in his actions. Our cries, our pleas, would not be heard. My father could not give the gentle loving care that my mother needed to survive. Because his own responsibilities grew, and his own needs—were they met? It was easier in his frustrations to give up and give into the demons of his past. I don't think it was his original intention, but actions stemmed from dejected futility and his own disillusion. My mother was not getting stronger, but it seemed too frail and delicate for the constant demands and expectation of our father, not to mention the tremendous responsibility her young children. My mother's medication seemed to put her in a stupor when she should have been aware, a deep state of sleep, not even to waken from the cries from her children. Where was our mother? Who was going to protect the children?

I remember the anger from somewhere coming from my father. I don't know why. Maybe it was one of those times that I couldn't eat my dinner. That was not unusual, for not too many food appealed to me. I always picket at my food, which I know not must have been frustrating for my parents. I would usually be the last one to leave the dinner table. My father would insist that I could not leave until I finished all my dinner. I would be sobbing, for it seemed impossible, sometimes getting sick, which did not help the situation. Many times Mary Belle would come and check on me. "Patty, can't you finish your food?" I must have really looked sad and forlorn, for it didn't matter if the food was mashed potatoes and peas or spaghetti. She would put the food in her pockets and then empty the contents in the garbage or toilet. I loved my sister, her courageous heart. How many times comforting or coming to the rescue?

I could not eat my meal one too many times. My father dragged me from my chair at the dinner table, so frustrated with me. It completely caught me off guard, not knowing what to expect. I was like a rag doll. My feet flew from under me. I must have been around four, maybe five. It was the first time I had experienced this kind of anger. I remembered my big brother getting disciplined, but I was a girl, too little. Something in my cries changed and he stopped. "I'm sorry ... Are you okay? I didn't mean to ..." Hearing his words softened my cries. I said through my tears, "My arm hurts. I can't bend my arm." The concern on his face was so visible and so real. He rubbed my arm gently, wanting desperately to undo the wrong. He then carefully wrapped cool cloths around my outstretched arm, for I could not bend my elbow. He was so deeply distressed and sorrowful that I felt bad for him. Seeing his anguish instilled the consequences within and I realized I could never or ever lose control that I hurt anyone, for I would not want to live with that regret.

There has to be a release, something of worth to have even a momentary sense of pride, to be able to see what other facet or dimension that has not been honored but suppressed, but would have been the saving grace if acknowledged and addressed. I remember the few good memories, for there had to be. My father played the violin. That is one of the things he had learned. My mother played the piano, the guitar and could sing at the same time, which impressed me and stayed with me. Memories of my mother and father playing together, the intricate rhythms and modulations as the bow was drawn across the violin intrigued me. The sounds could be wonderfully melodic that seemed to touch my heart, honoring my soul. Sometimes my father would burst into a piece so rhythmic and fun, which would surprise us children, for we never saw that side of him. Music can be a way to express emotions or bring a sense of momentary job or release, if no other way is found or known. I am grateful. I saw that side.

Music came naturally for my mother. She was taught but also had an incredible ear. I think that irritated my father eventually because he had to work a little harder, where for my mother it came easily. She could hear a piece of music and play it. My father would study the piece and get perturbed in the process, if not to his perfection. I always hoped that he would get it right the first time. I don't remember when the music stopped and I don't know why it ended. My father put his violin away. My mother now played piano or guitar for herself, sometimes my sisters and I would gather around her to sing. Our own voices blending together in a natural harmony that sisters share. That was my natural gift. One day, I would grow up to be a singer.

My father was a builder of houses and tall buildings throughout the states. Because of that, each of us children was born in a different state. I was fortunate enough to be born in Neptune, New Jersey, on the seashore. At least that is what I would tell people, as if I were a mermaid born to the sea. Except I have a fear of water, as fear that should not be for I am also drawn to the beauty and mystique that a body of water can offer.

Our family was growing up. I would be going into the seventh grade when my father decided that we were to move from the city and into the countryside of a small town of Crete, Illinois. Hopefully, my mother would get stronger and healthier and our father would find peace and contentment. But I was uncertain.

We had very few neighbors around us now that we lived on the outskirts of Crete. I had an ominous feeling. I liked having neighbors. My brothers liked the openness of the land, the big yard with the big shade trees. But it was also close to a small cemetery. I didn't like to look at it. Wasn't this unusual?

The big old house sat on top of a small hill. A big open porch covered the length of the house. There were large bay windows on the lower level that would be the dining room and another bay window on the second level, which would end up being my bedroom that I shared with my two sisters, Sandy and Ginny. Ginny was ten years younger than I. There were four bedrooms upstairs. My oldest brother Rammy took the first bedroom at the top of the stairs. It was long and narrow. I chose the next bedroom with the big bay window and large walk-in closet that also had a big window. Because it was so big and I did not want to sleep by myself, my two younger sisters would share my room. My brother Billy had the bedroom next to mine. His was not quite as large and had a small walk-in closet. Mary Belle chose the tiny bedroom at the opposite end of the staircase. Her walk-in closet was almost as big as her room. It could have been a nice little bedroom, except one of the windows overlooked the small cemetery.

This old house had high ceilings. There was a large living room with a small foyer and doorway leading to the front porch. My mother had her piano against the wall in the living room. The dining room was large with the big bay windows that gave the room an added interest. To the right of the dining room would be the master bedroom. Across from the master bedroom presented the long staircase, the stairs not carpeted but a reddish golden smooth wood. Off to the living room was the large country kitchen with a big pantry. Next to the pantry was a large bathroom that even held a free-style bathtub like an antique. My father would eventually replace the old linoleum floor with individual tiny mosaic tiles. He seemed to enjoy this project, even though it was long and arduous, placing the tiny pieces one by one, perfectly. It was one of the few times that I saw my father do anything around the house and it seemed to soothe him.

The yard was big with pretty green grass and a few large trees. There was also a border of slender trees that tried to obscure the cemetery that was too close. Way in the back, there was a big white barn with a hayloft. We also would get a couple cats, for my sister Ginny loved cats. Sandy too, but not as much. My brothers would get a collie dog that they named Prince.

One day my father bought a cow. My mother would actually learn how to make butter and process the milk from the cow for us to drink. By this time, I really did not like milk. That was too bad for me. My mother learned to can fruits and vegetables. She seemed to really get a lot of satisfaction when she had her rows of canned jars lining the shelves in the pantry. We also had a big freezer that she would freeze certain fruits and vegetables. I liked to help her freeze the corn. She would precook the corn, but not all the way and then she would scrape the corn off the cob with a relatively sharp knife, not too big and put them in a little plastic bags. That was about the only thing I had to do with cooking. Mary Belle was always experimenting in the kitchen, creating some type of edible dish. To me, I stayed away. When I grew up, I would hire a cook, for it seemed too dangerous in the kitchen, things boiling on the stove, grease splattering from the pans, sharp knifes, hot plates to take out of the hot oven. One would have to be very careful not to get burned or cut.

Here we were from the city, now on a ten-acre farm, with a cow. Rammy would get up every morning to milk the cow. He gave her the name Daisy. She was black and white. She seemed gentle enough, but she was so big that I kept my distance. We had a small garden that we would learn how to grow our own vegetables: lettuce, tomatoes, potatoes, pumpkins, cucumbers, string beans and snap peas. There was a lot of hard work in having a garden. It was the girls' job to garden. Sometimes the boys helped. I decided I would rather be a housemaid. Actually, it was not too bad, for we would make it fun, but if our father was home, fun and work together was not allowed. Work was work. That is where I disagreed.

I wish I could say that my short life on the farm was wonderful, but it was everything but a trip to the farm. Now it seemed our father became more controlling and possessive. We would take the bus to school, for we lived at least five miles from school. My brother was limited in playing his beloved baseball. My sister and I were not allowed to participate in after-school activities without a certain amount of pleading. School dances were rare for us, but sometimes we would stay after for sock hops. We both loved to dance. My sister had light hair with green eyes, perky and pretty. She loved having a certain amount of attention. We were kind of similar except my hair was dark with blue eyes. I was more reserved. I didn't want the attention that my sister would seek. I loved learning but I also rebelled if I was forced to take a class that I had no interest. I would say, "When I grow up, I am going to be a singer, dancer, artist and missionary." I would not need the skills of a bookkeeper or accountant. Now I realize we need a little knowledge in almost everything—and, almost anything can by interesting if presented in the right way. It is important to know why that subject or lesson is necessary or beneficial.

My sister and I were growing up, maybe a little too cute, a little too pretty. My father would not like the attention we would receive. I liked boys from a distance, but if they showed an interest, it would scare me, especially if he had whiskers. I still felt so young, and not ready to grow up and be serious.

Rammy was growing up and was as handsome as a movie star. He was oblivious to his good looks, still having his dream of being a baseball player. The girls could not help but have a crush on him. Not only was he good looking, he was modest and kind hearted. He was a good dancer and could carry on a conversation for he was well read. He was interesting and interested.

My father should have been proud of his children, teaching them, guiding them, encouraging them to have all the experiences that would help them achieve the success opportunities of life. Prepare them, not hold them back. He gave us shelter, food and clothing, but he instilled fear in his violence that was always so eminent. His violence would grow, along with a look in his eyes that was not really understood, but knowing to avoid. My mother at the crucial time in our lives became absent—too medicated. I would dread going home from school. I never knew what to expect when I came home. My mother became a shell of the mother we once loved and depended on, but never really could. But we didn't want to give up for she was our mother.

I was between fourteen and fifteen when I came home one day from babysitting. The house was empty, quiet, but not for long. My father walked into the room. I was uneasy. He looked at me with this strange look, wanting me to give him a hug. No way was I going to go near him. I looked at him. I could not trust him. I ran upstairs as fast as I could. I ran to my room, slamming the door that held no locks. I looked around frantic. Where could I go? Sandy was in the room. Her eyes wide. "Patty, what's wrong?" I shook my head. I was speechless. I ran to the window and pulled it wide open. I then climbed on the windowsill and sat on the ledge.

I could hear him laughing as he opened the door. My sister was pleading with me not to jump. I was crying, "If you come near me, I'll jump." And I knew I would. He stopped in his tracks, backed up and left the room. I sat on the ledge, looking down before me. It was a long way down. I don't know if I would have made it alive. It was not until I was certain he would not return that I allowed myself to release my grip and step down from the ledge. My little sister was as traumatized by that scene as myself. My sister put her arms around my neck. We stayed in our room until we knew that our mother was home. Where was our mother?

It would not be too long after that incident that my father was in a terrible accident, while working downtown Chicago. He was on a tall building, standing on some scaffolding when a huge crane accidentally picked him up in the air, swinging him back and forth. The crane operator could not hear his screams of fear and agony, until he looked up horrified. My father would be extricated from the viselike grip, so close to death. He was rescued. Not knowing if he would live or die. He would be in the hospital for nine months, most of that time lying in traction. His body weakened, broken and in shock, his malaria returned.

When my mother got the phone call from the hospital, Mary Belle and I were both in the room. The telephone sat on a small table near the dining room. When my mother answered the phone, she was silent, listening intently. I could hear her gasp. She slowly sank to the chair. Mary Belle and I looked at each other. From our mother's demeanor we knew it was something serious. She spoke softly into the phone as if in shock and disbelief. When she slowly put the phone back on the cradle, she said, "Your father was in a terrible accident. He's in the hospital but he might not make it."

Mary Belle started crying hysterically. I didn't know what to think for how to react. But I knew he was too mean to die, but if he did I still didn't know how I would have reacted. I couldn't cry and for that I was ashamed. The memory of the window ledge was still too raw in my mind. I stood there in disbelief, trying to comprehend the ramification of the whole thing. One of the neighbors would take my mother to the hospital for she did not know how to drive a car. Rammy would give my mother a couple lessons in order for her to finally have the freedom and independence to drive herself to the hospital. She would drive every day for nine months even though the hospital was well over thirty miles away.

I remember the time my sister, brother and I went to the hospital to see our father for the first time since the accident. My mother drove. She was so proud and very cautious as she drove below the speed limit, looking this way and that at every crossroad, steady and calm in her concentration. The hospital was a long ways away. Seeing my mother driving the car seemed to instill a confidence in her that I never saw before. That was a good thing. Eventually, my mother would even get her own job that would give her an added dimension to her world. When we walked into the hospital room and saw our father in traction, his body encased in white wrappings to, I imagined, hold his body together. His legs were suspended. I was amazed at this predicament more than saddened. He survived and he would continue to make progress, but his malaria would return. Mary Belle ran to his bedside, once again crying. "Are you okay? Does it still hurt?" My brother and I slowly approached his bedside. Was he still the same? Would this close encounter magically change him? He responded in a weakened voice that validated his misery. I felt a pang of sympathy, not just for his misery, but also for the regrets of his actions that affected us all. Our father was human after all, with feelings that were now exposed.

The tears would surface but would not come for me nor for my brother. Seeing all the tubes and IV needles was a jolt to me. I'm sure for all of us. I was till processing the whole scene, but I realized that I could not just stand there. I touched my father lightly on his shoulder as a sign of presence. "I'm sorry this happened to you. I hope you are not in too much pain." The words spoken were with sincere regrets. It seemed to lift his spirits to see us. He was a fortunate man to have survived and have his family surrounding him.

He would be in the hospital for nine months. For the first time in all our life, we were not under the storm within waiting for the next outburst. For me, I could breathe freely. I was fifteen when that happened. When Mary Belle realized that her father would survive, she seized this limited opportunity. This time would give her a reprieve of sorts. It would be a time that she could explore her feelings. In fact, we all could. I was not as bold or daring. My actions would be more discriminating, more discerning in my thoughts, words and actions. It was as if the constraints of bondage were broken and she could now experience life on her own terms.

I had never dated before. That was not my first and foremost desire or thought. I did want to learn and experience all that life had to offer, in a way that held no regrets. One time we had gone to the hospital, my sister told me she had met someone, and she had invited him to come to our house. He was a few years older, maybe a freshman in college. He was going to also bring a friend for me. Ooh, that made me nervous. But I was curious too.

The two older boys came over to the house. They were nice looking. His friend that was to meet me, I could see already could shave. Right away, I felt very reluctant with the whole idea. He was very nice looking but this was not what I wanted. My guardian angels must have been whispering in my ear and my date's ear, for he was so sweet and polite. Our mother had gone to the hospital to visit our father. That was another thing that did not seem right to me. I looked at him, searching for an understanding. I think he could read my mind. "Why don't we take a walk outside?" he gently said. "Sure, we can walk down to the bridge. It's just down the road from here." I felt as long as we kept moving it was a good thing.

By the time we reached the bridge, I realized what a nice young man he was. He was soft spoken, considerate and wise. Now that we were at the bridge, we talked a little about my father's accident and school. He looked at me intensely and said, "You are very young." I looked younger than my years. I didn't mind at all that he said that. "I know," I said quietly. "You know that you are very pretty. I want you to know I am not going to take advantage of you. One day you will grow up to someone special," he said. Soft warm tears fell down my face. Not because of fear or frustration, but because he understood and cared enough. He did kiss me tenderly and I let him. But it was of the experience of expectations ahead, when the time was right. I was quietly thankful and relieved that we kept our dignity and respect intact. I would think about my first date, my first kiss. That held hopes for a promise of something greater than a fleeting memory.

It was as if that young man came into my life for a reason. I would never see him again. Not that I wanted or expected to. For what he gave me was more valuable and precious, instilling the gift of hope, belief in myself and not compromising what I value and cherish the most. In some ways I was a very fortunate young girl.

That would be the end of summer. I would be going in my sophomore year at Crete-Monee High School. My father was still in the hospital. My mother was still driving to the hospital every day but never taking the expressway for the traffic was too busy and the cars too fast. My brother told me that the only reason my mother was given her driver's license was of her determination. She failed the test so many times that they finally broke down and had mercy on her and gave her a driver's license. She would take Torrence Avenue and all the side streets all the way to the hospital.

One of the times we drove with our mother, she stopped at a red light. She waited. The light turned green and she still sat there waiting while the cars were passing her and honking their horns behind her. My brother, not losing his patience, asked, "Mom, why aren't you moving?" "Well, those other cars were here before me." That was the gentle character of my mother, too kind and too patient, would never impose her will. Her sheltered life even showed on the road.

MEETING RICK

THE YEAR THAT OUR FATHER was in the hospital for all those months proved to be also a turning point for all of us. I was happy to be going back to school. This year I would take a typing class. That class happened to have a mix of sophomore, junior and senior students. I remember where I sat, in the first row and about the fourth seat. There would be this skinny boy with dark curly hair for some reason would turn to look at me as he was in the second row. I didn't pay much attention. I needed my attention on my typing. Then he got in the habit of borrowing my eraser. That was okay too. Then we would maybe talk before or after class. Then one day he asked me for a real date.

The boy's name was Rick Zona. He was a senior and I was a sophomore. I liked that he wasn't real tall and that he really didn't shave yet. Maybe he did, like every three days. Since my father was still in the hospital, my life became more normal. We might go to a football game, the drive-in movies or an occasional dance.

Rick would walk me to my classes carrying my books. We would linger outside my classroom door, until just before the bell and then he would tear down the hall, hopefully to make his next class in time. First love runs deep. In some ways seems more real, no pretenses for everything is out in the open. Young and in love gives the courage to conquer the impossible. To me, Rick seemed bold and fearless. But he was gentle and loving to me. He had a fun-loving side, but also a practical side. I felt safe with him. After a date, before he would take me home, like all teenagers we would park, making out with fervent kisses and embraces. He always respected my wishes, or when to go no further. That was important to me. I was not ready for an intimate relationship. I wanted to be courted, swayed and won over without any doubts.

I would still go to the hospital, occasionally to see how my father was faring. Each time, along with his body healing, I prayed that his ways would change for the better also. One day, going into his hospital room, I could hear my father yelling at the nurses. Then I noticed how he would look at me or my sister and I decided I would not go back. I had a sinking feeling things were not going to change. I would learn my father would be coming home soon and it turned out to be on my sixteenth birthday. I would think, surely he would change his ways, since being so close to death. Now he would be thankful and grateful for life and his family. Evidently, it would take more than a close encounter.

I remember coming home from school. My father was home. When I walked into the room, I caught my breath. There were other members of the family around too, but when he said, "Aren't you going to give your father a hug?" I cringed. I wasn't going to show him my fear. Maybe if I gave him a daughterly hug that would suffice. Hugs should be given freely, not requested. I did hug him, but then he would not let go. He should have been weak. But it was as if a pretense. I pushed him away with all my might. I looked at him with such anger. He laughed. That was my birthday. The first day of February. Again, as always, I kept my distance.

Now since my father was back home, I could not see Rick as often. Usually once or twice a week. Friday or Saturday. That did not deter Rick, but it didn't surprise me for I never questioned his feelings. Rick had several part-time jobs that kept him busy. Life became more bearable with Rick. I knew once I graduated I would have my own life. I could fulfill my own dreams. Meanwhile, I would focus on my studies. Now since my mother learned to drive, she decided to go to work for the first time outside the home. She would work at one of the hospitals. I'm not sure what she did. But that meant there would be times that my younger sister Ginny might be home alone and she was ten years younger than I. This gave my mother another newfound freedom and dimension in her life. Meanwhile, our father had not changed a morsel. I could not believe it and was disappointed to no end. During this time, he also bought himself a new car, a Porsche. A little sporty red car that seemed incongruous with our large family of six. The only person that ever drove that little toy car was our father. That is one of the things he treated himself to after his close encounter.

It seemed that our father was trying to make up for lost time in the disciplinarian department. He would have us do insurmountable chores that seemed unnecessary and mean. My brother felt that because his life was so miserable he wanted us to have the same experience. Who knows?

One day he came home in another foul mood. It seemed he would provoke Rammy unnecessarily. This time, he went to a room and came outside with a shotgun. He told Rammy that he wanted him to shoot Daisy. My brother grew to love this gentle cow. This did not make sense. Our mother again was not around, but my sister and brother Billy and I were outraged.

Rammy vehemently refused. We could not understand how anyone would make such a request. When my brother refused, he grabbed Rammy forcing him to get Daisy and bring her from the barn. We all started crying for our brother, pleading, "Please don't do this." Our father would not listen. So cold hearted.

Rammy walked out with Daisy, his face distorted with grief. Surely, this would not happen. My father then demanded my brother to take the shotgun. My brother refused for his love of Daisy was greater than his fear. When my brother refused, he put the gun to his shoulder to shoot Daisy himself. I was horrified. I ran away not to see, not to hear. I heard the shot. I sank to the ground, sickened with grief. We all cried in disbelief and hopelessness for our unbearable situation. I saw my brother kneeling by the dead body of his beloved Daisy. "We hate you. How could you do this to Rammy?" The effects of that incident, the way it was done, was cruel and senseless. Rammy would plan his escape.

We also had a few rabbits that we kept in the barn. After that incident my sisters and I opened the cages and let them out. They were used to us for we would play with them. "Run, little rabbits. Run," We pleaded as we picked them up and cuddled them in our arms one last time. It took a long time for them to disperse for they forget about their freedom. We saved those little rabbits. I can't remember the consequences for that deed. It must have been so horrendous that I blocked it out. Or maybe our father was filled with too much shame since Daisy. I do not know. He wasn't too happy about the gardens, for the rabbits were feasting on their vegetable of choice. But what did he expect? We did not grow up on a farm. This was foreign to us. Our animals were our pets. After writing about this, I called my brother Billy in Texas. I felt a need to talk to him. He told me, "Patti, we did let the rabbits out. They were hopping all over the place. Dad would get his shotgun and shoot them from the back porch." Hearing that just made me sick. I will never understand cruelty of any kind.

Rick was not afraid of my father. We were going to go to a school dance and he was to pick me up in his car. My father—and it is difficult to call him that—was angry that I was going with this "wild boy." I had filled the tub to get ready for my bath and had set my hair in large rollers. My brother said something and he started getting really angry with my brother. I thought this could escalate into something really ugly. I stormed into the room, partially pleading and demanding to stop.

"Do you always have to fight? Please stop."

Well, my father did just what I told him. But then he grabbed me, and dragged me over to the filled tub. Threw me down and pushed my head down into the water. He would hold my head under. I tried to fight him off, shaking my head, pushing my arms. Mary Belle ran, grabbed a broom and started pummeling my father on his back and head. "Stop! Stop! You're going to kill her," she screamed. My sister saved me. My father backed off. I was sputtering water. I was in complete disbelief. When would this tyranny end?

Once again, my sisters gathered around me. Rick would be coming in a matter of minutes. I towel dried my wet hair. I put on a pretty light blue dress. My hair just flowed down my back. I was ready by the time Rick came to the door. My sisters gathered about me. "Patti, you still look so beautiful." I didn't know. I just wanted to present myself as if nothing of significance had just transpired. A pretty blue dress can do wonders. The further we drove from that big old house, I let that experience fade from my thoughts as I felt Rick's arms gently around my shoulders.

One day, my big brother would fight back for he had had enough. Now that I think about it, I think our father was angry because we all were growing up and he was losing his control over his domain. I think that he also felt threatened and jealous of his sons. They were not at all like him. They had a sense of humor. They did not carry the anger or simmering rage of our father. They had healthy interests, sensitivity, compassion. I think our father had too many regrets and gave in to his demons. I remember my father provoking my brother as if daring him to react. After all the years of abuse, my brother would not take anymore. This time he hit back and he connected with a powerful shot that knocked our father down. Just what my father bullied him to do. My brother stood his ground. At this time, he was now taller than our father. Our father was five foot ten inches. I hoped he had no remorse, for his action was justified. Still, he looked at my father, shook his head in dejected indignation and walked out of the room. He would pack a bag and join the army at eighteen. Fortunately, he had just graduated. It takes a very special person to overcome severe trauma and obstacles. There is a time when we have to address the cycle of abuse and understand why it is critical to all not to be repeated or ignored. But abuse still continues in every form and I will never understand why when it is obvious. When overlooked or ignored, it will be allowed to perpetuate.

We all were affected when my big brother left. I think we all felt more vulnerable. We missed him, especially my younger brother Billy. Now he was the only boy in the family and in the middle surrounded by two older sisters and two younger sisters. Now that Rammy was gone, he would beg my sisters and I to play baseball with him. We were not good but feeling our little brother's loss, we of course would throw the ball so he could practice hitting. That is probably one of the ways I developed my own good hand-eye coordination. This is one of the memories that was precious to Billy when I called him in Houston, Texas, to gather some tidbits of his own memories and insights.

"Oh, Patti, I'm so glad you called. We all miss and think about you all the time. Candice still talks about her 'Aint' Patti," he said in his Texas drawl. Mary Belle and I went to Texas when his wife Shirly died of breast cancer. Once she was diagnosed, it was fast and furious, catching everyone off guard, with hardly any time to absorb or prepare. They had four children: three handsome boys and little Candice who loved to dance. She was like a little ballerina, thin and wispy. She was five or six when Mary Belle and I went to visit. We stayed several weeks to help them through this major adjustment in their lives.

It was great talking to Billy, who is like a gentle bear. I told him about my book.

"Patti, that's great. You've always been the one that faces things head on."

I told him I wanted to confirm with him some facts for accuracy.

"Sure, Patti. I'm glad you're doing this. In fact, we all should, but you can speak for all of us."

I told him if he wanted I would read a few paragraphs to let him know where I was at, setting the scene. "I would be honored to hear,' he said amicably. I told him that I was writing for understanding, basically the same thing I told Mary Belle and Rammy. I read to him several paragraphs about what I knew of our parents. I also skipped some pages that would go into some memories as we were as children and teenagers. As I read, he listened intently. I could hear his sighs of expression as the memories came tumbling to the surface.

"Oh, Patti. As you were reading it all came back. But there are some things that I do know. One is that," and then he chuckled politely. "Dad wasn't in Africa. He was in Panama, the Panama Canal."

"What? How could I have thought he was in Africa all these years? I pictured him lying sick in the jungles with malaria, among the wild animals, peeking through the thick jungle vegetation waiting for their opportunity. I pictured African drum beating in the background, way in the distance."

Now I was going to have to picture him suffering along a canal in Panama. I was going to look at my map.

"But, Patti, you were right. Dad did have malaria and almost died. He also ran away from the uncle's house at the age of fourteen and joined the army, saying he was older. But he was probably about fifteen when he joined. He also boxed in the army and evidently was quite good."

Well, I imagine with all the pent-up rage and survival skills that it was a natural release for him.

"Billy, thank you for setting me straight." I was slightly disappointed because Africa to me sounded a bit more exotic, but I'm sure the Panama Canal has it's own fascinating history.

"You know, Patti, as I am thinking, are you going to include some humorous things also?"

"I'm trying to."

"Gosh, Patti," he said in his slight Texas twang. "I'm racking my brain to think of a fond memory, but the bad ones are more prominent."

"I'm sorry. We don't have to dredge anything else up."

My brother was supporting me one hundred percent, encouraging me in this venture.

"Patti, do you remember when dad bought boxing gloves for Rammy and I to teach us to box?"

"Vaguely."

"Boxing was not my forte. I was always interested in the creative and humanitarian aspect of life. Well, Dad thought we boys should learn the art of boxing. The only thing was, once he got into it, Dad would not hold back."

I shuddered as faint memories came back, long ago forgotten.

"Dad would sometimes forget he was teaching. He would force Rammy to put on the boxing gloves. It seemed he had a vendetta and he was always the hardest on Rammy. One time, Rammy hit back and connected. Dad got so angry and started hitting so hard and fast that he knocked Rammy on the ground and kept hitting him. Rammy's face was bloodied and he still kept hitting him. Mary Belle started screaming at him to stop. He was in a frenzy and he was aware of nothing around him. Mary Belle ran and took a flying leap and jumped on Dad's back and started pummeling him. Boy, could she ever run fast. She also could jump higher than nay girl I ever knew. She really was athletic.

"Dad finally stopped realizing the damage he had done and skulked away."

Picturing my precious brother on the ground bleeding, my sister leaping to his defense. It was too much to comprehend, but I know it was true. Mary Belle saved Rammy. That was just a way of life for us. Never knowing who would be the next target. What a way to live.

One thing we all knew was that once we graduated from high school we would be free to have our own lives, free of the abuse. Anything would be better than what we had to go through at home.

My brother and I talked for quite a while, Billy telling me that he knew that writing about all this could not be easy but in some way also cathartic.

"God, I don't know," I said. "I just hope this book can make a positive difference. Somehow. Some way."

I remember the time it was a very hot summer night. We didn't have air conditioning. It was so hot I slept with my legs off the bed and just had a light sheet. I could never sleep without some kind of cover over my shoulders. I was feeling the slight coolness on my legs when I heard a piercing scream in the night. I jumped and pulled my legs, arms and head under the covers. The screams continued. The lights came on in the hallway and I could hear my mother come upstairs. When I saw the light, Sandy and I got up and went in the hall as our mother came toward us in the long hallway. Mary Belle ran out of her room, saying a man, a ghost, walked out of her closet and stood at the end of her bed. She was hysterical. Since the lights were on in the hallway, my mother walked in my sister's small bedroom and turned on the lights.

"Mary Belle, you must have had a nightmare. This is no one here. You just had a bad dream." She tried to assure a shaken Mary Belle. All I could think of was that little cemetery that was on the other side of her room. That night all four of us slept in the same bed on that very hot night.

I often wondered about that house.

One night after Rammy left for the army, Ginny was sleeping in my brother's big room. She would sleep with her two cats. She started screaming in the night. My sister and I ran into her rescue. She was sitting up in bed, shaking.

"Ginny, what's wrong?"

"Something jumped on my bed and woke me up. I was so frightened I couldn't move or speak."

"It was probably one of your cats."

"No," she protested. "They were right by me, asleep, but woke and hissed. It was a hard bounce."

Ooh. I didn't like that. Again, we all slept in the same bed. Later in the week after I wrote this piece I called Mary Belle to confirm this occurrence. She got very excited and said, "Patti, you know that house was haunted. Remember we could hear voices in the night? Doors slamming shut or thing mysteriously missing or misplaced?" Maybe that explained why I should stay up so late. I didn't want any unpleasant surprises. My sisters and I would talk sometimes in the wee hours of the morning. I tried to keep my mind on positive things and I always said my prayers. There would be many nights that all of us girls would sleep in the same room, for there is safety in numbers.

As Mary Belle and I talked, she lamented her anguish and regrets when our father moved us all out to the country. She remembered how our father would paint a picture of a wonderful life on this little farm. Instead of a safe haven or a port of leisure and serenity, it was as if a terrible mistake and there was no way out or a bad dream that goes on and on. No one hears the cries in the night for we are too far removed. Mary Belle told me of times that our father became so enraged and out of control that she ran outside for help, standing in the middle of the road in front of our house.

"Someone, please help us!" She screamed in the day, in the night. Her screams turned to tears of frustration and hopelessness. No one came to her futile attempt to rescue her brothers or sisters. That was my sister, protecting her siblings before herself. I do remember those times. No one would come to help us, which made us realize even more our very vulnerable existence. Our survival would depend on each other and our own will and determination.

When Rammy left for the army, the loss for us all was almost unbearable. I felt the buffering walls of protection crumbling and weakening, feeling almost defenseless, but I also felt time was on our side. That this might force our father to reevaluate his behavior and actions toward his family and hopefully turn a new leaf. I was forever hopeful. But what I have learned is unless problems are addressed, they will continue. Apathy for whatever reason—illness, ignorance, stoicism or just plain disregard—will perpetuate the madness to out of control, creating chaos, turmoil and feelings of futility. Stifling the spirit and mind, harming the body and soul. No one has the right to have that kind of power over anyone, especially a child. My own sisters and brothers are forever grateful that we had each other to intervene in each of our defense, validating our experiences as real and so unwieldy that we knew would and could impact our whole lives. Would we be able to grow up unscathed, unaffected, emotionally healthy and productive? Would we be part of the problem or another problem or would it be possible that we would overcome the obstacles thrust upon us? There is strength in acknowledging the really difficult issues that would help build and restore the mind, body and spirit that helps become the solution.

* * * * *

CHAPTER 13

LULL BEFORE THE STORM

THERE IS ALWAYS A LULL before the storm. I don't know why. Maybe it is the gathering of the energy that has culminated from the far distance, eventually making its presence known. Some are aware and are vigilant, watchful, anticipating the unknown. Many choose not to know. They close their eyes, cover their ears and avoid what they cannot understand or undo. Until they gather that courage. Some never will.

My dear friend Jill just called as I was getting back into my writing this morning.

Our background is somewhat similar, with artist and musicians in her family. She has a deep love of nature and the outdoors. She also came from a family of six siblings. She was the oldest and still is, while I was insulated in the middle of my family. I still like that. We both were divorced about the same time, married the same number of years. We both had two sons and a daughter. There are many similarities in our personalities. We both are passionate about our families, our ideals and life.

"Jill, would you like to hear the last two paragraphs I've written? Tell me what you think."

I love the fact that she is always so enthusiastic. "Sure, I'd like to. I always like what you're doing. It makes me think of my own life. How I grew up."

Jill grew up in Canada. I learned my father's father would be exiled to Canada. There is the difference. Her life fortunately was not quite as tumultuous.

"Patti, I was thinking all of your sisters and brothers turned out so well. There must have been something in each of your parents that you and your siblings gleaned onto that gave you a coping mechanism."

I needed to hear her worlds of wisdom and insight.

"Thank you for recognizing that, and that is true. I do think that our mother's gentle loving nature was predominant especially in those formative years. I believe also that we understood our father's tragic background and our compassion was always evident. But I believe that we chose to take the best part that our parents had to offer themselves. A strong desire of learning, achieving and a gentle spirit from our mom."

"Yes, Patti, but what I could see is that none of your judgments were clouded. There never seemed to be problems with drugs or alcohol that many people rely on to escape or cope."

Well, yes, to a certain extent that was true. Except my younger sister Sandy shortly after I had left home did raid mother's medicine cabinet, taking the meds herself to try and understand our mother's behavior. Why was our mother so oblivious to what was going on around her? How could she be so calm, as if in a fog or drugged? Was it the medicines?

"Sandy was also always a little different. She never learned to ride a bike or roller skate. She never would dance, but she wrote beautiful poetry."

As I grew older, I wondered if she didn't have some form of autism that was never known. She was probably too sensitive. She loved our mother so much that she put her on a pedestal, but the reality was too hard for her to bear. By taking our mother's meds, it became a downward spiral in her thinking and thought processes. She ran away from home just weeks before she was to graduate from high school. To support herself she went to work as a go-go dancer, which led to a drug addiction. Uppers to get her motivated and downers to bring her down. Since she did not feel comfortable with herself and never really danced, that we knew of, the people who hired her would encourage her to drink. She never liked the taste, but evidently was pushed on her to help her relax. Because Sandy was so young and vulnerable, her life escalated rapidly out of control.

I will get on with my story. Before I go too deep too soon.

I had an interesting conversation with Billy when we talked about Rammy's departure in the army. I would have been sixteen at that time, or almost. Rick was in my life. That gave me a sense of security and confirmation. I didn't quite feel as vulnerable, probably as the rest of my siblings. Billy did tell me that when Rammy left, he would plan his own way out. He would save his money from his part-time job to get a car. But his plan was great than just a car, for it offered him a means of independence. He would continue working and finish his education. In his senior year of high school, he left home, found an affordable apartment in town, continued his senior year and graduated. After graduation, he joined the army and was stationed in Germany. I remember when he would write letters, sending pictures. He looked handsome, happy and confident in his uniform. I did not know of my brother's plans for at this time I was married and going to be a mother myself.

Rick was in my life. He would be in college. I would be a junior in high school. Our feelings were dependable, never questioning or doubting. Rick was the one constant force in my life that I could turn to. He had no fear of my father and my father somehow knew that. For Rick, I was the girl that he wanted to be in his life. I had no one else really to compare. But did I need to when he had almost all the qualities a girl would want? He was devoted to me. To me, he seemed brave and worldly or I should say streetwise. He drove a white car with red interior. He also rod a motorcycle for recreation. He grew up surrounded by his Italian family, mother and father, Grandpa Mike, Grandma Gilda, his aunts and uncles from both sides, with lots of cousins always around. Rick had one sister and then himself. He was the first grandson in his clan and he would be pampered and adored. His world was his to command for he grew up with no fears. What a great and wonderful difference.

When Rick graduated from high school, he would attend the Roosevelt University in Chicago. He would study business, which would become his area of expertise. This was very helpful in life. That is what I've learned. Now I think that everyone should have some business background and know what it is important, for we use some form of business in every aspect of life. Rick's life never skipped a beat. He did what he chose to do. He had a master plan and he knew what he would need to achieve his dreams, and the people that were necessary and important in his life who would help give him the incentive to achieve it all. Rick was fortunate to have all that in his life from the beginning and even in his marriage that would never change.

Rick and I would date throughout the summer. He had quite the schedule going to school, several part-time jobs, plus the fact that we were dating. I would be a junior in high school at Crete Monee. Even though Rick was in college, he never lost interest in me and because I was not allowed to date that much anyway, the times we shared were special. I was sixteen going on seventeen when I noticed more expectations coming from Rick. We would go out, maybe to a dance, a movie, a double date with friends. When Rick would take me home, he would want to park. His sweet kisses were being replaced by an urgency that I could not understand, nor was I ready for. I know that it was a natural part of life, a normal rite of passage, but I had fears. I was hoping that he would be content with loving me, loving him knowing that when the time was right, but I had not idea how I would know. It seemed he knew already. I pondered this question. But I didn't have anyone to turn to for information, advice or how to approach such a topic.

Rick and I were going on a special date. It was my seventeenth birthday. I can't even remember what we did, but I think it was a dance for I wore a pretty blue dress. But I also know it would be a time that I know would never forget. I remembered we stayed out later than normal, for I always had to be home before midnight. On the way home, Rick parked the car on the lonely country road. He kissed me so fervently, telling me that he had wanted me for so long, that his desire was so strong that he could even die from this strong desire. It was my birthday. I didn't wan him to die. I was seventeen now. He was in college. Maybe the time was right. Our lovemaking went further than I wanted. It happened. I did not feel the thrill that everyone talked about for my fear was greater than my desire. My tears were soft. Rick comforted me seeming relieved and at peace. What would all this mean?

I gathered myself together as much as possible. I would have to go home. I would get in trouble for it was too late anyway. Rick drove to the back of the house. The back porch light was on. He kissed me goodnight at the door. I walked inside the enclosed porch and into the kitchen. A small light was on and the house was still and quiet. When I went to go upstairs, my parents awakened. My father was stern, but more tired. Thank God, more tired than ready to discipline. I quietly went to my room; my sister's sound asleep. I took off my pretty dress that I would never wear again and placed it on a chair. I got ready for bed. I needed to talk but I couldn't. I wanted to go within myself to think this whole thing through. When I went to get in bed, Sandy woke up.

"Did you have a nice time, Patti?"

I wanted to cry. Could my sister see that I was different now? "I'll tell you in the morning." I stifled my feelings and tears. I quietly said prayers. But did I deserve them to be answered?

Strangely enough, not too much happened that next morning. What was that when any other time the slightest provocation would be harshly addressed? Life would continue pretty much as normal, but for me I felt a stirring difference. I know that I was quieter than normal. I tried to act the same, but I found myself wanting to withdraw from the world. I needed time to process and understand the significance of my life. Each day that went by was quiet agony. Time is telling. It was only once. Didn't I have to feel something other than pain?

I was approaching March. My periods were like clockwork, brazenly making their presence known. What was happening to me? There were no signs of aching that turned into throbbing cramps that released the heavy flow of blood that came from somewhere in my body. I would dread that time, for my periods were harsh and long, lasting up to eight days. They were never easy, but now that was what I desperately welcomed. It would not happen. I was in disbelief. But I knew I had to face my fear and the consequences of my first time. I knew that I would be a stigma to my family. I would hold on to my dignity and face the consequences. What would possibly happen to me? Would I be given the scarlet letter? Would I be beaten and fed to the wolves or ostracized from life? I could not imagine having a baby. That never entered my thoughts. I wanted to experience life unencumbered without such heavy responsibilities and I did not know if I was prepared.

For some reason, I have always faced my challenges head on, if there were to be consequences for my mistakes or actions that was justified. I would face them with as much courage as I could gather. Hopefully, I would learn and evolve a better person because of what I experienced without too many regrets. I would have to tell Rick. I felt he had a right to know of my suspicions. He picked me up from school and we took a walk. This was in March. I remember the day. We walked along the parkway. The grass was just starting to come back from the winter. The sky was hazy with a slight breeze. There was a feeling of melancholy in the air or maybe it was my own feelings. We walked slowly. Rick held my hand. I quietly told him my concern.

"I think I might be pregnant."

He listened quietly, not interrupting. Maybe he was too stunned to speak. I had no expectations, other than I felt he had a right to know. He stopped, turned and looked at me and said, "Well, we'll just get married."

He said those words with such brave conviction that I was slightly thrown off guard. I was not expecting such a chivalrous attitude.

"Are you sure that's what you want to do?"

"Patti, you are the girl that I was going to marry anyway. It is just going to be sooner than expected. We'll be okay."

With those words, he put his arms around me to reassure me. I had never pictured myself getting married while still in school. I always felt that I would be a singer, dancer, also an artist and because I was so appreciative of my gifts of talent and abilities, I would also be a missionary. Those interest and abilities always helped me get through difficult times and gave me something to hold on to. I would have to alter my picture and my dreams when Rick said he wanted to marry me. He even wanted to be with me when I told my parents, but I was afraid of my father's reaction to Rick. I would tell them myself. Sometimes fear of the unknown is greater than the reality, keeping us in a state of uncertainty and limbo. We all make mistakes. No one is invincible in that regard, for to err is human. What is important is to learn from that lapse of judgment or transgression in order not to create an even bigger problem.

Rick never wavered when he said those worlds and for that I will always love him. Those words to me epitomized the courage and character that would hold him always dear to my heart. For me, that was the characteristic that was paramount to me at that time for I knew about living in fear. I would not know and it was certainly unforeseen but Rick would be the catalyst for my escape and I would be the catalyst for the successes in our marriage. I do not say this to be arrogant, but as a fact or a phenomenon that occurs when people or situations are compatible. We would have a small wedding. I was still going to school. To be going to school one day and come back to school after a long weekend married was surreal. I would not be allowed the time to process or prepare. I really did not even know how to begin, for a marriage was maybe something in the far future if and when I truly fell in love.

I remember Rick and I going to get our marriage license at city hall. When Rick told the kind woman behind the counter of formality that we needed a marriage license soon, she turned her head from Rick and looked at me squarely. It was as if she could read the future. "You do not have to do this. You are so young. You've got your whole life ahead of you." She said this with such genuine sincerity that I wondered what she saw in me that would provoke such a passionate plea that her words made me realize I might have a say in this whole thing. I was too young and to make it worse, I looked younger than my years and to top that off I had so much to learn. I was wide-eyed innocent. It was almost reassuring knowing this kind stranger cared to speak her mind, her thoughts. I wondered what Rick was thinking. This interaction made me realize even more the seriousness of all that was to transpire. We could get our license. I didn't have much recourse, at least that I had control over. The only thing that I knew I could do and be was to do and give the best of my abilities. I would be young, Rick too. But I do know back then we both were willing to give our best.

My life from the beginning would not be typical. Needless to say my wedding would not be ordinary either. After all the necessary formalities were addressed and attended to, we would be married at St. Rocco church on April 27. My future mother- and father-in-law would take Rick and me shopping for a bedroom set first. That was thoughtful but awkward also, when Rick too me aside and whispered, "Don't select the most expensive set. I don't want my parents spending a lot of money." When I think back, the monetary issues were always prominent and foremost in every decision made or carried through for Rick, but also his family. They all had a natural aptitude for business. Money was to be made to save.

Mary Belle was mad at me. She was older than I, but I was the one getting married first. I know my older sister entertained the idea of marriage but that was never in my thoughts. Here I was the one to be making this tremendous step. I was the reluctant bride. Now I was going to have to find a fitting dress to mark this special day. I remember wanting to just get the whole thing over with. No one told me, I could not or should not wear white. I made that decision myself. I did not want to start my marriage with pretense. I chose a two-piece dress of the softest pink, with spaghetti straps, the bodice fitted snug to the waist. The skirt softly gathered with a crinoline of netting that made the skirt flounce. This dress had a fitted jacket with short sleeves that was cropped at the waist. I wore a small oval type hat with delicate netting in surround. I wore soft pink open-strapped heels, but not too high. I had never worn heels before. I was surprised at the result. It seemed appropriate and I was thankful that I looked pretty in my soft pink.

The bridal party was small, just Mary Belle and Rick's older sister Cynthia. Rick would have his cousin and best friend Frankie Maine and his friend Dennis stand up for our wedding. Dennis was also was dating my sister Mary Belle at that time. I remember feeling calm. I had resigned myself to trust providence. For me, since I had no relatives that lived near, I would just have my own immediate family. I remember the feelings as I was preparing for the wedding, my older sister still slightly miffed that I was getting married. I knew for reasons that went deeper than the magic order. Sandy would break out in sobs. I was her rock of hope and reassurance, the one person who seemed to understand her. Ginny would be seven, not quite understanding what was going on, but she would look at me with doleful eyes silently wondering. She was an astute child, quietly observing, knowing that things were changing. Billy kept a respectable distance, his own feelings to himself. I know he was missing Rammy, who was now in the army. He would not be able to be at the wedding. I'm sure even more so, he was thinking of the changing dynamics of our family and how he could eventually make leave of his own in a more dignified manner. I loved my sisters and brothers. If only I could gather them all with me.

Throughout the ceremony, I could hear Sandy trying to stifle her tears. As we were pronounced man and wife, loud wailing permeated the church with heart-wrenching sobs coming from Sandy. It seemed tears were a part of the scene at weddings. But this was my sister and I knew it was tears of loss for her, something else in her world that she had no control. As we gathered outside the vestibule of the church, people greeting with extended wishes that I took to heart. When my own family came to me, I felt sadness for my mother. I wished she could have been a stronger presence in my life, in her children's lives. I think my father in his heart didn't think that he had a right to be at the ceremony, for he offered his children nothing but fear. Fortunately, he did have those rare occasions that we chose to remember that instilled a certain value and strength in times that were needed. When Sandy came up to me with Ginny, I put my arms around each to try and comfort and reassure both of them. Rick was looking on. I'm sure never seeing a reunion quite as this emotional scene.

Dating once or twice a week, under very structured conditions certainly didn't give me an accurate concept of life. For even through all the turmoil I would maintain an idealistic way of thinking. We were definitely made up of two entirely different components. Rick was ravenous and I needed loving tenderness. So I was very much surprised at the intensity of our honeymoon. It was not at all what I expected. Now that we were married, it seemed that all his sexual energy was released with an insatiable appetite. Maybe that is normal for many on their honeymoon. I don't know. It is just that I was inexperienced and would have preferred a more gradual, tender introduction that was romantically sensitive and thoughtful. We hardly slept. Rick would make love at every turn as if there would be no tomorrow. There would be no sleeping in either, for Rick set the alarm clock so we could attend the six a.m. mass that was in Italian and Latin. I remember the strong scent of the incense making me feel nauseous. I was so sleep deprived that I felt like I was going to faint. We would have to leave the warm, cloistered church for the coolness of the early dawn.

That was our one night honeymoon. Rick would return to his routine of work and college. I would return to my classes at high school. The only girl that was now married which surely imposed provocative questions to some. Most were oblivious. Thank God. But to some I was even more an enigma, even to myself. I wondered the first day back at school if I looked different. I prayed that I could go through each day with a certain amount of dignity. Through my whole pregnancy, I only gained eleven pounds. But I was naturally healthy. I had never touched a cigarette, drank or did any kind of drugs. For some reason, I always felt that if it smelled bad, tasted bad and a person had to acquire a taste for it, it could not be good or healthy for you. I could always only eat in small increments for some reason. If I tried to eat more, I would feel sick. So I just didn't. For some reason, I loved oranges and orange juice that was my favorite. Still is. At any rate, the only noticeable change was my bosom. My breasts kept growing. I was skinny, but it was hard to conceal the fact that I was more endowed than I wanted to be, much to my chagrin. Also, a very heavy sleep would overpower me, to the point that I could fall asleep as if under a spell. I would fight the sleepy spells at school, but at home doing my homework, I would fall asleep while sitting up with my head on my paper or book. It was that overpowering. I was either trying to catch up from my one-night honeymoon or the fact that Rick prided himself on his sexual virility that was becoming his favorite prelude to each day.

We would live with my in-laws for a little over two years. It was their way to help us get a start. It would also be the time that we shared together. My mother-in-law would use this time to teach me to cook Rick's favorite meals, plus just how to cook. She taught me to iron shirts and pants, keeping the creases in the proper places, and how to do laundry, sorting the darks and colors from the whites. She taught me like a child and she was right, for those skills were never taught to me. But during this time we also developed a friendship, a bond that would deepen through the years. Diva became like a mother, a best friend and a mentor. We could not help but become close, as she was with me throughout my pregnancy. When I would get sick, she worried and would care for me. During this time, Rick was happy, content, moving forward with his studies and doing well. I was thankful to be surrounded by my new protective Italian family. What a wonderful change for me.

I will be getting back to my wedding. Sandy would continue crying her tears even at the reception. The music at the reception that brought frivolity to our guests would not be heard or felt by my younger sister Sandy, who was in such desolation. Rick and I danced a few dances, but Rick wanted to leave for our honeymoon. I couldn't understand why he was so eager to leave when our party had just begun.

When we left, the young people were still dancing. I wanted to stay until the last dance. A week after the wedding Ginny called me wanting to know when I was coming home. When I told her I was married now, she quietly said, "Does that mean you can't sleep here anymore?" At this time, Rammy was in the army and I was married. There seemed to be a lull. I wanted to think that it was a change of heart, or that close encounter or the sheer fact that it was time to change the miserable ways for my father. I was pretty self-absorbed at this time, with processing my new life, school and homework, while the silent pregnancy was a constant reminder with tremendous changes. I was hoping that life everywhere was worry free and peaceful and that applied to my own family.

My in-laws lived on the outskirts of town, so now instead of the long ride on the school bus, I would walk to school, which was about a half mile. Perfect for me. I would start out walking by myself, but by the time I would arrive at school I would have collected a small entourage of friends on the way. By the time I would leave from school I would start out with my friends, eventually going our own separate ways. I would have a few blocks to myself, which was a pleasant way to start and end my school day. I liked that. That brief moment of time gave me reprieve from the solemnity of my life. I also would focus my thoughts on achieving a new destiny that would include a bright future that inspired in a positive way. I would help make it work.

That was my humble and tumultuous beginning. I knew all I had to know about survival, about avoiding precarious situations and overcoming fear for that is what I grew up with. I was thankful for the time that my mother-in-law took, teaching me in a way that brought us close. I knew in the beginning it had to be difficult for her, so I did everything I could think of to show my gratitude. If she would be gone for the day, I would surprise her with dusting the furniture, taking the rugs out of air, vacuuming the floors. I liked things to look nice. If there were coins, earrings, buttons or odds and in pieces lying on the counter or desktop, I would dust or clean and then arrange the items in a decorative display. She liked that and I was happy that those simple things surprised, delighted and pleased her. When the weather was nice, I would open the windows to let the gentle breezes flow through the rooms. I loved seeing the wispy curtains gently waving in the soft breeze.

I called my mother-in-law Diva for that was her name. She almost from the beginning wanted me to call her Mom. She was Rick's mom and she had a daughter Cynthia, so it did not feel quite right. I did have my own mother. But my mother-in-law gave me something that my own mother did not know how to do and that was to teach, to care for and protect. I knew when the time felt right I would be able to probably when I finally had no doubts and felt deserving. My mother-in-law would get her hair done once a week. She prided herself with her meticulous dress. She always wore her hair short and curly and colored her hair a shade of red. She was a spunky, energetic woman. She was the older of her two sisters Elda and Lorraine. Their hair was dark brown in fact closer to black. I think they all colored their hair, but I could be wrong. I loved having this family around me, hearing the sisters with their lively conversations. They all had their distinct personalities. But the fact that they were all so close was what was important to me. To me it was like having that strong nucleus that circled and kept the family strong and apparent.

Diva reminded me in some ways of Mary Belle. In the fact that she had that high energy and was not afraid to say what was on her mind. Sometimes surprising or slightly shocking those around, but she also had an endearing quality that made people overlook, if they knew her well. They lived in the same neighborhood all their life, so that helped. I immediately liked her sister Aunt Elda, she was married to Uncle John. For some reason, I found it easy to call my new family aunt or uncle, and really easy to call Grandma Gilda and Grandpa Mike by their titles. Well, Aunt Elda had a commanding presence, but also the most welcoming and warm smile, with the biggest heart. She would take charge when she had to, for she had a lot of common sense, most of the time. Aunt Lorraine was the youngest. She was married to Uncle George. Uncle George and Rick were buddies. He was a big guy that would do anything to help those that he cared about. He must have really cared about Rick and me, for he would help us move and build with meticulous care a tool and garden shed for Rick, and when we had our two boys, he would come over and cut their hair. Now back to Aunt Lorraine. She was more reserved. She would come into a room with her calming presence. She would sit back and listen to her sisters and then with real authority set the record straight if she had to. In that respect, she was strong but she was also smart and sometimes that is a difficult thing to be contained and she knew it. So life was interesting and good.

Finally, in my life, I would experience what it would be like to have grandparents around and what an incredible experience bringing such richness of history of life experience and knowledge, laughter and joy. Grandpa Mike was always so playful with the grandkids and Grandma Gilda ample arms ready to hug. Her pride and joy was her family, teaching her daughters well for they all were expert cooks, making their own pasta and delectable Italian dishes that were fit for royalty. The wonderful aroma of the perfect blend of spices filing the air and whetting the appetite. They both opened their arms to me and I loved them immediately. They were no longer living but their memories will always be with me.

My first son Mark would be born into this family on Rick's birthday, November 4. It wasn't quite like what I read in the books. I would read about the false labor that can happen and helps prepare you for birth. I had that. I learned that in the beginning stage the labor pain could be fifteen to twenty minutes apart. I had that all night, but not to worry for the contractions have to come about three to five minutes apart, before the baby comes. When I thought this was finally the real deal, the twenty to fifteen minute contractions would stop altogether. Sometimes I wondered if I was really pregnant that this was now my real body shape. I knew I was in real labor when my contractions didn't stop and it was November 3. That was my due date, just like Dr. Parizzi said.

So far, like clockwork. I was up all night with my twenty, fifteen and now ten minutes apart contractions. This must be it. They were getting stronger too. Rick was pretty calm and so was his mother. I think my father-in-law was a little nervous, but everyone was anticipating. I called my doctor and he said, "Now, Patricia, since this is your first baby, it might be a while. So don't come to the hospital until the pains are three to five minutes apart consistently." My contractions continued throughout the morning along with some bleeding, which alarmed me but was also another part of real labor. It was evident at this time that this was for real. Rick would take me to the hospital, which was only a few miles away. Since it was Sunday the driving was easy.

When the nurse saw me, she didn't think I was full term because I was small, only gaining eleven pounds. After settling in the hospital, my pains drifted apart for a while, but would gather in momentum and intensity. I thought once the labor pains became three minutes apart, the baby would naturally come. I never expected the pain to be so hard and relentless that I could hardly catch my breath. Rick stayed with me the whole time, sometimes walking with me through the night until I could walk no longer. I was delirious and exhausted. I hadn't eaten for so long I felt I needed some nourishment to give me strength but I could not even have a cracker. Eventually, my thirst overcame my hunger. I was parched. How could this be happening? Rick tried to soothe me by putting cool compresses on my forehead. I begged for a small sip of water. I felt that would help me, maybe my thirst was making everything worse. The nurse finally said I could have some chips of ice in a cloth. Somebody cared after all, but I wondered how anyone could endure such pain and live through it.

I didn't know if it were day or night, just a series of long wracking pain. Finally, I would be wheeled into the delivery room. The nurse so kind and gentle kept telling me to breathe like a puppy. "Just breathe like a puppy," she would repeat softly. I couldn't remember how a puppy breathed. I told her, trying to catch my breath through the pain. She started this panting. "Oh yes. I remember.

I can do that." I started to imitate the breathing, trying to feel like a puppy, anything to end my misery. It worked. Finally after thirty-six hours of labor, our first son was born, weighing six pounds two ounces and seventeen inches long. I was so exhausted that as soon as they told me I had a healthy baby boy I fell sound asleep. There would be poking and prodding and pushing on my belly. What were they doing I needed my rest so I could be a mother.

* * * *

GALLERY III

We were invited to sing in Washington DC . We sang in seven different venues, most of them we sang acapella. Governor Mark Dayton met us at the airport where we gathered for photos and good wishes. In the front row is Polly, Jane, Chris, Gov. Mark Dayton, myself and our accomplished Music director Tom Paulson. This was an incredible experience in many ways to add to our repertoire in life.

Unless the peace that follows recognizes that the whole world is one neighborhood and does justice to the whole human race. The germs of another world war will remain as a constant threat to mankind.

*No country, however rich, can afford the waste of its human resources.
Demoralization caused by vast unemployment is our greatest extravagance.
Morally, it is the greatest menace to our social order.*

*They (who) seek to establish systems of government based on the regimentation of
all human beings by a handful of individual rulers...call this a new order. It is not
new and it is not order.*

We must scrupulously guard the civil rights and civil liberties of all citizens, whatever their background. We must remember that any oppression, any injustice, any hatred, is a wedge designed to attack our civilization.

The test of our progress is not whether we ad more to the abundance of those who have much; it is whether we provide enough for those who have little.

Aeschylus wrote: In our sleep, pain that cannot forget falls drop by drop upon the heart and in our despair, against our will comes wisdom through the awful grace of God.

What we need in the United States is not division, what we need in the United States is not hatred, what we need in the United States is not violence or lawlessness, but love and wisdom and compassion toward one another and a feeling of justice toward those who still suffer within our country, whether they be white or they be black, let us dedicate ourselves to what the Greeks wrote so many years ago to tame the savageness of man and make gentle the life of this world. Let us dedicate ourselves to that and say a prayer for our country and our people.
–Indianapolis 1968

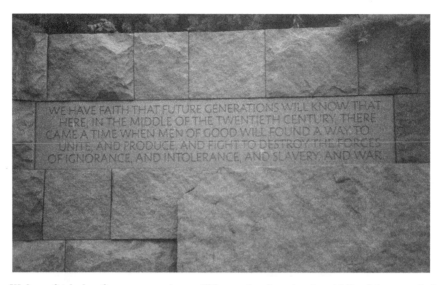

We have faith that future generations will know that here, in the middle of the twentieth century, there came a time when men of good will found a way to unite, and produce, and fight to destroy the forces of ignorance, and intolerance, and slavery, and war.

I HAVE SEEN WAR

I have seen war on land and sea. I have seen blood running from the wounded. I have seen the dead in the mud. I have seen cities destroyed. I have seen children starving. I have seen the agony of mothers and wives.

I HATE WAR

194

CHAPTER 14

FEBRUARY 7, 2006: LOST REDRESS

IT IS AMAZING HOW THE legal system works or doesn't work in some cases. We have become a very legalistic society, making it now a very profitable form of business, consisting of designer laws, loopholes to create exemptions for those that have learned the ropes and can avoid consequences. These special exemptions and allowances or favors slowly and insidiously become a normal part of the process left unspoken, obscured or hidden but raises its head in compliance when the price is high enough ignoring the unjust consequences sometimes spiraling out of control with long-term ramifications that are far reaching. Yet no one has to be responsible and they know it, for no one is looking at them to be held accountable. I thought the laws were to protect the innocent, keep the criminals and the criminal mind responsible, in check. I never thought that the offices that we hold in the highest esteem would be part of the biggest problems, creating a dysfunction and corruption within.

I will continue with this part of the my story, only because it is another pivotal period in my life as a recently divorced woman set free to experience the side of life I was denied. Now would be my time to acquire the sophisticated exposure in life, pursue my talents in painting and music. As painful as it was to be divorced, I felt at least I still could pursue my own dreams that had been encumbered by the restraints of the necessary responsibilities that were thrust upon me so early in my life. A priest once told me in counseling that the men in my life that I should have trusted the most had also hurt me the most. This was just before my divorce, when my husband was so affected by the successes of all the years of the mergers and acquisitions that consumed him, to the point that he became hard and indifferent, critical and demanding. Instead of being grateful for what he had and what he had accomplished, he turned forgetting his reason and purpose. His world became all about himself for now it was out of sight, out of mind.

It was so easy for him to forget those who helped him accomplish his dreams. The techniques and skills he learned in the ruthless world of mergers and acquisitions would be carried over in our family, including his oldest and dearest friends. For now, his wealth would buy his needs and his new friends who were so impressed. In his mind, he was entitled and deserving and would be reluctant to part with the spoils from his so-called successes. When Rick turned his back on me, and our family at this time it was another awakening for me. I guess I needed to be sure. I would never be able to count on him for anything. It would be up to me to figure it all out for I had no family here and now my children were grown and struggling in their own paths. This divorce would place an extreme hardship on our children and myself. Rick would be spared and rewarded.

For two years the Eichorn-Hicks would intrude on my life as the bothersome neighbor. There was nothing I really could do except wait this whole thing out. During this time, Rick was in the midst of doing his appeals and he also made the decision to do the annulment. Meanwhile, Mrs. Agent was told to contact an attorney, as she could be in serious trouble for her part in this unnecessary predicament. So I was caught in a legal quagmire, in a game that I never wanted to play or participate in. But that did not matter, for now it was about the rules and the protocol designed to prolong and antagonize.

Shortly after I learned that the Eichhorn-Hicks did not have the means to buy my house, I had a bizarre encounter with my neighbor Mrs. Agent. She had contacted an attorney for fear that she could be in trouble. He told her not to speak to me or have any kind of contact as she might say something that could or would be used against her if I ever decided to take her to court. At this time I believed it was an honest mistake or misjudgment. All I wanted from her was an apology and her support along with Edina Realty. We could work this out together. But what I didn't know at this time was she had been let go from her previous position at Burnett Realty for creating and causing much havoc for that company. The important factor was Burnett could not state why she was released from the position, because of a disclaimer clause preventing any disclosure of misconduct or wrongdoing. I found this incredibly careless and thoughtless, problems never resolved but handed over to some other unsuspecting company or victim.

Of course, since Mrs. Agent was told not to talk to me, and if she apologized or anything else it would be acknowledging her part in some way. Now that is hard to do when she was my next-door neighbor. We were in close proximity.

I was stymied by this strange development and I finally confronted her. She told me, "I'm sorry, Patti. My attorney told me I had better not have any communication with you, until this all resolved."

I was shocked, stunned and disappointed that she would even think of resorting to such measure. How can there be any understanding or reconciliation of any kind once a lawyer is in the picture making this convoluted and adversarial? I really wonder who creates the laws or rules, and whom do they protect?

One bright sunny day for some unknown reason Tara called. Maybe it was a momentary awakening of her own conscience or a need for her own closure or just curiosity. I was a bit apprehensive but I listened wanting to hear something that made some kind of sense or explanation. Our conversation was going nowhere, for she became defensive and verbally out of control. I finally hung up the phone, but she would call back ranting her abuse. She would wait every few minutes and call back. This was my home. I suddenly felt a fear and I wanted to flee from the voice. I grabbed my purse and my keys and left my house away from the madness.

I would be gone for several hours and returned that afternoon. I felt a reluctance to go inside. My house was now strangely quiet. I walked into the kitchen with the pretty wallpaper and wispy curtains wanting to dispel the harsh memories. I could see that I had some messages on the phone. When I turned on the machine to listen, I was astounded to hear Tara's sharp, sarcastic voice, relentless and out of control. There were messages on top of messages. Finally, I could not listen anymore. I called a friend. She came over and said, "Patti, you've got these calls on tape. Bring them to the president of the realty company. They should know about this kind of behavior." Of course, she was right. In my shaken state of mind, I had not thought of that.

Immediately, I called Edina Realty and told them I needed to speak with the president of their company. That it was important. I was able to set up an appointment the following morning, as he seemed to be concerned and wanted this taken care of promptly. That morning a friend called. I told him about my experience with my neighbor and he was shocked. I told him I was okay and I had set up a meeting with the president of Edina Realty, Ron Pelteir. He said that was a good thing. "Is anybody going with you?" I said, "I'm going by myself. This just happened. I can handle this myself." He didn't think that was such a good idea. "You know, in cases like this, it is always good to have someone with you, especially a male figure."

I told him I really didn't have time to ask anyone. It seemed an imposition and a rather sensitive issue, that I could do this myself. I would bring my tapes. He said that he would go with me that he wanted to. I told him I had to leave within the hour and I could not be late. "If you can't be there on time, I'll have to leave without you." He was a little late. I left with the noxious tapes in hand. As I was turning onto Wooddale Avenue, my friend's car come toward me and lightly honked to get my attention.

"Pull over. I'll park my car over there and get in your car."

I guess it was meant to be. At least I had some moral support, if nothing else.

We were directed to Mr. Pelteir's office. There was an undercurrent of seriousness that permeated the room. Mr. Pelteir was formal and polite, wanting to get down to business. I was glad that I had someone with me, as he had his own attorney seated in stern professionalism. Now since my divorce and all my encounters with all these different attorneys I am more skeptical than impressed. I let my male friend introduce himself, as he immediately surveyed the situation for what it was. We immediately went straight to the purpose of this meeting, for I had no desire to prolong. I was calm and relatively poised as I gave him my background, my experience and what I had learned from people that knew Mr. and Mrs. Attorney and Mrs. Agent. I also had the tapes. They said it all.

On hearing the condemning tapes, Mr. Pelteir was even more concerned and his attorney was more conciliatory. I really cannot remember what was accomplished with that meeting, for I was still going to court for the appeals and anything else Rick and his attorney could invent. Also, during that time, Rick wanted the process of the annulment. Therefore, this encounter with my neighbor and the two attorneys were a real irritating annoyance, more than anything. I felt at least this company was now forewarned and what they did with this information was up to them. I felt a strength meeting with this president of such a well-thought-of corporation. Yet I cannot say that I was so impressed. It bothered me that he must have felt an overriding anxiety about this problem that he felt the need to have an attorney at hand. What I could see was they had a big problem that they must not have been aware of, and now they knew. What would be their solution?

Life would go on amid the ongoing legal games that were improvised in order to bring to motion regardless the intent or credibility, just blindly moving forward. The purpose to distort, convolute and prolong. Two years after this experience, I would sell my house on Edgebrook Place. My plans were to move to Tucson, Arizona. This would be the end of summer 1994. There were several significant and bizarre occurrences during this time. This move would be more complicated and disconcerting than the past as now I had many things from my children now grown yet needed to be saved.

When Rick left, he took very little for he did not want any reminders. He did take his trophies, plaques and mementos that seemed precious to him, from golf tournaments and business recognitions or achievements. He took his custom-made business suits and monogrammed shirts for business still goes on. He would not want any family photos, at least not yet for he was moving on, wanting no remembrances from his past. He looked at the furniture and said, "Just keep all the furniture. There's nothing I want." That didn't surprise me but it did sadden me. His shallowness was so apparent. This seemed so easy for him, in his arrogance.

While going through storage in the lower level, I was dismayed to find his hunting and fishing gear along with some scuba supplies. What was I to do with this stuff? Do I discard it? I decided to pack all his things in boxes and decide later. I had so much storage in this house. It really was a long and difficult task for this time I was alone. But again I was so busy. I really could not dwell on my loss. As I was going through closets, cabinets and drawers, I could not help but reminisce on the past. It seemed everything I touched or picked up brought me back to another time and another place. Needless to say, it prolonged the process. It was continuous work, from morning to late at night. I came across some old movies that my sister-in-law had given me. She had combined them all on tapes, in hopes that watching the old family movies would reunite a spark. That was a thoughtful gesture. But when I told Rick what his sister had done for us, he said that he did not have time to watch movies.

I decided I would call and tell Rick to pick up his things. He said he didn't want anything. "Just throw everything away." Some of the things I could have given away and I did. But seeing the hunting equipment was a dilemma for me. How do you dispose of hunting rifles and the shells? It bothered me that this was now my problem and it was his. I decided I would just drop everything at his house, boxed up. He could sort through his stuff and decide for himself. I then decided since he didn't take any pictures of our family I would give him the movies that his sister had given us. The movies started from when he was little. I thought for sure he should have them, since his grandparents were no longer living, and they were important to him. There were movies of his family on holidays and vacations, showing the passage of time, up into our marriage and family. I was reluctant to part with them, but I felt he would one day want these precious mementos.

It was a Sunday afternoon, late summer. I called his house. No one was home. I left a message saying I would drop off some things of his, that I was sure he would want. I carefully placed the videos in a prominent place, in consideration. I also tucked the bright yellow snorkeling mask and fins, a reminder of happier times and a sign of a possible truce. I just knew that since my house was now sold, I could now start my new life in Tucson. I felt that distance away from the constant reminders would help me heal. After our divorce, Rick bought a big mansion on Lake Harriet Parkway and Penn Avenue. That did not surprise me for he loved to jog around Lake Harriet and was close to his office downtown. His girlfriend would move in with him. She was a career woman, never married and never had children. This was the same woman he would flaunt at the country club just before we were divorce, as if stating to the world that he was a man free of moral responsibilities for now he had proven he was entitled.

Actually his house was not that far from my house. Occasionally, my friends and I might bike from my house to the lakes, stop and have an ice cream or a bite to eat. My favorite thing to do was just walk around the lake and sometimes walk to the lake and talk with good friends. If I were alone or by myself, I would walk and sprint. I loved the energy, bringing out a feeling of contentment and vibrancy. Now as I am taking this short drive to deliver Rick's belongings, I could not help but feel a form of finality. But it was not as it should be, not like this. This was so cold and indifferent. I would drop off his things and leave.

I approached the large Tudor house and pulled in the driveway. This was not a house I would have bought. It needed a family. I knew this place would not last, for there was no warmth, just big and gloomy, meant to impress, but they didn't know how to impress with grace or dignity. I got out of the car, hoping Rick or someone would come out of the house, but that did not happen. I took the three boxes out of the trunk and placed them in front of the garage, so when he came home he would be sure to find them. I felt funny, just dropping them off. I decided to run up the stone steps and ring the bell just in case.

No one appeared to be home except ... I heard a large dog barking inside the house. The dog was barking so loud and when rooms are large with high ceilings the sound travels. Since no one was coming to the door, except the guard dog, I left. As I was walking down the steps and there were several, I heard a noise above my head. I slowed down and stopped just before the landing. I looked up and saw a flash of light in the window high above me. As I was looking up, rather perplexed, the light flashed again. At first I thought it was some kind of security. A female voice then said, "Stand right there. This will make a good picture." This all seemed so ridiculously surreal. I couldn't believe it. What in the world was going on? This seemed like a bad movie, a bad joke or worse.

This was unbelievable. I knew her name was Janice B. But I preferred not to acknowledge her. Finally, I said, "What is wrong with you? Why are you doing this?" With her heinous voice, she sarcastically countered, "We're going to take you to court and this is evidence that you are trespassing on our property. In fact, your husband—I mean, your ex-husband, is calling the police." Then she proceeded to yell: "Rick, you can call the police now. Do you have the phone?"

I could not believe that Rick was part of this. How could he stoop so low? Since, I was in such disbelief, wondering what was going to happen next. Would Rick suddenly appear and speak up, show his presence? I noticed I was standing in front of a large window of a sunroom with the old lead-paned glass. It looked dark inside, but I could see a figure stooping low, skulking about not wanting to be seen. Was it shame? Janice ordered Rick again to get on the phone and call the police. "I am. I'm calling now." Would I be sick, faint, scream or commit hari-kari right there on the spot? Should I stay here and wait until the police came? I came to my sense. I looked up and said, "You are out of your mind. Both of you!" I left. No way was I going to stay here. If they wanted me, they would have to come and get me.

I drove home. I could hardly breathe from this horrid experience. There were no sirens or police cars, just the fear. I pulled in my garage, went inside my house and called my friend Pete. He said he would come over if I wanted, or I could come to his house. I told him I could not be here. I needed to get away, away from this nightmare.

I felt the comfort of his arms around me, holding me close. His eyes were so tender and loving for the first time in so long. I felt safe and secure. Yet this relationship was so new that I felt bad, burdening him with this bizarre problem. What a way to start any kind of relationship. He reassured me that I was going to be okay. Then he said, "Whatever you do, just avoid your ex-husband. He will just hurt you." Well, I certainly knew that now. How could I ever forget that image of Rick trying to keep from sight, not daring to make his voice heard? What kind of hold did this woman have on a powerful, broken man that he was under her control? Was it shame or fear?

True to his word, he would try and use this against me. He could not hurt me himself but he could find others that would do his bidding and keep his hands clean. He would use the legal system for that was his style. But there would be others that would try and profit from his games. It would be easy, if I were the invisible or unknown woman, a woman not to be heard.

Each day, after that incident, I held my breath. What would happen next? The only thing I could do was try and keep to my routine, keep packing and preparing for my big move. One of my neighbors suggested I have a big garage sale. I had never had one before, but Karen said she would go in with me. We would do it together. Make it fun. I liked that idea. We had also planned Monica's and her daughter Kim's graduation party together. We put balloons on the iron railing going down to the lower level of the backyard. The backyard was filled with colorful streamers and balloons. It was almost magical with the flowers and bright colored tablecloths. The bright sun peaked through the filtered shade of the leafy trees, sparking like jewels. The backdrop of all this was the Mill Pond, rippling in splendor. This was a perfect summer day for a graduation party.

Karen would help me again. Having this garage sale with a friend made it bearable almost a normal occurrence. Karen was very organized. I think she could do anything. She seemed to bring out the best in everyone with her friendly style and grace. She was quite creative, a gifted artist that was unaffected by her talents for it was hers naturally. By all standards, it probably was one of the better garage sales. Between Karen and myself, our items were placed creatively, showing our wares in a dignified fashion. It was almost like a department store, in some areas a dollar store. For me, it was like cleaning closets and storage areas, except this time I was moving. The thought of moving again made me want to sell almost everything. I decided to put the small miscellaneous items in unique bags or boxes and label them. For instance: Bag of Wonders, Surprises Inside, Box of Goodies, or A Box of Treasures, etc. It's amazing what you can sell when the display or presentation is inviting and the price is right. Everyone should have at least one garage sale in their life, just for the sheer experience.

When Rick and I were married and we had our new kitchen installed we kept the cabinetry for they were in excellent condition. I even saved the closet that held the dropdown ironing board. We used the cabinets for further storage in the lower level and the garage. I did not just want to throw these things away. Someone had recommended I call the Free Store. I called them. They gave me the number of a Vietnamese family that had moved into a house that needed cabinets for their kitchen and for storage. When she told me they had children, I gathered up some toys, etc. That following work day, the family came in an old van. They were excited about this find as they packed everything tightly inside.

They asked me if I had cleaning supplies, paint or tools of any kind. Boy, did I ever. Mr. Wells had left antique cleaning supplies. Plus I had some of my own.

When we walked through the lower level storage area, I was surprised at their find as if a cache of riches. Some were of the oldest cleaning and painting supplies untouched for decades. I never discarded them for they seemed to belong to this old house. They were excited about old buckets and empty cans, cans of stuff, turpentine and cleaning supplies for which labels no longer existed. I had a big box of rags, rags from the past that Mr. and Mrs. Wells collected. I would donate a few my self through the years. They spotted that box. It was like a goldmine for them.

When I saw the small children, I asked them if they would like the box of toys I had gathered. They looked at their children and smiled: "Yes, thank you very much." As they were getting ready to get in their very stuffed van, I wondered if they would all fit. I saw my boxes of articles I was to give to Goodwill and on top was a delicate heart-shaped wreath of baby's breath. I carefully picked it up and asked the father if he would like to take this wreath home for his wife. For many women and mothers like to have something pretty in their home. But he was much too practical. "Oh, no thank you. We'll take the toys for the children to play, but the delicate wreath is not necessary."

I felt sad for them, starting out from scratch, taking the remnants of the basic necessities, but not having time for the beautiful things in life. But then what did I know of their world? The heart made lovingly from the delicate dried baby's breath—probably was too fragile and they recognized that. At this time, they needed a heart that was dependable and strong. I wish them well.

The following Monday morning after the garage sale, a dear tennis friend Lois Clark stopped over my house for a short visit. We had met several years ago, while being on the same tennis teams. She was a great shot maker and fun to play with on the courts. Her enthusiasm for the game upheld and inspired our whole team. We eventually became tennis partners. One day while drilling to prepare for a match, Lois stated it was her birthday and that she was now older than the speed limit. We all laughed and I said, "Do you mean fifty-five?" She said, "No, the new one. Sixty-five." We all were impressed and inspired. I was grateful to have this time to share the love of the game with a friend of such presence. She and her husband Bruce were avid players, also actively involved in coaching young kids to senior citizens. They truly gave back to the community in so many ways. This was a good time to see my friend other than one the tennis courts.

As she was leaving, Lois noticed my boxes that were marked in front of the garage for the Goodwill pickup. The delicate pretty wreath stood out among the items, so out of place in its humbled state.

"What a beautiful wreath," she said. "You're not giving that away are you?"

"I don't really want to, but I'm afraid it will get crushed in the move." I then exclaimed, "Lois, would you like to have it?"

Lois was delighted and so was I when she told me she already had a prominent place in mind to hang it.

One day, I was invited to Lois's house for lunch with the ladies. It was a perfect summer day. As I walked to her entryway, I saw the pretty heart-shaped wreath in its place of prominence. A wonderful message to all that entered her home.

I am thankful for those truly good moments that would continue to come into my life during those difficult times, for those moments would continue to give me hope and strength.

* * * * *

The end of summer 1994 was approaching rapidly. My friendship with Pete continued to grow ever since the incident with my ex-husband and his girlfriend. He offered me a safe place. He gave me the challenge of adventures to flying in his small plane and sometimes letting me take the controls, teaching me, guiding me, having the confidence in me, knowing that I was capable. He taught me how to let the plane rise and turn direction, how to dip down slowly and gradually let the plane rise until we were again linear and smooth. We would always be in contact with the ground control, keeping us informed of changes in weather. He taught me how to detect rain far in the distance and how to avoid the ominous weather patterns. Of course, we had to be on the watch for other planes that occasionally would be in the distance.

One time, we planned a real adventure. We would fly to Colorado and see my daughter Monica. She was attending Regis College. Our final destination would be Sedona, Arizona. Before we would make our way to Sedona we would fly to Tucson to see my friend Judi White, a cousin through marriage. We would spend a few days, visiting and hiking the canyon trails. From there we would fly over the magnificent Grand Canyon. We had to be sure that we had plenty of fuel. So we would stop at small airports along the way to refuel and catch our breath. Before we would begin the engine of our plane, Pete would make sure that I had my headphones and the speakerphone on properly so we could both hear and have communication once in air. I felt like a child again as Pete would look at me and grin, sometimes taking close-up snapshots of me or both of us with our headgear on and smiles ear to ear. I will never forget the wonder of flying over the Grand Canyon and the excitement of seeing the brilliant wooded greens as we came upon Flagstaff. What an incredible country we had, the contrast from deserts, mountains, streams and valleys, all the rivers and lakes, rich farmlands and mighty forests. To see all this from this little plane was beyond my imagination.

We flew over Flagstaff. Our mood became quite and awe inspired. We knew this was the buildup of even more wonders. We flew slowly to savor the contrast of the awaited anticipation. We rose from the mountain of trees, now over the spectacular red mountains of Sedona. I had been there before with my cousin Judi. We drove from Tucson and I knew I would have to go back. Now I was flying in this little plane, having the experience I never dreamed possible. Surprisingly, Pete had never been to Sedona. He had traveled all over the country. Now here we were, flying from Minnesota to Arizona. My eyes were wide with wonder. I heard Pete draw in breath. I looked at him to see if he was okay. He was excited, but still fortunately in a controlled state. "Get the camera," he said. I started taking these incredible pictures that I still have to this day.

There is nothing like the red mountains of Sedona. I have heard that Sedona is one of the spiritual wonders of the world and it truly must be. We slowed the plane again to savor this experience. The brilliant rusty reds to various shades of the paler pinks to the deeper shades of the mountainous canyons was a wonderment. We knew we would have to land soon. We spotted the small airport on top of one of the mountains, where we would land. Pete circled the mountain several times. I thought that he did not want to let go of the experience. So I was giving him this moment. I did not know he had never landed a plane on a mountaintop before.

Finally, he took a deep breath and headed straight for the runway. I was holding my breath too. Pete has good concentration. With strong will and determination, we were going to land. I had a feeling this was rather critical, but I felt confident and I knew this was a spiritual land. It was okay. The wheels touched the runway. Wow, that was done. We were going pretty fast. We kept going. The end of the runway approached. What was going to happen if the runway was too short? I held my breath, my eyes wide open. I looked at Pete. His face showed a serious concentration. I knew we were going to be okay.

Surely we would. We seemed to be going faster than we should be. The end of the runway was coming up. I thought we would probably fly off and swoop in the air. Fortunately, that did not happen. With all Pete's willpower, he managed to stop the plane.

People came running from the control building. I thought to greet us. But it was to see if we were okay. We learned that because the airstrip was surrounded by mountains and the direction of the swirling winds, we should have come in from the other side. Since Pete had never flown on this mountain, he was unaware. Now he learned something new. Pete did very well. Coming from the Flagstaff side, we had to ascend to the landing strip, which meant we had to gather momentum. If we would have come from the other side, we would have to descend then we could have slowed down, which would have made the runway seem longer. Needless to say, we were here standing on the edge of the mountain overlooking the winding trails and roads leading to the town of Sedona. Sedona, drawing in many artists and craftsmen by their love of beauty and inspiration that the glorious red mountains provided.

By the time Pete was directed to where our plane would be stationed and paperwork complete, dusk was approaching. On the edge of this mountain high above the small city were small cottages where one could stay. But they were all reserved. That was okay because this little airport also provided a small restaurant where we decided to have dinner and make our plans. From the small airport, someone drove us to pick up a car. It would be an all-terrain vehicle, which could climb the steepest sides of the mountain and climb over the rockiest paths. I was not planning on driving this one. I was on vacation plus an adventure. I was thrilled, happy and excited. What more could I want?

One of the first places we went was to the Chapel on the Hill. A small chapel built high on the mountainside, blending in with the pristine landscape. The first time I had been to this very special place was with my cousin Judi. It had not been that long since her divorce that came out of the blue, and shook her world to the core, for John was the love of her life, the father of her two children. Judi is probably one of the most loving and caring persons I know. Now she wanted to help me through my own divorce. We were close in age, close in height and probably since we both were married too young shared a special bond. When we would get together, our playful side would come out, releasing an infectious joy and energy, our enthusiasm not to be contained.

As we looked up at the mountain leading to the Chapel on the Hill, I pointed out one of the natural phenomena, a stone figure of a Madonna. Stone figures of the Wise Men. And, if you looked from a certain angle, a whimsical Snoopy. We would walk up the mountain trail to the chapel. The first time I went inside that little chapel I was deeply moved. In fact, the closer I came, I could feel this incredible spiritual energy and an intense sorrow. Inside the chapel, as I knelt in prayer, quiet tears streamed down my face, as if through an understanding and cleansing. I felt for my cousin Judi, for my broken marriage and the effects of that breakup on my children. I wanted the world to be better and do better. I wanted forgiveness and peace.

Going to Sedona with my cousin Judi will always be a special memory for me. I will never forget as we approached the red mountains of Sedona by car. This trip would be a healing journey. Every scenic marvel we passed lightened our hearts. When we looked in the distance seeing the beautiful red mountains against the brilliant blue also appeared a double rainbow. I had never seen one before. Evidently, this phenomenon occurs when the conditions are right. I interpreted this as a good sign for both of us.

This trip with Pete would be an incredible adventure for me, for Pete had a way of embracing challenges, conquering fears, testing his skills on daring feats be it on the black diamond ski slopes and moguls to hiking in the mountains. Going the distance, the steep and rocky inclines did not deter him. One time we were on a mountain ledge. As we climbed higher, the ledge narrowed. Eventually we were hugging the mountain. I was getting fearful, for to look down into the valley spiked with huge rock and crevices bristling with huge fir trees brought me back to reality. If one of us would fall, we would never be found. I realized it was up to me to speak up. Pete probably would have kept going. But for now this was enough adventure for me. He agreed reluctantly. I breathed a sigh of relief and once we were on safer terrain I was thankful I knew my limitations and my spirit of adventure was still intact.

Pete of course preferred to park as far as possible from the Chapel on the Hill in order not to miss anything as we walked up the mountain trail. I was pleasantly surprised and pleased that Pete wanted to savor even the smallest detail of this trip, making this a once in a lifetime memory. I liked the fact that we would start this first trip to this very special picturesque chapel. I was drawn inside this wonderful sanctuary, remembering my last visit with Judi. Pete quietly and respectfully looked around, walked over to the front of the church where the lit votive candles were displayed. He seemed in deep thought, a need to reflect and make his own peace with himself and his master. Pete did not consider himself a religious man. But when I would see him feeding the birds with such loving care, I saw that gentle side. His love of the outdoors and his consideration for people in need, he would be the one to help. There was a genuine goodness in him, also a sorrow he could not escape.

Once we were outside the chapel, Pete looked up and I knew he was eager to explore the rocks and crevices and climb as high as we possible could. There would be plenty of flat plateau areas hidden behind large boulders offering a place to rest in a shaded or sunny area, providing the most glorious views above, our curiosity moving us forward and upward. The further and higher we climbed, the fewer the people. It would be so quiet, so peaceful that we could not help feel a deep contentment as we looked around. After we explored to our heart's content, we started to descend from the mountain of the Chapel on the Hill. I thought to myself, "What a wonderful way to start our adventure."

Pete in his expertise and daring would drive our Jeep, an all-terrain vehicle, on some of the steepest inclines and maneuver over the rockiest impossibilities. I thought for sure we would topple over, for what I knew of the law of gravity. I gritted my teeth and watched Pete with his look of sheer will and determination. By myself, I never would have even considered such a daring feat. We were heading for the Seven Sacred Ponds and Pete would study the map fervently when we would stop and rest and marvel at how we made it thus far. At least I did. The higher we climbed with our Jeep, there would be more and more trees, usually kind of scraggly fir trees, then gradually getting thicker and more plush. The trees offered a sweet coolness, for it was very hot that day. We learned it was 102 degrees. It was a good thing we didn't know.

Surprisingly, we really didn't bring enough water. Before we began this venture, we happened to stop and both ordered a large orange drink. That is unusual for me because I usually order a small, maybe a medium if I'm really thirsty. This time I thought whatever I don't drink Pete probably will. Finally, we came through a clearing and it was like we were on sacred ground. We parked our Jeep and were excited to explore and hopefully find the Seven Sacred Ponds. We had no idea what to expect. It was interesting because we seemed to be the only people on this mountain. Behind us were the trees. But ahead of us were huge boulders and expansive plateaus of various levels. They looked like shale, which is soft and flaky but these were hard and smooth. The colors were of the softest pinks to the deeper shades of terracotta, depending on how the sun or shadows played upon them.

I wanted to savor the whole experience, this quiet sacred place. It was not an easy place to get to and so unexpected, which made it even more special.

We could climb up plateaus and then have to jump down to another level. Pete spotted the first pond. It was amazing where did the water come from? Was it from underground? Some were quite large and then there would be a small pond. The water looked pure and refreshing. We wanted to find all seven ponds. As we were going up and down the plateaus, we had to be careful because there would be prickly cactus coming up from the crevices of the plateaus. Sometimes you could not see the cactus because it might be tucked underneath a ledge. I jumped down from one of the ledges and felt a terrible sting on my leg.

"Ow! I exclaimed. "Something bit me." Blood was streaming down my leg. Pete looked and said, "Patti, you got stuck by this cactus." It stung like fire on my leg. It seemed that I wasn't that close to the cactus, but it was like it reached out and stuck me when I jumped from the ledge.

Pete wrapped my leg with a colorful red bandanna. I was surprised how my leg stung and the pain seemed to expand. Darn. Why did this have to happen at the sacred pond? That saddened me more than the sting of the cactus. Now I hobbled around the plateaus, feeling frail and vulnerable. We continued exploring but not with the same intensity for me as my wound was always a reminder. We went back to the Jeep and took out our orange drinks from the cooler. To this day, I love anything orange. The pain in my leg was beginning to ease. We decided to try and find the ancient Indian ruins that were on the highest part of this mountain.

After driving the Jeep on the tricky mountainside, lo and behold, we found it. The ingenuity and foresight to build their homes within the mountain amazed me. They would be able to see for miles around. That would have been practical and advantageous as a lookout for predators, storms, hunting and for the sheer magnificence of the vistas lying before them. I tried to imagine people living within the mountain. There were Indian artifacts of cooking utensils, tools and pots and ladders made to get to the upper berths. Steps were carved to get to the upper levels. Overall, it was quite amazing, so intact. We were practically alone, except we saw a couple exploring the ruins in the distance.

By this time, we were running out of our orange drink and reluctantly decided to head down the mountain. It was difficult leaving this mountain. Yet, we didn't want to be there when it became dark. Besides we needed to allow enough time, in case of problems. But all was well as we traversed our way back to the base of the mountain and the hearth of the Seven Sacred Ponds. Now that we were back on solid ground, we realized that not only were we thirsty but we were borderline famished. On our way back to our quarters, we found a 50s art deco style diner off the side of the road. What a contrast from the serenity of the mountain that we had to ourselves. This little diner was bustling with locals. They were in good spirits, but how could they not be? Playing in the background was the old 50s classics, which immediately put me in high spirits. The aroma of freshly grilled hamburgers and fries wafting through the air greeted us at the door. This is where we were going to dine.

I loved it. As we looked around, all the tables were filled with happy contented suntanned people. We decided to sit at the bar and share a chocolate malt with a grilled burger. It was the greatest. I don't know what they did to the hamburger or malt, but the feast was delicious. The malt tasted so good we decided to share another. We could not have been more content. I felt I was in my element as I looked around me. The women wore their shorts and sundresses. It was fun seeing some of the men with their cowboy hats and boots. It added to the ambiance. I was happy I brought my own cowboy boots. They were my favorite boots, off white with leather fringe on the side. I would put them on as soon as we got to our room. It was like we were transported to that wonderful space of time that was free of complications. All the wonders and grandeurs deeply appreciated and the locals valued this priceless treasure they had before them and would keep it that way—simple and pure.

We hiked and explored and took lots of photos, shopped for souvenirs to take back for family and friends. Even when our trip was winding down, we still had our flight back to Minnesota. I remember I brought a little journal with me to record this flight and other points of interest. On the way back from Sedona, we would again stop in Tucson to see my cousin Judi. That was another thoughtful gesture from Pete, helping me through this transition. Actually, we helped each other for no other reason than we both cared.

I will touch briefly on how I met Pete. I had been divorced now for over a year. I was new to the dating scene. I basically wanted friendship that might grow into something more meaningful if not we could still be friends. I wanted to have fun, be spontaneous and occasionally playful, but I also wanted someone in my life that would have a compassionate side, along with wisdom and a loving heart that was brave and fearless. Not afraid to speak the truth—not only for him self but speak for the oppressed and broken. I wanted a man of real substance and character that had strong convictions and integrity. I wanted someone who was not afraid to admit a mistake, for we all make them. That is how we learn, but only if we own up to our errors. That is not easy. It is also humbling but we have to remember that we are only human.

* * * * *

It was a Sunday on a perfect summer day in September 1993. I had just returned from a tennis event held at Flagship that my friend Cammy had persuaded me to go to. We had a great time seeing the familiar faces of friends and some of our favorite coaches as we made our way to our seats in the stands. There was a festive quality to the air. I felt at last there is life after the Big D. This tournament would be outside on the clay courts with ranked players. We would be home early afternoon. I felt at peace. Content. I was pleased that so many of my friends had not forgotten me and seemed genuinely happy to see me.

I was home for a short time and the phone rang. It was Rick. I always hold my breath when I hear his voice on the phone. I listen intently, for I never really know what his purpose is. He wanted to see me, he said. Because the way the divorce was done, in my mind, I felt he had had a breakdown. That he had regrets but didn't know how to express them. Maybe now was the time. At any rate, he sounded kind. Maybe he was a little tired. He had just finished playing golf and said he could be right over. I have a curious nature and am forgiving. I also am forever hopeful for the best outcome. What did he have to tell that it was so important that it could not be told over the phone?

Rick came to the door. He automatically smiled when he saw me. It was a gentle smile that appeared on his face and it seemed genuine. A natural response. When he stepped forward he went to embrace me. I stepped back to look at his face. What did this mean? I did not understand. It was not a look of a cruel man, but a man wanting to please, to be accepted. I let him put his arms around me. I wanted to feel his embrace, a loving embrace, but I still could not understand what this was all about. It was so confusing. He went to kiss me. I wanted to respond, but dared not.

"Rick, what is all this about? What are you doing?" I said. My words jolted him into reality.

"I'm sorry," he responded gently. "I just wanted to give you some information and wanted to do it in person."

We were still standing in the foyer. I asked if he wanted to go and sit in the living room. We slowly walked into the pretty room. He was drawn over to the larger corner windows and stood for a while looking at the Mill Pond below, the flower gardens on the hillside brilliant with color. My neighbor had extended the land that the years of erosion had taken away. She had also landscaped the hillside with flagstone steps to go down to the lower level by the pond. At the landing was a walkway of flagstone with the most delicate mosslike grass that Tara herself had planted in between the flat walking steps that led to the southern-style gazebo, painted white with a rough sawn cedar roof. Going down the hillside, done in feng shui, perfection would be stepping stones to rock gardens where water gently trickled to the lower level into a small manmade pool. The results were spectacular. Gardening was her passion and her labor of love. It was also one of the few things that seemed to bring her any peace or comfort and softness to her character.

Being surrounded by the beauty of the waters, the majestic trees and the colorful gardens inspired me even more to beautify my own home. That would also be a productive and positive project. On the upper level of the backyard stood the biggest old oak tree that made it impossible to grow a decent lawn. I decided to put in a patio. It would be kidney shaped to suit the contours of this level. I would also add a walking path leading to the side and front of the house. This gave me just enough room to have my own manageable flower garden. I would plant different bulbs that would come up in the spring, some perennials and colorful annuals, and since I loved moss roses I would border the patio with the colorful little flowers. I also loved stones, the feel, the color and texture. I would also plant chicks and hens and place the suitable stone or stones close to the moss roses and chicks and hens for they liked being near the heat of the stones.

I also decided to make my one-season porch that led to the master bedroom and the living room into a year-round sunroom. I added a door and talked the builders into building curved steps leading down to my new patio. They seemed to like the idea of a more creative touch. Overall, my small changes added comfortable and pleasing results that were functional and inviting.

As Rick was taking everything in I wondered where his thoughts were taking him. He turned to look at me and said, "You've done a great job. Everything looks really nice." I remembered when he practically cut off my funds when he found out that I was going to do some needed repairs with some added remodeling. I told him, "It needed to be done. It was time." He seemed a little embarrassed. I asked him if he would like some tea or lemonade and then we could talk.

We sat down in the living room on the oriental key designed curved sofa. He brightened and eagerly started telling me about some stocks that were to be exorcised. He then explained the purpose of his visit.

"When these shares of stock are exorcised, I am going to give you"—and he stated a generous amount of money. He explained that his share would be larger, but mine was free and clear, meaning what I received would not be taxed. He looked at my face to see my reaction. That was not quite what I had expected to hear. Yet, Rick seemed so proud and happy with his generous gift that I thanked him. I definitely could use the money, mainly for financial security. But I could not help but be a little disappointed that it wasn't a gift from the heart.

We sat and talked. I felt his regret. He seemed torn and wanting to linger, a part of me wanted the same. Twenty-eight years of marriage is a lifetime. The ringing phone brought us back to the present. I told him I didn't need to answer it. "Go head," he said. "It might be important."

It was Cammy's ex-husband telling me he hurt his ankle and could I pick him up at the fair.

"What fair?" I asked.

"The State Fair."

I told him that I was busy and besides I did not know how to get there. I figured he would find a way without asking me. I was a little exasperated at this interruption and told Rick about the call. We pretty much dismissed it, but the moment was broken.

A few minutes later, the phone rang again. Cammy's ex-husband.

"Patti, I really need your help."

This whole scene was starting to frustrate me. I repeated I had no idea how to get to the fair. How could I possibly find him among the crowds of people? I had never driven to the fair before. At this time in my life, I wasn't a native Minnesotan. He wasn't deterred. He proceeded to give me step-by-step directions, even down the color of his shirt to his gimpy ankle.

I went back to the living room and reiterated the weird conversation that I had with Cammy's ex. Heaven only knows what he was thinking. Rick said that was okay, he should be leaving anyway. Before he left, Rick told me I would receiving the check from the stock sale. If I didn't receive the check within a week, I was to call him.

Why did I not want him to go? Why did I now feel the progress made was now on shaky ground? Why couldn't we go out to dinner, talk and be friends again? Oh no. Now I felt a sorrow within and I couldn't even take time to feel the depth of it, as now I had to try and locate the State Fair and my needy friend. It is amazing what we ask our friends to do for us, and more amazing that we sometimes say yes. I gathered up my purse, clasping the directions in my hand. Oh, Lord, give me strength and discernment.

I was not familiar with that part of the city, but the directions were good. I knew I was getting closer when lines of cars were in front, behind and on each side of me. There were people out directing traffic. I knew I was going to have to mosey to the far left, for that was closest to the entrance. But the traffic controllers kept moving everyone slowly but always forward. I saw no one that looked like Gunnar. I looked every which way that my head could possibly turn. I had to circle at least three times. One more time, I said to myself. If I don't find you the next time around, I'm leaving. This would be my last try. I was scrutinizing everyone, stretching my neck to the left and right. I was getting exasperated and was about to speed up when this crazy man jumped in front of my car.

"Oh, my gosh! It was Gunnar. I'd found him, or he'd found me."

Gunnar then ran to the passenger side of my burgundy relatively new Honda Accord and jumped inside. He was in good humor, proud of himself and never minded being the center of attention.

"Patti, you passed me three times," he said. "I yelled, waved my arms, jumped up and down to get your attention. You would stop, but by the time I got to your car you would speed up."

I know my concentration was good, so were my ears but I still managed to be oblivious. He laughed. I could not help but laugh myself, envisioning this grown man jumping up and down, flailing his arms. He certainly had determination. When we settled down to seriousness, I said, "Gunnar, you jumped right in front of my car. You could have been hurt."

"Well, I got your attention, didn't I?" he said.

As we were making our way through thick traffic, Gunnar exclaimed, "Turn down this street. Let's go to the fair. I have some friends I want you to meet."

Was this some kind of pretense to get me to the fair? "You told me you had a bad ankle. That you can't walk on it."

"I did twist it. But since we're here, we might as well meet my friends."

I must be a marshmallow because I relented.

I was exasperated with all the shenanigans. The games people play. What a day. This now seemed all too surreal as we were making our way through the hustle and bustle of the fair. What happened to my Sunday that had started out so perfectly quiet? Now it had descended into the hullabaloo of the State Fair. We were to meet his friends at a jazz show. It was already in progress. Gunnar pointed out his two friends sitting in the front row—Bobby G. and Pete. I wasn't going to stay there very long. Not at all. There were two empty seats next to

Gunnar's friends. They were both personable right from the get go. They were both also into the music. We sat down in the empty chairs.

Strangely, it felt good to sit down and relax. They were obviously happy to see us. They introduced themselves in a friendly and gracious manner. Bobby G. was tall and slender, toned and tanned with a strong presence. Pete had a rather dignified and warm manner, his eyes crinkled when he smiled.

Pete looked at me. "Congratulations," he said.

"For what?" I said.

"For getting braces."

I felt self-conscious. I had forgotten about my braces. They made me look way too young for my years. It was an interesting comment. But I liked Pete's easy candid manner.

We settled in to listen to the concert. I allowed myself to relax. For some unknown reason, I felt like resting my head against Pete's shoulder. I didn't know why. He was a stranger. A gentle, kind stranger.

That's how I met Pete. At the time, I didn't know the direction and depth our friendship would take on. Although, I did think he was an interesting and kind man. I also thought he might be someone perfect for my good friend Barb to meet. They were closer in age.

* * * * *

I must get back to Rick's unexpected visit and what that was all about. As soon as Rick decided that he wanted the divorce, he distanced himself even further. He planned and plotted his strategy as if I was a business to be destroyed, or to be kept in subservience. For him, it was always about money. Money would buy him his power, his connections, respect and his absolution. He was known as the financial expert in the world of high finance. He was also known as ruthless, and it carried over in our marriage. It is not a people friendly or family friendly type of business. Unfortunately, we would be caught in the crossfire of misplaced values and indifference, corruption in high places, unspoken and sealed, convoluted to the point of exhaustion and confusion. Who would want to go there to defend the innocent against those who can influence the outcome with all the knowledge, power, connections and resources they are allowed to hold in their pockets.

I felt with time after the divorce and all was said and done, I felt he would have moments of listening to his conscience, and he would feel the pangs of regret and remorse. It was obvious he held all the cards. All at stake was in his hands and he controlled his destiny by the skills he learned in his rise to victory, discarded and sacrificed his most precious while other looked on, but did nothing. I wondered how he felt now and was it worth the cost? I actually saw Rick a few days before this visit. He came over early one evening. Again, I felt the turmoil that he was struggling with, his guilt and his cruelty. I guess I never really blamed him, for I felt he had an addiction as bad or worse if it had been alcohol or drugs. I know now that I forgave too easily as I had done throughout our marriage.

Rick came to the door. His face lightened when he saw me. He walked in the room and he reached out to me and I knew he needed comforting. He held me lovingly. He seemed so torn, so lost that I could not help but reach out to him. Reach out in a way that would heal the pain. I wanted a gentle love. He loved in desperation. I felt sad. I felt hopeful. What was this all about? It seemed strange to be in our bedroom together, almost as a long fretful dream and waking to a feeling of disorientation. As we lay in each other's arms, it felt right. But when he said he should leave, I could not understand. Why? I could not understand why he would come here in the first place.

"It's not right that I stay here tonight," he softly explained. Then for sure I could not understand why he was here. Hot tears streamed down my face. "Don't cry," he said. "Don't cry. Otherwise I can't see you again. It hurts too much." As he spoke, I was trying to understand the meaning behind everything he way saying.

* * * * *

I never did receive the money from the shares of stock that were exorcised. Every day that went by, I felt once more that Rick would conveniently forget or just ignore. Why would he go out of his way to inform me of the stocks that would be exorcised when it would never materialize at least not for me. I did call him at his office as he told me I should do. Everything seemed copasetic as his secretary put me through to him. He was pleasant saying there was some delay, but to call back in a few days. I was beginning to feel like a business. Because he was so busy, he told me to call him in a few days, if I did or did not get my share of the stocks. Each week that passed became more awkward, but I would notice an attitude change, or an abruptness. One day, when I asked the secretary if Rick was in, she seemed distressed and said that Rick was not in the office. I decided I would not call back. If he had any news at all he could call me.

Meanwhile, I thought I should call my attorney, Larry Katz, and tell him of this latest exchange, not only with the stocks that were to be sold but also with Rick's untimely visit. Since, shortly after we were divorced, Rick replaced his former attorney Bob Zalk with Ed Weiner, one of the most notorious and ruthless financial attorneys in Minnesota to appeal my settlement. Larry was still representing me at this time. I met with him at his office at the IDS Center. He seemed upset that Rick had exorcised the stock. There was some form of legality that was not proper. I also told him that I was confused about Rick's behavior, about our making love. Telling this to my attorney was uncomfortable, but I felt it was significant. Was it meaningless for Rick? Larry seemed visibly upset and said that what Rick had done was like emotional rape. Now I felt sick. He was my husband, the father of my children. We were married for so long. I didn't know what the consequences were for this kind of behavior.

As I was writing this segment of the story, I came upon the journal I started when first separated from Rick and continued through the divorce. I wanted to check the dates as I am searching. I could not help but read once more, bringing me back in time. It is not an easy place to go, but made me realize even more my need for closure and that I cannot just accept an injustice of this magnitude not only for myself but also for other women and families. I decided to use these pages from my diary in this story to help enlighten and show that without consequences that are no boundaries. It was interesting my thoughts back then, have not changed that much except may be more pronounced. The reality is nothing will be done unless these issues are heard and addressed.

[Diary entry]

July 16, 1992

It's still not over—been divorced. Rick has appealed the settlement once. Now he has changed lawyers and has appealed a second time. He has also filed for an annulment. Never realized that I lived with a man for twenty-eight years, but never knew the extent of his coldness or cruelty. I am better off and I know I will be.

Duane was married Saturday, July 11. It felt awkward, almost as if it were not real.

I had not seen Rick in almost a year, and the few times we talked on the phone he was verbally and emotionally abusive. I had no idea what to expect. He was cold and arrogant. He wanted to exclude me from family pictures. Like they did at Lisa's wedding. I was not going to let it be repeated. So Monica and I went in together. She knew Rick said some words in anger under his breath. Cynthia said I had a lot of nerve.

They just do not get it. Is it arrogance or sheer delight in another's misery? I do not want to be part of anyone so cruel. I guess I am learning there are all kinds of cruelty. My father in his rages and living in fear. My own husband very subtly using me, abandoning and discarding in a most cruel manner and then having me ostracized from his family, the country club, any social setting. He wants no reminders.

That is too bad, for I am here and he has lost the best thing that ever happened to him.

My house is going on the market Sunday. I feel good about that. I want to heal. Make a new life. I'm not sure where I will go. Depends on my feelings with Jack. Maybe Minnesota is too harsh for me.

In August, I am going on a retreat sponsored by the Basilica of St. Mary's. I need God's guidance, and this too feels right. This retreat is for separated and divorced people and it is to help with closure. I called today and talked to a very nice woman and she wanted to know what brought me to this stage. I gave her a brief synopsis, some of the most poignant or significant details. And she felt this was very timely for me. I hope this can also help with my new beginning.

I am also going to plan a trip to New York—business—to talk personally to Bob Kelly and maybe Mike Grobstein too. I want them to understand why I will have to write my book. At this point it is necessary.

218

I feel I should backtrack on the annulment before I forget.

Rick has filed for an annulment. The ultimate insult and act of humiliation to me. He says he wants to become more actively involved in church and to take the sacraments. Yet he still will not drop the appeal or his harassment of me. What is his motive? I know. God knows. And Rick also knows.

There would be no way that I would have married that man for twenty-eight years if it were his intention to abandon me. Then he should have encouraged, allowed, me to have a career, and we would have shared equally the responsibilities of the home, raising and taking care of our children.

Either way, if this annulment goes through, I will expose him and the hypocrisy of it all, and I will consider legal action. I have not worded this very well. I'm tired of expending all the energy directed on this.

When I realized that Rick would not take time to work at our marriage, and Larry Katz said, "Patti, once you are divorced, then you can get on with your life. You will know what to expect and Rick will also." It has not happened. Rick has just become more embittered and finds more ways to be destructive at any cost.

I guess what surprises me is that he has been able to get away with it and people seem fearful to confront his actions. But yet shake their heads in disbelief. I'm very disappointed. I have an excellent lawyer, for that I am thankful. But I wish it had not come to this. Rick being so angry, sick that he is obsessed with his destruction of me. What does it matter? How far will he go? And will he ever realize what he has done?

I just do not want to be around such hatred. It hurts too much and holds me back. So for now I will remove myself and surround myself with better things, and kinder and more compassionate people.

March 1, 1994

It has been a year and a half since I have written and I am still in my house, not by choice. When Rick filed for the annulment, I ended up doing a lot of writing and had several meetings with Sister Paulissa, a very gentle and sensitive nun, but protected and not really in touch with the realities of all that occurred in my situation or the impact.

She saw me as someone that was better off being annulled. She would say, "Patricia, think of it as your annulment." She could not. Nor could she ever understand the annulment was done to hurt, not to help, not even Rick himself." The process was long and arduous. Again Rick and I were isolated throughout the process, never saw or spoke. That is the way he wanted it. What I wanted was immaterial. I wrote and he verbally talked to Sister Paulissa privately. She recorded his statements and then typed them.

I never knew what he said. He did it as easily as possible for himself. I wrote many pages because twenty-eight years is too much history, as if a lifetime, to be erased, pretending never to happen or exist.

The whole process was extremely painful. I had to go back to the beginning. My family, growing up, how I met Rick, dating, our marriage, honeymoon, our life together for twenty-eight years. It was not easy. It took its toll emotionally, and through it all I held onto my being, my beliefs. During this time, Jack and I broke up, so that was meant to be.

I also was in such a vulnerable state and I became unknowingly a prey for the neighborhood's opportunist. Which left me in a costly legal nightmare for over a year. Also, through this process, I did tons of writing and although these people—and I hate to put their names in this—but since it is all fact, so it must be. Tracy and Mary Eichorn Hicks intruded into my life to create again an enormous amount of havoc—two attorneys with a sordid history that slipped through the cracks. I would be their next victim. So much has happened here in Edina, the place where everyone wants to live and never to leave. But I never wanted it. And I do want out, away from here.

I do not want to write about that part of my life because it is so separate. Sometimes I wonder the reason that I have been through all this. I was not just divorced, but appealed and I'm still waiting for the outcome. But to also go through an annulment is the height of insensitivity. Tara B. brought these two attorneys into my life and then dropped out of sight. My house and my life were tied up in legal technicalities for over a year because I would not allow them to commit fraud or extort money. That is what they wanted to do. I still find it hard to believe. Does the criminal have more rights and protection than their victim?

Last summer, I must add, it was July 10. 1993. Rick called. I did not know what prompted him to do so. He wanted to see me. He wanted to make peace.

CHAPTER 15
ANOTHER VIOLATION?

*H*OW CAN PEOPLE BE SO heartless? How can people be so cruel? Easy, so it seems, especially when in business it is all about profit. There is a song with those questions, but I also wonder how people can be so indifferent, untrustworthy and unreliable. Yet many do not have to be responsible or accountable. The solution to many corporate or legal problems are: Never admit a mistake, distance yourself, avoid at all costs, do not have any communication whatsoever, and get a lawyer that is not afraid to fight dirty. But what about the person who cannot even find representation? That is forced into this dysfunctional charade, all for the misplaced values, inflated egos or just playing the game because they have the means and the audacity. The money trickles down.

Rick would not call me back, even though that is what he wanted me to do. It was as if he vanished, at least from his office. I would be in the grips of his unwarranted legal appeals, forever holding me back, stressed to the max. I believe that he was disappointed that I was not freaking out or out of control, just trying to move forward with my life. I don't think he liked that. He wanted me to suffer. He was not going to make anything easy for me. I believe that is why he decided to try and have our marriage annulled, during the appeals to keep me emotionally distracted. But to have the Eichorn-Hicks come into my life fraudulently and try to extort money from me, and Rick turns his back on me, wanting not to see, hear or acknowledge? For what reason or purpose?

It was the summer of 1996 that I finally sold my house on Edgebrook. My plans were still to move to Tucson. Somehow, I was able to stand my ground and not waver in my convictions. I guess I was even more stubborn than even I thought. I just thought that Rick would eventually come to his right mind eventually and if not the courts would just stop the madness. During this time, I was fortunate that my friends stood by me, keeping me at time busy and distracted with activities that I never would have necessarily chosen to do, but now I'm glad that I had the experience. We would bike twenty to twenty-five miles at a time. That was a lot for me. I am reasonably athletic, but my passion was really for the dance, the arts, but now it seemed I was being super jock—within my limitations.

I traveled more than I ever had when I was married. I finally skied those mountains, taking me to breathless heights—the thin air and the daring of it all. I preferred the long runs with an occasional challenge, but sometimes I found myself on the bumpy moguls looking for an escape. For some reason, I enjoyed skiing through the trees. It was all in the timing, traversing and concentration. Most of my skiing I did with Pete. He would encourage me always to go beyond. These occasions gave me fragmented spaces of time where I could be me, free of the reminders of all the legal turmoil that was infringing on moving forward with my life. The worst part was knowing that was the intent.

I think back when my attorney Larry Katz told me things would be better after my divorce. I always thought once a person was divorced that was it. I also believed that we would always care for each other, if not marriage, at least friends. After all, I was the mother of his children. I'd known him since I was fifteen and we were married an incredibly long time. I didn't expect him to change to this degree. It seemed once we were divorced he lashed out at everyone. But I was his main target. I could not understand how he could hate me so. I wanted him to be happy. I encouraged him to follow his dreams. But I never know that the successes that were too many would destroy him as a husband and father, even as a friend. Now I realize that our world revolved around placating my husband's every want and need. This is not a good thing, especially if it becomes one-sided.

Now I have to get back to the events that happened before my move, shortly after the encounter with Rick and his girlfriend. There are so many things in between the days, weeks, months and years, even the moments, that come back to remind me. My emotions are all over the place and the memories rampant, spilling into the now. I really don't want to go back, but the injustice is too vast and I know I can't rest until I make some sense of it all.

One early evening just before my move, Pete picked me up for dinner. Since I was so busy, it would be something casual and fast. I originally was going to meet him, but he called and told me that he was going to be in the neighborhood. He would just pick me up. This would be the first time we would be solo, for we had always done things with friends or a small group. We decided to go to the Convention Grill since it was close. Pete always, even when we were friends, was very attentive, and rather protective. I felt special when I was with him. I felt he was worldly, confident and kind. I knew it would be fun when he picked me up in his vivid blue Jeep with the top down and clear skies. I remember feeling the special connection with Pete. I wasn't sure what that was all about but I knew it was mutual. As we were eating our hamburgers, just talking and feeling good, I found myself thinking, What a sweet nice man.

When we came back to my house, Pete walked me up the long steps to my front door that I had painted dusty pink on a Labor Day weekend. Since my divorce, I usually do a special project on Labor Day to commemorate all that labor. Of course, I could not just do an ordinary paint job. I decided to do a Monet pointillism work of art on the door frame to complement the door. I liked the results. It actually also complemented my kitchen wallpaper. So I had a Monet theme going. He was one of my favorite impressionistic painters. Pete and I were both in a lighthearted mood. It felt so good, like this was meant to be. Pete was to be in my life somehow in a positive way.

The lights were on outside. I asked Pete if he would like to stop in for a minute, for I knew he had to be at the office early. I opened the front door and the security system did its little chime just to let the person at home know someone was coming in the door. "Beep, beep, beep," it sounded. I explained to Pete that we had a security system installed several years ago, for our house was broken into in the middle of the night.

It was very frightening to wake up and find a strange man walk into the bedroom, telling me not to look at him, that he had a gun. Rick was sound asleep. It was dark. I pulled the sheet up over my face, saying, "I didn't see you." He had a flashlight that he shone in my face when I first sat up. I was startled but I could still see a scraggly reddish hint of a beard with hair coming down by his ears, almost like sideburns.

I was surprised that Rick was so sound asleep, snoring away. I could feel this man's presence in the room. I could also hear his breathing as I tried to shield my face. I could hear him walk about the room. It is amazing what one thinks in times like this. But I thought if Rick should wake up, he might panic or jump up and try and save us all. I knew if he got too excited and got shot, he would want to know what happened to himself. How did he get to heaven or the other place? I gently nudged him several times. "Rick, you must wake up. Someone is in the room. He has a gun, so don't panic." With that he sat upright and said to the man, "What do you want?" Well, he must have had a certain amount of authority, for the man didn't shoot him or me. I still had the sheet to my face.

At the sound of Rick's voice, the man moved over to the door. "I've got a gun, so don't look at me." Again the flashlight was directed at our faces. "Don't hurt us. What can I give you? I've got money in my wallet."

"Where's you wallet?" the man said.

"Over on the dresser." Rick pointed.

"I want you to get it. Then get back in bed and toss me your wallet."

I had lowered the sheet from my face at one point, but covered my eyes with my hand. I left enough space so I could see Rick scramble to his dresser, grab his wallet and quickly get back into bed. I could see him toss his wallet toward the man.

As the man was going through the wallet, Rick pleaded: "Would you please not take the credit cards or driver's license?"

I thought Rick was going to say, "Please don't shoot us."

As he rifled through Rick's wallet, the burglar seemed pleased. He tossed the wallet back to Rick. Then he looked at me. "Where's your purse?"

Oh my gosh. Where did I put my purse? I looked around and I could see my bag sitting on the floor by the double doors leading to the sunroom. "It's over there by the door."

"Pick it up slowly and hand it to me."

I was thankful I wore my pajamas that covered almost all of me. I still remember them, white with little red polka dots and stripes on the cuff and collar, small buttons on the front. I handed him my purse, not looking at his face. I thought he would be disgusted with the little money he would find in my purse and shoot me. But that was just my overactive imagination thinking. "I never carry much money with me," I told him so he would know.

I returned back to bed and hugged the covers up to my face. He started to approach the bed. I pulled the covers over my head as not to see. Rick was telling me, "Watch out for your head." I thought the burglar was going to shoot me or knock me out because of my meager allowance. He was standing by my side of the bed. He grabbed the phone and started pulling the cord. Well, it went on forever, for we had an extension put on the line that reached into the sunroom. He finally managed to pull it from the wall.

Rick and I looked at each other as the burglar stood by the door surveying the scene before him. "Don't get up. Stay in bed for twenty minutes."

Rick spoke up. "Our daughter is upstairs. Please don't go up in the bedrooms."

I was upset that Rick would mention our little girl. "Please don't go upstairs," I pleaded. "My daughter would be frightened." My oldest son was also home at the time. I thought if he should wake up, he might overreact and try and do some karate moves.

"I like children. Don't worry," the burglar said quietly. "I would never hurt a child."

I held my breath. He still had the flashlight in our faces but I knew he could see my pleading eyes. He left the room. I was listening intently. My heart beat sharply. I would be able to tell if he was going downstairs and out the door or if he was going upstairs. I could hear the steps going down to the lower level. I could hear another voice. I could hear the door downstairs quietly close. I could hear a car as it backed away. He had said there were two others, one in the car as lookout and the other ransacking the lower level.

The house was now very quiet, a stillness in the night. I felt such relief. I whispered to Rick, "I think they're gone." We both slowly got out of bed. The first thing we did was go upstairs and check on Monica and Mark. Rick had forgotten that Mark was home. They were sleeping, undisturbed. I was so thankful. We went downstairs into the kitchen, found a working phone and called the police. It was around three in the morning when they broke in. Dawn was rising. We were up all night giving all the information to the two officers. They said there had been a series of break-ins that evening. We were very lucky. Mark was bummed when he woke up and realized he'd slept through it. Monica listened with wide eyes and couldn't wait to tell her friends at school.

Life goes on. Rick went to work as usual. Monica caught her bus for school and Mark left for classes. It was a traumatic experience, but more than anything I felt so thankful that no one was hurt. Our tennis teams were in the playoffs. I almost thought I would not be able to play, but once the police had all the information they needed there was nothing else to do except wait. There must have been something in the stars, the moon or the air, for there were three of us on our team who had had unusual experiences that evening. One had a small fire in her home. The other had water problems. Mine was probably the most dramatic. The adrenaline carried over into my tennis match. I was totally focused much to my opponent's chagrin. This was the end of the season's final of the Women's Daytime League. There were six on a team. There would be hundreds of women competing. So to be in the playoffs was what we all strove for.

One of the men who broke into our house was caught. He was trying to break in another house a few days later in another town. They found various stolen goods in the trunk of his car, with names and articles that could be identified. This incident changed I believe both of us. I noticed that Rick now had an anger and obsession. I think I was in shock for I had to be so contained, calm, say and do the right thing. Not anger anyone. I had to be a calming factor. I was more frightened for my family than myself. I was so thankful my children were asleep when this transpired. Rick was now adamant about locking the doors. He called a security company and we had a most comprehensive security system put in. All the windows and doors with beeps and other intrusive sounds and small laser beams set to go off with unusual movements. I did not like this feeling. This was my house, my neighborhood. We should not live in fear.

I believe that I have delayed reactions when I encounter stressful situations. Sometimes it may take a few days longer. I'm not aware of it at the time. I am usually pretty calm, but one day about a week after, my youngest son Duane was playing some videogames on the computer. It was about battles, scary things. Rick all week had expressed his anger openly. I guess he got it all out of his system and he did what he thought he should do to keep his family safe. I went downstairs for laundry or something. Rick was doing his paperwork, finally content. The house was peaceful but for some reason I could not stand to have those violent games in my house, even though it was the popular games that many of the kids played. I practically went berserk seeing my son so immersed in those games that served no positive purpose, at least to me. I started crying, beside myself with frustration, a feeling of helplessness and I was angry too.

I think I had a twenty-minute breakdown. After I sobbed hysterically, I managed to calm myself down. Rick tried to say some words of comfort. My teenage son was probably scared speechless and I was now looking and feeling rather foolish. I pulled myself together. "I'm sorry. I'll be okay," I said through my tears. Everybody must have breathed a huge sigh of relief for me. But I know that it was part of the unraveling of our marriage. I wondered if Rick would or could really protect his family, and I wondered if he had the same thoughts but projected rage instead of communicating his feelings or taking the time to comfort each other. Even to be home for one day instead of rushing off to the office.

* * * * *

At any rate, that is how we were greeted as we opened the door, the sound of the beep, beep alerting. Most people thought that the alarm would go off, so they would step back. As I stepped in the door, Pete asked me if the alarm was going to go off. I told him that the alarm was set to alert if someone was coming inside. When I went to bed or was going away for the day or on vacation, I would set it differently where it would go off and report to the proper authority. He looked at me and smiled so tenderly and gently put his arms around me in an affectionate embrace. We both felt lighthearted as we playfully kissed inside the foyer. Since it was all so sweet, we kissed at little more and I let him, for that is one of my favorite things—if the kissing is done with the right person. With each kiss, Pete would take a small step forward and I would take a step back.

Next thing I knew, we were in the hallway leading into the master bedroom on the main level. It must have been close to nine o'clock for it was dark. Pete was sweetly amorous and I was feeling dreamy contentment. At this point, we were now in my bedroom. The bedroom was dark, but the large windows brought in a softness to the evening. Pete was facing the bed, but my eyes were drawn to the closet doors. I thought, Patti, that's not like you to leave the doors open. Then I stumbled on something on the floor.

"What's this?" I said.

We both looked around. My closet doors were wide open and the clothes strewn about the floor. The drawers to my dressers were wide open, some totally emptied with the drawers lying on the floor. I literally felt sickened seeing my lingerie tossed so casually about. Letters and cards among all my personal effects scattered at my feet. My jewelry box opened and emptied.

"Not again," I cried. I couldn't breathe. Pete held me close, protective.

"You're okay. That's the main thing," he said.

The time I could not be so brave or stoic. Pete was holding me tightly to calm my shaking body and my tears. This time I felt a chilling fear. Who would do this? My doors were locked. My car was in the garage. The lights and the stereo were on. Was someone watching my house? To all appearance, someone had to be home. Then I remembered I had gone down to the garage so that the door was not locked. Since I originally was going to meet Pete, I was going to drive. So I did leave the garage door unlocked and the door to the lower level. But still, just seeing my car and seeing the lights were on, and the security system on alert. I felt a sinking feeling that it was someone who knew me, who knew this house. They knew where to go, where to look. I was not gone that long.

Finally, I was able to gather my composure. What would have happened if Pete had just left? The thought was too horrific for me. Once again, I would have to call the police. This time as a single woman.

The police came and I filled out their report. When they left, Pete asked if wanted him to stay.

"I don't want to be here. I'm sorry. I can't sleep in this room. At least not tonight," I said quietly, mainly to myself as I shook my head. Where can I go that's safe?

Pete gently put his arms around me. "Patti, you can stay at my house. You can stay as long as you need."

I felt like a child who had been traumatized one too many times. I felt safe in his gentle presence.

When we arrived at his house, he was very gracious. He showed me around his town house. It was pleasant, relatively neat and tidy, as I would have expected. I felt a little awkward. I wondered if he felt regrets now that I was here. "Oh, Pete, I didn't bring my toothbrush. I don't have pajamas." I was in such a haste to leave the dreaded scene that I didn't even think beyond the moment.

"Patti, I'm a dentist. I've got plenty of toothbrushes. And I'll find you something to sleep in."

I guess I wouldn't be such a burden. One night would be okay.

Pete showed me an assortment of colorful toothbrushes and let me choose, as if I were a child. He showed me where the bath towels and other necessities were and told me to make myself at home. I brushed my teeth with my new clear-colored toothbrush, gently washed my face. I filled the tub and allowed myself to luxuriate in the warmth of the refreshing water. My thoughts were scattered from here to there. As the bath water was starting to cool, my thoughts turn to the present. I let the water out and pulled the soft beige towel from the bar, dried myself off. There was a robe hanging on a hook. I folded the damp towel on the edge of the tub and put on this gentle man's robe. I looked in the mirror to see the effects of this day, this evening on my face. I was okay.

When I opened the door from the bathroom, it led to Pete's bedroom. The lights were dimmed. He turned around with a gentle smile on his face. "Patti, you can sleep in my dentist smock. It's my favorite." He laid it out on the bed. I loved the print. It was of a leopard print that was of teal greens, gentle brushings of grays and blacks leopard spots with touches of off-white. Then he said he was going to get ready for bed. But he would sleep on the couch.

"Okay. Thank you." I didn't know what else to say.

I took off the robe and slipped the smock over my head. I looked in the mirror. I liked the effect. When Pete came into the room, he slowly walked over to me and put his arms around me.

"Precious Patti," he said softly. That was what I would become to Pete, his precious. And he would be my gentle sweet Pete. Neither of us planned or expected this. It just happened. Like it was meant to be. We would sleep together, lying in the gentle embrace of his arms. He was gentle and loving. I felt protected and cherished and I wanted him to feel the same.

Our relationship would take a dramatic transformation for both of us after that evening. People would say they could see the difference in Pete, a happiness that could not be contained. They could see a difference in myself as well. I know I felt different in a positive way. I would go back to my house the next day to face my fears head on. I had someone in my life who would protect me and who would be there for me. That helped give me a certain amount of courage and control over my life.

Sometimes people recognize the pain and trauma in others. They can identify and relate. Reach out in quiet understanding, bringing comfort and a normalcy back into their life. That was what we gave each other. The first night back at my house, Pete would stay—stay until the fear was no longer.

This incident occurred shortly after my encounter with Rick and his girlfriend. I would move from my house. It was a long and laborious process. Pete helped me find a new place. It would be a temporary place at the Cliffs in Minnetonka, for Rick's appeal was still pending. A few days after moving into the Cliffs, I learned Rick again was taking me to court for being on his property when I dropped off his stuff. Unbelievable. It was all a sham. But it was allowed. He had the means and the moxie. All his money, all the successes would never compensate for what he gave up and he knew it. Shortly after that incident, he and his girlfriend broke up. That did not surprise me, for she brought out the worst in him. At least, he had the strength to know it. But how could he extricate himself from his conscience? All the hostile takeovers, the meditation used for the wrong reason and self-hypnosis to dispel his emotions and conscience still had a powerful hold on Rick.

* * * * *

It would be much easier for me to linger on the experiences that would finally bring spontaneity and lightheartedness to my life that I had never known. For a brief moment of time, I would experience the tender love and nurturing that I had been denied in my childhood and throughout my marriage. Growing up, I knew about fear. But I learned that emotional abuse and verbal abuse were equally hurtful. My way of coping with fear, fear of my father when he was many times too angry—I would avoid it. I would hide or escape. But I also would be the one that many times would stand up against my father in his rages. Being married so young, I was so thankful being away from the fear that my gratitude carried over and beyond. I would be the best wife possible, forgetting myself in the process. I didn't mean to do that for I did value myself. I knew my strength, my abilities, my strong determination and my deep desire to learn, grow to be the best that I could be, but to also give the best of myself to others.

I would prove to myself and to others even though I was a young mother, my determination to overcome any and all the obstacles was greater than failure. It was easy in the early years of my marriage. I equated love with gratitude, providing and giving the best in each other, encouraging always to grow for that to me was exciting, not just for myself but to see my young husband's potential and encourage him to achieve his dreams that would be my dreams too. We did complement each other. I knew when he came home that was where he wanted to be and that was known and respected. I was the girl he chose to marry, the mother of his children, giving him reason, purpose and an incredible incentive of a loving life together. That was my vision. That was also my dream and what I held onto through the difficult times for the difficulties are part of life. We can't avoid them. But it is how we face the problems—that is important in growth.

I loved my husband. How could I not? He saved me from fear. He was the father of our children. But it wasn't until I had my first child that I felt the depth of that love. I now had this little life, depending entirely on me for all its needs. To me it was an incredible awakening. Now for sure I had to be the best wife and mother possible that was my reality. That held the determination and power of my conviction. Rick was the most loving when I was pregnant. That was when he was the most gentle and tender. He was a proud husband and father and it showed in his character and his drive to provide for his family. But something slowly shifted along the way. Values became misplaced. Interlopers knowing no boundaries or limitations, finding their weakness and insidiously luring the unexpected, permeating thoughts and draining the energy until there was nothing left to give.

I did not seek recognition. I did not need it, for I was always confident in my own strength and gifts. My happiness and contentment came through my family. When my oldest son played his trumpet with such passion that I would have to stop, listen and take notice—I understood that passion. My youngest son excelled in practically everything he did. He also had a passion for music and would compose the lyrics to pieces that he had captured in his dreams. We would have intellectual and wonderful philosophical discussions that would even open my eyes in surprise and admiration. Then having a daughter, a little sister, who introduced a much needed feminine softness to our household. My husband was a fortunate man. He had everything in his midst to achieve his dreams. Our children gave him a reason, purpose and incentive, a positive direction. I was his catalyst. I helped make his dreams a reality. Wouldn't the success that was borne from the beginning of a union be equally acknowledged?

I remember the night Rick and I were sitting in bed. Our children all sound asleep. They would not know that there would be a big change in their lives. But Rick and I were in deep contemplation on a dramatic move that would enhance his career. I knew he struggled with the decision for our sons were both teenagers, and that is never an easy time to uproot a family. The timing was not right either. Rick wanted his family with him while he was working on this project in Minnesota. The name sounded so cold to me, so far away. Yet I could feel, even in his apprehension, that Rick felt this was his opportunity to excel beyond his own expectations. Could I deny him that? I was torn and so was he.

We decided that we would tell our children the next day, so they could be part of the process and deciding factor. I guess in reality children always want to please their parents. Rick would expound on all the virtues of Minnesota, the great education, all the lakes and the music programs. Rick was eager to have us with him. He also had a "brilliant idea" of moving the kids and me just before Christmas. This would be a pivotal period for our family and our marriage, this move to the land of extremes.

Our divorce was not done with any kind of dignity or consideration and even after the divorce I would be thrown into the appeals that would be allowed, unnecessary and excessive court hearings for no reason, except that was how my husband would maintain his power and control over me. And his way of healing for himself. He needed to be validated and he was not going to take time to feel his loss, for now he was turned loose to test what all his money, position and power could buy. That was what he learned as well as many that love, money and power had done the same. Because I trusted and I knew the value and importance that I gave in our marriage. I thought after Rick got what he wanted in the divorce, he would let me be, set me free to build my own life. I knew we both would be saddened and have to take time to heal and adjust. It would not be easy and it would take time. But we were married too long. We had our children together. There would always be a responsibility and a connection. We owed that to our children. But our divorce was meant to crush the spirit, demoralize our existence and erode our financial and future security.

Even now after the divorce, I would not be allowed to pursue my dreams or my passions for my life would be held in court. Rick leading the way as the Pied Piper with his group of followers that would benefit him testing his limits. How could anyone heal or move forward to rebuild when under the control of the madness? I found fragments of happiness, glimpses of another kind of future but would be thrust back into a legal nightmare, not of my making. My creative spirit would be put on hold. But my strong deep-rooted desire for justice and freedom would dominate my thoughts and existence now. I would have to make my own stand. My own way.

CHAPTER 16

THE CHAISE

I LOOK IN THE LARGE empty room with the sun pouring from the large corner windows. My eyes are drawn to the inviting oriental key designed chaise, at one time a lovely shade of blue but now well worn and used.

I walk over to the windows to see one last time the view. It is peaceful and serene, a beautiful sunny afternoon. The sunlight filters from the giant trees and plays with the rippling pond below. I know this is a very special place, once filled with lots of laughter and good times where family and friends would congregate and enjoy the wonderful home with a view.

I feel a weariness. The chaise is so inviting in the warmth of the afternoon sun. It inspires me to sit for a while and rest. Maybe reflect a bit and maybe, if I feel inclined, have a replenishing nap. Sitting back.

I look at the landscape, the neighbors' beautiful flower gardens, which slope down to grasslands and gentle pond. I am mesmerized by the grandeur. My mind skips to another time and place, as if in reverie. The chaise is so comfortable. The place where I am drawn as others before me to ease into a moment of luxury before I begin my journey into the unknown.

Even though it is an unusually cold day in March, it feels more like winter. That is okay because right then it is a beautiful sunny Saturday afternoon. The sun feeling warm and inviting, and the air fresh and clear with a still, peaceful quality that makes me feel content and languid. This is a treat for me, even in the solitude, for it has been a very busy week and the gentleness of the day seems a reprieve to quiet my mind, body and soul. I have been trying to gear myself up, to delve into my story. Yet I am also reminded that I should savor this moment also. I decide to take a walk, before the sun goes down to gather my thoughts and reflections.

Although it looks much warmer than it is, I was out earlier and felt the biting cold, so I was preparing for a somewhat vigorous walk, with all the necessary warm layers required for a cold Minnesota day. That had never been easy for me, and it brought back memories of when my husband and our three children moved to the Twin Cities.

It was a corporate move and that was a week before Christmas in 1978. It was the coldest winter that we had ever experienced. We had bought a house in Country Club where the streets were tree-lined and mounds of snow had built layer by layer and impacted so tight what looked so soft and inviting, was hard, frozen as a deep freeze. It crunched with each step, sharp and crisp. This would be our new home, beautiful but daunting and challenging.

My husband had been working in Minneapolis for several months before the children and I came to live also. We had decided that maybe the transition would be easier if we moved in the middle of the school year and he was eager to have his family with him. Our two sons were in high school at the time and our daughter was in the first grade. I remember my friend and next-door neighbor Kaye driving us to the airport. Our house had been sold and packed, the movers on their way. So it should have been an adventure, but I remember feeling a strong, overwhelming sense of sadness, and I would break out in heart-wrenching sobs. I could not understand as this was not our first move. We had done it before, but this was different. This time, it would be farther, colder and Rick had said that this would change our lives. Those words played in the back of my mind. The boys were quiet and my daughter clutching her Raggedy Ann doll and a handmade Christmas stocking, almost as big as herself, a going-away present that she would treasure.

I tried to think how our lives would change. Our life in South Bend had everything that we needed. My oldest son Mark played first-chair trumpet in the high school band. He had a private instructor Mr. Lovin, as Mark seemed to really have a passion and gift. We would go to his concerts. The music would consist of jazz, classical and pop. I know my children got their musical, artistic side from me, but I could see that their father was impressed with their ability to perform with such passion, flair and charisma. Our youngest son chose the trombone, even though that instrument was bigger than he was. His real area of expertise seemed to be in the sciences, history and you name it. He had and still has the energy and determination that amazes. Someone had asked him once how he could do so many things and so well. He said, "I got that from my mom." Some things you just don't want to forget.

My sons loved having a little sister. To me, she was like a special gift. It was nice having another female presence in our home. She loved doing all the things that little girls like to do. She loved her stuffed animals actually more than she liked her dolls. But she loved playing dress up. I would fix her hair in curls or braids, ponytails high on her head. She would taker her little dance classes of jazz, tap and ballet. And we would go to the recitals. There would never be any pressure, just to have the experience, learn the art and grace of dance, and mainly for sheer fun. She made friends easily, and was like a social magnet. Her friends gravitated to her and her circle of friends grew and grew, for she seemed to embrace everyone. I really did not worry that much about Monica. She had just turned six. Yet I know that for my sons it may not be as easy, for they were of that age of transition and changes and that did play on my mind with some apprehension. But still, this could be another positive move.

When our flight touched down at the Minneapolis airport, we were to disembark this lonely venture, as Rick could not be there to greet us as he had important business to attend. But there would be a special shuttle that would transport us to the Minneapolis Athletic Club where we would stay for a few days until we moved into our new old house in Country Club just in time for Christmas. By the time we got off the plane, staying pretty close to each other, as we did not want to lose anyone, we had to get our luggage and since we had just moved we did take quite a few things. As we were to go down the escalator laden with gifts and luggage, the escalator seemed pretty formidable with all this stuff. How was I to do it without losing somebody or worse? The boys stepped on. I was standing there with Monica and because my arms were full of her precious things, plus my own things, I somehow stepped forward. Monica was supposed to take my arm, but she panicked and I started going down. She started to cry. I tried to go back but could not. Her brothers were very concerned on the bottom landing. Seeing my daughter frightened distressed me terribly. Thank goodness a kind man took her hand and brought her down the escalator. Now all we had to do was find the shuttle that would take us to the Minneapolis Club.

Well, we did get to our cozy room all by ourselves. But it left us little time to spend together as we also had a black-tie Christmas party to attend, which meant leaving my children along the first night in Minneapolis. They did not seem to mind, but it did bother me. I knew it was going to be pretty cold in Minnesota and I had found a wonderful deep turquoise, full-length sweater dress with long sleeves. It was warm and pretty. I felt in this I at least made a good practical choice and still looked elegant.

The dinner was held downtown in a very nice hotel. I cannot remember the name right now. Rick was happy to have his family finally with him. And he was proud to introduce me to his coworkers. In these situations I was pretty much at ease, even though I was much younger and the newcomer. I still felt comfortable and confident but I was surprised that I was the only one with a full-length dress. The other women had street-length dresses or pant suits. That surprised me for it was cold. A long dress seemed more practical and appropriate for this occasion. I didn't let this fact bother me, for I just wanted to be myself and experience the moment and this adventure that would bring new friends into our lives.

The Christmas and introduction party was a success. We left happy and eager to get back to our children. It was pretty late and we all were very tired from all the emotions of this big move, our first flight by ourselves and having to leave the children the first night here to attend this big extravaganza just did not seem right to me. I did not really know what to expect when we unlocked the door to our room. But it was a sweet sight. Monica had decorated the room with Christmas touches. Her big homemade stocking hung in a prominent place, along with cut-out colored paper chains, and cards left to her wonderful imagination with the help of her brothers. That is a sweet memory, and now we would begin our sojourn together.

* * * * *

We moved into our new old house just a few days before Christmas and in that first day the impact of a long-distance move was obvious. We had no family in Minnesota. With a growing family, especially young teenagers and a small child, there is a tendency to accumulate and need space and storage. There was an incredible amount of boxes, plus gifts for Christmas. Rick was determined to get a tree for the kids, but we had to make the space first. I look back and I wonder how we ever did it. There was so much to be done. The emotions were there. This place was so cold. When you opened the door, the cold hit you. I wondered were the winters always this cold here in Minnesota.

We eventually unpacked the boxes. We even had a sad little tree that was thrown together in a state of exhaustive determination. It looked as if it would topple over at any time, but it held steadfast. Things were looking up as we had good neighbors. We were still unpacking boxes, discovering that closet space and storage was going to be a problem, as this did not have the space for a growing family. One day, as I was backing out the driveway, and it was not easy as there was a wall of snow, I turned my wheel and hit what I thought must have been a hidden brick wall, but discovered was just hard-packed snow. I was surprised snow could be this hard. The snow we were used to was soft and fluffy. The winter was not five or six months. Now I lived in a place where people shoveled their rooftops. It was amazing to me and I thought Rick was not going to like this.

The boys started their classes in high school. Back then it was called Edina East. They would come home many times silent, sometimes angry. This move was not going to be easy in this new town. It was the first time I felt that our family could unravel and by a move that was to secure our family's future. The timing did not seem right or fair for our sons. I felt overwhelmed at times, wanting to give this move a fair chance. The music programs were different here. My boys were used to classical and jazz. Here they wanted marching band music. Mark began to lose interest in his music. He didn't feel challenged or needed in this big band, in this big school. He did not feel part of but eventually stood out by submerging himself in his religious studies. He decided he would become a priest. I know part of that decision came from frustration and a need for challenge and attention. Many of his questions and search for answers were not encouraged. Through his studies there was a program that was connected with the synagogue. The rabbis would encourage his questions, and he felt a connection. By the end of his senior year, he converted to Judaism.

Having an older brother or sister that stand out does not always make it easy on the youngest brother, especially if they are only two years apart. Both my boys were very bright. But that did not make their life any easier. Duane would openly rebel and challenge his adversaries, even his teachers. He would be openly defiant and stand his ground. If he found an error in a textbook or a test, he would show the teacher and sometimes they did not appreciate this observation or fact, but that did not discourage him. He loved knowledge. Actually both my sons did. He was bored in schools and it was easy for him skip class or classes and still ace the tests. It was all I could do to keep him in school. Sometimes in the most unexpected moments, we would have a heart to heart talk that would connect us again as mother and son. During these most formative and informative years, my sons needed their father's guidance, attention, reassurance. But that didn't happen. Rick was now submerged in his career, and that seemed to be taking precedence over his family.

* * * * *

Shortly after we moved here, Rick was made a partner of Ernst and Ernst, a CPA firm, which should have been a time to celebrate instead was bittersweet, as he was the only person to achieve this honor or position that year. Maybe it would not have been so bad if we would have been from the Twin Cities, but Rick was a newcomer. The other partners and staff made it clear that they resented this new kid as a partner before their own. Rick was clearly distressed, for this was never what he intended. Sure, he wanted to be a partner. That was a dream he realized could happen, but not like this. He wanted to feel acknowledged for his hard work along with his peers. I tried to comfort him and reassure him, to give it time. Eventually, if it was right they would realize that he was deserving of this position.

If we had been in Chicago or South Bend, this promotion would have been acknowledged and celebrated. That would not happen here. The head partner of Ernst and Ernst, Bob Kelly, and his wife Joan invited us to their home in Edina. It was a quiet and subdued dinner, just the four of us. I was surprised that no other person from the firm was attending this recognition dinner. I felt for my husband and was disappointed in the turn of events. Rick was hurt, and determined to prove his worth, and he would make millions for this company. His determination eventually turned into a simmering rage that fueled his relentless quest for recognition, power and money.

I could see the change in my husband. His work now took precedent over everything, including his family. Our sons were growing up, but their father was now on a different mission, and he had no time or energy left to give to his family. I felt everything that I and the children had given up was too important. I wrote Rick a letter telling him I felt like a single parent, that the children were growing up without knowing their father and their father not knowing them. I did not feel that we were a priority any longer. That the children, especially his sons, needed a male's guidance. If we moved back to Chicago or South Bend at least we would be close to grandparents and family and the familiar. I also knew that I could eventually earn my own money.

Rick wrote me back telling me that he loved me. He loved the children. That we should be patient, things would change. And that he was doing all this for us. He did not want me to leave. That is all I needed to know, was that he loved us, that we were important and necessary in his life. I stayed, determined to be the best wife and mother possible. For a while there was an obvious improvement and difference. Our sons were not that easy to forgive or forget, for they were asserting their independence. Mark would throw himself into his newfound religion, but that would not surprise me, as he was his father's son, born on his birthday, November 4th. And Rick would do the same—immerse himself totally in his choice of passion. To me it was too extreme. I felt it was a cry for attention from a male figure. It should have been his father, but now it would be in the form of respected rabbis who would influence and shape his life. I did think that maybe this would be a temporary fascination, but that was not to be so. During his senior year, he started observing the kosher rules concerning food and holy days, wearing a yarmulke to display his faith at home and in school. He read and studied the Koran. He was my quiet studious child, growing up, searching to find his own way that he felt would bring him admiration and respect somewhere, somehow. Maybe even his own father would be in awe or at least show an interest. He grew his beard and side curls, wearing black or dark clothing, no longer the typical teenager, but expressing his own individuality.

My son stood out among his friends and family. Mark was not one to make life easy on himself. It was as if he was testing the loyalties and depth of friendship of everyone, no exception. This did not make Duane's life any easier at school, although he never really expressed his real thoughts. I think that maybe he understood his brother's rebellion or search and respected his decisions. I think back and I would like so much to do things differently. But I was a young mother, learning the skills of life and parenting. I never thought that the task of parenting would be mine alone. I had a husband whom I thought would want to share in parenting. But Rick's work demanded and eventually became all consuming with no energy left to give. Between his travels and his long hours, Ernst and Ernst realized what a prize they had in this young partner. They would compensate him well, for he had much to give and he was willing for that was now his quest to prove his worth.

. * * * * *

I will close for now, as there is so much more. That can be overwhelming, but too important to leave out for understanding. The first is that I was married very young, not that I chose that for I had my own dreams and aspirations. I met Rick in high school. We were in the same typing class. He was a senior and I was a sophomore. He would walk me to my classes carrying my books, and linger until just before the bell would ring, and the he would tear down the halls to try to make his next class. When Rick graduated, he went to college at Roosevelt University. We continued to see each other.

We married. That is a story in itself. This was while I was still in high school and Rick in college. I had our first baby at the age of seventeen, on

Rick's birthday, Mark. Rick was a proud father and husband. At the age of nineteen, I had our second son. I will close at this because I have a tendency to go on for too long. But this story is about the value of family and corporations utmost loyalty at the cost of families, corporate and legal corruption, especially when money and power are involved. Twenty-eight years of marriage and the devastation of divorce during that time, the ultimate sacrifice and betrayal that continues with legal harassment led by ruthless attorneys for over ten years. There is much more. I want to get the message across of the importance and value of family, accountability and responsibility. We all have that responsibility for love, compassions and et cetera. I've got to go right now.

* * * * *

CHAPTER 17

BABIES

*I*FIND THAT AS *I* write about my life growing up and having my first child, putting all my hopes and dreams into perspective, believing and trusting that if I gave the very best of myself to my husband and to my dear little baby, which was so easy to do for he was so precious to me. I know Rick felt the same, although between his studies and part-time jobs, that left little time or me and even less with Mark. Therefore, Rick's father would usually be seen in old movies interacting with Mark. He would be the one holding Mark in photos. Our son grew to have an incredible bond with his grandpa Alfred, which was lasting to the end. Eventually, we would have our own little place not too far, surrounded by Italian family and old friends in a small section of town know as Hungary Hill. We would live just above Grandma Gilda and Grandpa Mike, in a red brick fourplex apartment. Our neighbor across the hall from us would be old friends of the family who owned this building with their extended family living across from Grandma Gilda and Grandpa Mike. The aroma of delicious Italian meals wafted through the air and greeted us throughout the day.

The Petraca family, good friends of Ricks' family, were well known and highly regarded in this little neighborhood. It was a family who worked together securing their family's future bringing different business to this little community. They owned the grocery store and meat market. They had the Petraca Launderette and dry cleaning business. They were generous with the church, their friends and neighbors. We were fortunate. Knowing that Rick and I were just starting our on our own, they gave us our little apartment for only fifty-five dollars a month. I never had to worry about laundry for I had a diaper service that did Mark's diapers and jammies and linens too. My laundry would be picked up and brought back to our apartment. Many times, my groceries would be delivered to my door. When I tell people how it was when I first married with all the help and support from so many different sources, they are incredulous. How lucky can one be?

I rarely went to the grocery story unaccompanied. I was very sheltered and protected, for Uncle George and Aunt Lorraine lived in the house next door with their two little boys, Kenny and Michael. Rick actually worked within a mile or two from our apartment as a bookkeeper. Many times he would come home in the middle of the day for lunch. I liked that. I would make his favorite sandwich, salami with mustard on fresh Italian bread, even taking out the black little peppercorns. There were four rooms in our apartment, each exactly the same size. Two bedrooms, living room and eat-in kitchen. The one bathroom must have connected to our neighbors across from us for the rooms were square. In the hallway we had our own broom closets that held mops and brooms, and various cleaning supplies. I took special care of the floors for although Mark was walking now, he still liked to be on the floor playing with his toys. We had a great routine, breakfast and maybe a visit with Grandma Gilda and Grandpa Mike and then a walk to the park for Mark loved the swing. Afterwards, we would go back to our little apartment to prepare for lunch, greeting our neighbors along the way. People were always friendly and Mark had a way of capturing every passerby's attention.

As Mark grew a little older and getting more hair, Uncle George would give him his first haircut. That did not please Mark in the least, but when he showed Mark that his own little boys received haircuts too, he was more receptive. That following year for Christmas, Uncle George gave hair clippers to Rick and gave him some pointers for cutting hair. It's too bad Rick didn't become a barber. But it seemed Rick's aptitude would be of the business nature and it would be a steady uninterrupted climb with a tangible reason, purpose and incentive—his family. Rick still was very much into his family and community.

One hot sultry night, our bedroom window opened in our little square room. We heard piercing shrieks from outside. It was a woman's scream in distress. Rick jumped out of bed with just his jockey shorts and undershirt on, tore through the apartment and out the door, bounding down the stairs to save this poor woman. I got up and put on my robe with the rose pattern. I looked like a flower as I stood at the top of the stairs. I could hear voices now just talking. Everything seemed pretty tranquil in the dark of the night now. The door opened. Rick emerged and bounded up the stairs.

"What happened?" I asked. "Is she okay?"

"Oh. That was just a neighbor yelling at her dog," he said in embarrassment.

I wondered who was more embarrassed or surprised, Rick or the neighbor. But I still thought that it was admirable that Rick's concern overrode his attire or lack of.

Another time, all was well. Rick was feeling relaxed and amorous. All was copasetic with the world. Suddenly we heard loud clamoring coming outside our apartment. Again, Rick jumped up to save the day or rather the evening. This time, he grabbed my short cotton leopard robe and threw it on over his shoulders. He grabbed a rolling pin from the kitchen drawer and stood poised to defend his territory. We could still hear obvious banging and rattling about outside our doorway. I was standing in the background on guard to protect my baby from mishap. Rick jerked open the door to surprise the intruder, when to his utter surprise along with the surprise of our benevolent landlord Rick was totally embarrassed and apologetic. I know Mr. Petraca took it very well and probably was thankful that my husband was so vigilant. It was not unusual for Mr. Petraca to work late in the evening for he was a night owl. I could relate to that. It was rather comforting knowing that my young husband would be there to defend what was important to him.

When I look back, even though we were young with lots of responsibility, we were deeply committed to each other and our family. How could we not be? We had all the loving support and guidance that it took to succeed. Rick and I were different, but our differences made up for what we both lacked. I was creative, bringing spontaneity and a touch of refinement that others were drawn to and sometimes wanted to emulate. Rick was proud of that. It was a good thing that I was around, for I would have to remind him that plaids and stripes really were not good in combination. He would want me to select his office attire, which was fine with me for I wanted him to look nice. One time, when we were out, we happened to run into a former classmate. Later he told me that marriage must really agree with Rick for he never looked better. I was happy to hear that. But isn't that the way it should be? Our partners should bring out the best in each other.

I loved the time that Rick and I shared with our baby Mark. We were protective, not taking any chances that our son, now a curious toddler, might get hurt. We probably were a bit too protective, even putting our first Christmas tree in the playpen for we did not want it to topple over on our son in case he tried to reach for the ornaments on the tree. I was not sure but there was a feeling that a woman or young girl knows if she is really in tune with her body. First, there is a sense of calm, a knowing that is quietly felt but too profound to acknowledge, unless certain, waiting for the right time. I finished cleaning up the perfectly square unusual shade of green kitchen, and went to the living room to see Rick lying on the floor with our little son, so contented in this arms. He looked up at me and said, "How could I ever love a child more than this?" Of course, I was so happy that he could feel that love so deeply for I understood that feeling. But it kind of saddened me and frightened me also. Was it possible my husband's love was limited? I shook that feeling off. I wouldn't let it happen. Days later, I would have to tell Rick that once again he would be a father. Once again, he accepted the news as if it were a normal step in his life, giving him added incentive.

Not everyone was as accepting, thinking that we already had too much on our plate of responsibility. I was almost nineteen, still too thin but healthy for I had a natural healthy lifestyle. I never developed a taste for coffee, rarely drank pop and I still preferred oranges and orange juice. Rick wanted to stay in our apartment for a while longer to save for a house. I knew that the new baby could sleep in the bassinet in our room until older. I thought we should at least paint Mark's room to prepare for this occasion. Rick came home with the paint that Mr. Petraca had given him for nothing. Well, that was very nice. I was eager to see the bright cheerful new color, but was so dismayed to see the deep battleship gray with a tinge of blue. Surely this must be a mistake for a child's room. Maybe if I stirred the paint it would lighten or brighten. But to no avail. Rick was adamant, saying it would lighten once it dried on the walls.

This was an apartment. We didn't own it and Rick didn't want to invest any money in paint. He said that with such gleeful conviction that I could not understand. His rationale disappointed me. I felt that a can of paint could not be that expensive. But if this were to be then I would brighten the room with white trim and lighter accessories. It was not easy to work with. I realized right then that Rick could never be a decorator or a color consultant. It was a good thing the he enjoyed the business aspect of life. One thing that was good when we would pay the bills for the first time, we would sit at the table together. Rick would be absorbed with each bill, checking the accuracy. He would write out the check, handing me the check and the bill to be sealed and stamped. That was my job. But I was learning all the time. I did my part and knew that paying bills was a part of life that I also needed to know. It amazed me, though, that Rick had no interest in learning cooking and cleaning. To him those chores were like magic. They just did themselves.

This pregnancy was very different. This was a very active baby. I could feel the kicks, which seemed like somersaults in my tummy. My doctor Dr. Patrizzi said I was going to have a ballerina. That would've been nice. But I wasn't sure about that. Probably more like an acrobat or gymnast. This time I would gain seventeen pounds. I had about two weeks' worth of false labor before the real thing. By the time my real labor started I was so exhausted that the doctor gave me relaxants to sleep and told Rick that he could go back to the office, which was close to our apartment. This was in the middle of the day. I was disappointed that they just didn't keep me, but evidently I still wasn't quite ready. I fell in and out of sleep, waking with pain, falling back asleep. My mother-in-law had Mark during this time. The contractions became harder and stronger, relentless. I was so groggy. I felt sick. I tried to conquer the effects of the relaxants. Did I take too many unknowingly? I was afraid I would have my baby in bed alone. I struggled to my feet, the room swirling around me. I made it to the living room, and another piercing contraction buckled my legs. I sank to the floor. It was hard to focus my eyes. I found the phone and managed, really concentrating, to dial Rick's office. I passed out from the pain. Rick did get the call and took me to the hospital.

I was in real labor. But again it would take time. I would deliver another healthy boy, over seven pounds and eighteen inches long. Our new son was beautiful, born October 13. I was nineteen at the time. I would name our new son Christopher Paul. I liked the sound of that. The third day, Rick came to the hospital. He said he would like to change our son's name to Duane.

"Why would you want to do that? I like Christopher Paul," I said.

"I would like to name him after Duane Strum."

"Who's that?"

"He's a man who owns the fishing resort in Minnesota where my dad and Uncle George and I would stay on our fishing trips."

Duane Strum must have made quite the impression on my husband for him to want to name his son after someone he'd only known on week-long vacations to Minnesota. In my weakness, and probably my confusion too, I relented.

"Okay. But only if we name our son Duane Richard."

"That's fine."

It is amazing how a name or a request that has not been well thought out can impact one's life. Rick liked having his way. But that was also what he was used to.

I would have bleeding complications that left me weak and would have that problem for almost three months. Eventually, I healed. Our new baby would sleep in the bassinet next to our bed until he outgrew his bassinet. Then he would sleep in Mark's room. Mark now slept in a bed, lending his crib to his new baby brother. Since there were only two bedrooms, Mark shared his room with Duane. It was a good thing that Mark was a pretty sound sleeper, for his brother rarely slept through the night. He seemed to be writhing in pain, which turned out to be a severe allergy to milk. The pediatrician suggested we try goat's milk. My beautiful baby would be fifteen months old and numerous testing before we found the exact problem and the solution. It was not an easy time, for also if Mark got a cold it would go into bronchitis and sometimes pneumonia. His temperature would spike to over 104.

* * * * *

While the beginning of our marriage was unconventional, we both accepted our responsibilities at an early age. I'm sure Rick felt a certain amount of pressure to provide for his family. But in retrospect I believe that is what he needed to stay focused on excelling for now he did have a reason, purpose and incentive. We worked as a team. I knew for our marriage to succeed, Rick's needs would have to come before mine. I also know our children's needs, welfare and future depended on Rick's and my providing the most loving and nurturing environment possible. I was determined that my children would have all that. I knew about living in fear, the kind of fear that holds you back, preventing the best of yourself to come forward. I would not allow that to happen in my own family. To me it seemed simple. If Rick was happy in his profession, he would excel and feel good about himself and be a wonderful husband and father in return. I always would give back also, through some type of mission work. Now that I was married I would have to center my attention on my family, for to me that was of the utmost importance. I knew that I could grow in my marriage. I would not be stagnant, but a positive and vibrant influence in whatever I attempted. When you're young and idealistic, anything is possible.

Since I was such a young mother, I was a conundrum to friends and our neighbors for several reasons. I looked younger than my age and would for years, and sometimes people would make such a big deal of that fact that I felt a little embarrassed. So what. Most people would love to have that problem. Also, because of my tremulous years growing up, I was probably a little more guarded, cautious and more contemplative and a bit more forgiving for small discretionary acts for no one is perfect. But I did also feel that good examples and behavior should be acknowledged in its importance and bad behavior should always be nipped in the bud, not ignored. Another good thing was that I actually played with my kids, sometimes actually being mistaken for the babysitter. If people made a big deal about my age and my appearance, I just told them all my healthy habits. I never smoked, never did drugs, did not like the taste of alcohol or the effects that I saw when used in excess. I did like the sangria at the supper club in South Bend, though. I think butterscotch schnapps tasted like the real thing. I said I know it sounded pretty boring, but to me my good health was a gift. Plus, I had so many talents and abilities. I was rarely bored. I was truly grateful for my newfound life and family and that would always be my main focus.

* * * * *

Finally, I am getting back to my writing after a myriad of interruptions plus major and minor distractions in every shape, size and manner coming from every direction demanding their attention, pulling at me, intruding into my time, my space. Nagging me until I take notice. Whatever little time is spared to write, I feel weary at the thought of trying to regroup my thoughts. Do I even want to continue going back in the past for even when life was copasetic now has become bittersweet. The loss would not be rendered with any kind of dignity, sensitivity or regard. In that respect, it hurts too much and it scares me too, for then the onslaught will continue until the devastation becomes too vast or considered a normal pattern of life or behavior.

Rules made for the select few that hold the wealth, power and connections, regardless of who is hurt or ruined in the process. It is known but overlooked, unspoken. Apathy and complacency sets in. In hopes that time will heal all wounds. But what about the accountability, responsibility, restitution and admission? Does it even exist when ignored? How can we learn from mistakes unless acknowledged and understood? Where does our responsibility start and where does it end and what significance will in impact on the future of our children and society? Is it for our own good? Ours alone? Are we so deserving that we can disregard the cause and effect of harmful actions that permeate the lives of others, eroding their worth, livelihood and security? While the designer rules are made to protect the select few who had become uncaring, denying and avoiding in their gated communities of pretense.

Now that I've said my piece or my verbal rampage, bear with me a while longer and I will continue with my story.

Our children changed our lives forcing both of us to take responsibilities seriously. I was the stay-at-home mom. That is what Rick wanted me to do and to be. I could do that, but I knew I also had to grow I my own way. I knew that I needed to have a creative outlet and Rick respected that. Living with Rick's parents for the first two years provided us with a great start along with homemaking skills for me. Just before we moved into our little fourplex, I told Rick that I wanted to get a special gift for his parents. Something that was unique and special to both of them. He agreed but since his time was limited with work and finishing college, I had to devise my own transportation for I could not ask his mother to take me shopping for her surprise gift. I decided to call my good friend Maureen and told her my plans. Since neither of us drove a car, we decided to take the bus. This was also when I told her I now had a baby boy. She was surprised. "Patti, I didn't even know you were pregnant." That was somewhat awkward but also the way it was and something I could not ignore. This was my life now.

I had never been on a bus before, other than a school bus. So this was like an adventure. We would take the bus to downtown Chicago Heights. My mother-in-law watched Mark so he was in good care. It was my first time away from my baby. I think Maureen was still processing the fact that I had a real baby and I was just acting as if this was a perfectly normal experience. It was the only way that I knew how to cope with the situation. It was great being with a friend with whom I could share this shopping experience. On the bus ride, it gave us time to catch up. Hearing my friend Maureen express and sometimes try to suppress her giggles made this adventure lighthearted.

"Maureen, I want to get something really special for my in-laws. Something beautiful they can have forever. Maybe we can find a beautiful painting that would look great over the sofa in the living room," I said in my excitement.

We searched for the special painting and finally decided on a large picture: a mountainous scene with craggy rocks and boulders peeking through the scraggy pine trees. At the base of the mountain was a stream running through the leafy green woods. A majestic scene of nature yet untouched by human. My eyes traveled up to the mountain and through the trees to glimpses of bright sunny sky. From the gentle flowing stream below that opened up the skies free from the adorning trees that provided great light from the contrast of the cool shade of the bordering trees. This was the one.

"But, Patti, how are we going to get it home? It's so big."

And it was. But that was the one and I have always had strong determination.

We talked to the sales clerk and she wrapped it up. I suppose we could have it delivered, but I wanted Rick and I to present this gift personally.

"Do you need help carrying this out?" the sales clerk asked.

"No, thank you. My friend and I can carry it out ourselves."

Maureen looked at me in wonderment.

"Yes, we can do it. I'll take one end and you can take the other."

"Okay." Maureen giggled again.

We must have been quite the sight, two young girls—we both looked younger than our years—carrying this large painting through the aisles, down the escalator, out the door and onto the sidewalk, making our way to the bus, with Maureen breaking out into contagious giggles.

It was a little tricky maneuvering this large picture through the narrow doorway of the bus, but with a little help from our bus driver, we managed to do it. Some nice people gave us their seats in the front, offering us more room. We sank to our seats in relief. We made it so far. Now, Rick and I had limited funds, so this was not a real painting, but beautifully framed and would enhance the living room. But one day, I would paint my mother- and father-in-law something of my own. We placed the painting on the floor, leaning it toward us. I carefully braced my prized gift to secure and protect it from the jarring of the bus drive. It was meant to be. We made it home without detection as we placed the wrapped picture inside the garage. Little Mark was sitting on a blanket, like baby Buddha with his grandma Diva in the backyard. It was a perfect day. I couldn't wait to see their response.

They really liked the gift but they also like the story behind the gift, as Maureen and I were traversing through the streets of downtown, making it to and on the bus. What a surprise. They must have liked it, for they had just painted the walls and they liked the beauty of the bare walls until our gift that inspired. Diva and Alfred kept that picture along with the real oil paintings that I did for them for many years, sometimes telling the story, but always pointing out my paintings. I loved my mother- and father-in-law for opening up their home and their hearts and giving us that start.

I remember how difficult it was even though Mark was not quite two years old to move from his grandma and grandpa's house. It did help that Grandma and Grandpa Spalluto lived just above us and knowing that Uncle George and Aunt Lorraine lived in the little house next door with their two boys Kenny and Michael helped. But our little apartment was getting pretty tight when Duane was born, for Mark was not quite two. His little world was changing and Mark did not adapt to change very well. Mark would be four years old and his little brother two when we bought our first house, not too far away on Ingrid Lane. Again, Mark cried his uncontrollable tears, while his little brother took it all in. What was this all about?

We would move into our neat little red brick bungalow. It would have three bedrooms, a nice size bathroom, a mudroom and laundry room off of the bright colorful eat-in kitchen and nice size inviting living room. Perfect for our first home, and all for under twenty thousand dollars. That was around 1967. That was when the necessities of life were affordable. That included education, medical care and dental care. Banks back then offered a service to people and for the people. That would be the time that Rick started his steady display of capabilities in the business world. Rick passed his CPA exam the first time round, evidently a rare occurrence. We were all proud, but it also held a dilemma for him, for during this time he was working in accounting for Mr. Carlstead, who had two sons of his own working for him.

Mr. Carlstead's youngest son also took the CPA exam and failed. This now posed an awkward situation at work. Rick worked for this company that was family-owned. He now felt his future limited. Rick decided to work for one of the larger accounting firms. It would be between Arthur Anderson or Ernst and Ernst. He would make the decision to work for Ernst and Ernst where he felt he had better potential for growth. Now my young husband would wear suit and tie to work. One of the most trying lessons was how to make that perfect knot in the tie, and I'm telling you it was not easy feat. Rick was sweating bullets trying to look professional and dignified. He tried everything from bowties to clip-on ties to slip-over-your-head-and-tighten ties. Through trial and error, strong will and determination and lots of encouragement, Rick mastered the tie. Hurrah. But he still liked me to pick out his office attire. That would continue throughout the years, until he reached the time of custom-made suits, shirts and ties and hired a buyer for his clothes.

We would live on Ingrid Lane for six years. During that time, having our own house gave us real independence and opportunities. It would be here that I met my friend Irma Piattoni. We became good friends while walking our children to kindergarten. My little boy Duane had blond hair like Dennis the Menace on television and her little girl had pretty dark hair.

After meeting on our walks to school, one day this pretty woman with short blond hair and about the same height as myself, said to me, "My little girl looks like she belongs to you and your little boy looks like he could be my son." I laughed. I knew I'd found a friend through our children. Our children were the common denominator. But there would be so much more from this friendship. Irma would also become a mentor to me. She and her husband Don were both highly respected in the church and the community. They had four wonderful children: Donna, Raymond, Tony and Susie. To have someone that I could finally relate to in a positive way was a gift to me. Irma would teach me yoga and the spiritual aspect of life. We both had an interest in painting and in our spare time would do tole painting on wood and three-dimensional glass painting. Many of the objects that I painted I gave away as gifts. My mother-in-law still has some of these paintings, like the chopping block I gave here with cherries bordering the scripted words "Life is just a bowl of cherries.""Hm. Who thought of that and what does it mean? Sweet cherries are delicious, though. So maybe a sweet life."

I had another marvelous neighbor up the street from me who was a real artist, Carla Bullaro. She sold her paintings for $500 and above and this was in the late 60s going into the early seventy's, which was impressive back then. I asked her one day if she would give a few lessons to Irma and me. Just how to prepare a canvas, what types of brushes, a few techniques, etc. When she said "Yes, I could do that," I practically jumped for joy. Carla added a few more students, but I probably was her most dedicated and prolific. There would be talks of a big move "one day." So I decided I had to make the most of this opportunity for I wanted to learn to paint everything from flowers to landscapes to ships and sailboats, water scenes from placid to turbulent, crashing waves I wanted to capture and achieve the effect. I wanted to bring beauty to my life and to others.

I started with painting from the masters, reproducing their works. How dare I. But I loved the masters, their elegance, the history and the passion felt conveyed on canvas. I knew if I loved it, I could do it. I could achieve, go beyond my own imagination for now my life was free of fear. I could move forward. During this time, my love for music brought me back to the freedom of dance. I found a local dance studio. I enrolled in ballet and jazz. Ballet was for grace and discipline and jazz for the sheer fun and expression. I went to the studio of the Bonnath Twins. Although they were twins, they really did not look that much alike. One was lithe, the other solid and strong. What I learned from these teachers of dance would stay with me for life. One day, I will get back to my passions in life.

With Rick's busy schedule, his commute by train to Chicago, many times a lot of overtime, but that was part of the package. I knew it was important for him to be able to play occasional golf with his buddies. But also it was important to leave some time for our family. I also knew that I needed my own outlet, that would be my painting and I could do that at home. My dance class was usually one night or day a week, and I could also stretch out and practice short routines at home. When you are young, inspiration comes easily.

* * * * *

There would also be during this times a few significant issues that arose. Toward the last two years on Ingrid Lane, I would get distressing calls from my sister Sandy. She was on her own now. Three weeks before, she was to graduate she ran away from home. I was not aware. I was hoping that since I had married, life for my siblings would get better. No news is not necessarily good news I would learn. I would think about my siblings and wonder but with two little boys and an ambitious husband, I needed to take care of things at home. When Sandy's call became more urgent for her concern for our sister Ginny. My thoughts turned to worry, eventually affecting my health. I went to my doctor. In fact, he was also my baby doctor, Dr. Parizzi.

"Patti, you've got an ulcer," he said somberly.

I looked at him with concern visible on my face.

"Patti, what is going on in your life that would stress you out so much?" I didn't know how to tell him my worries. He was a doctor. I needed a protector. "You can talk to me," he said. "I can help you. But I can't help you unless you tell me what it bothering you."

I knew his words were true. Just the realization that he cared enough to go beyond, I broke down in sobs.

"I'm afraid I don't know how to begin."

"Is it Rick?"

"No. No, he's a good husband. He works hard, and he loves me and our sons. He's a good father. But I worry about my sister Ginny. She's ten years younger than I am. I'm afraid for her and I don't know where to turn for help."

There. I said it. He was patient and his words were gentle when he told me that his son was an attorney and he would tell him about my sister, my fears. Then he would see what could be done. He would give me some medicine for my gnawing pain that would rise and diminish.

"I will call you after I talk to my son. But meanwhile, you take care and try not to worry." Then he said, "I always knew there was something troubling you. Now, I can help you."

My doctor would call me the next morning getting right to the point. "Patti, I talked to my son and there are some things that can be done. You can call the authorities and tell them about the situation. That will take some time to go through the procedures and proper contacts. Or, now this might seem extreme, but if it's a serious situation, it would be most productive."

I was listening intently. "What else can be done?"

"How old is your sister?"

"Fifteen. She's fifteen."

"Well, call her. Ask her how she's doing. Tell her that you can get her a safe place to live or she can live with you. It would be like kidnapping."

I gasped for air for I was so stunned.

"The reason is this, Patti. If your father has done nothing wrong, he will fight for her and will not give up. But if he has things to hide, then he will do nothing. He can't take that risk of being exposed."

That made sense. But I knew I didn't have any choice.

"Also, Patti, it's important that you contact the police and the authorities after this is done."

"Okay. I will." That would offer us a vigilance of sorts and protection. "Thank you so much, Dr. Patrizzi."

"Good luck to you and let me know how you are."

I hung up the phone. The gnawing pain reminded me that something had to be done. It was the beginning of summer. Rick was now traveling for Ernst and Ernst, working to provide for a secure future for his family. I had to act quickly. I called Ginny. She answered the phone in her soft melodic voice, so much like our mother's.

"Ginny, this is Patti."

Her voice perked up. I pictured her sitting by the phone near the dining room, the same phone where our mother sat, when she heard the news of the terrible accident to our father.

"Ginny, how are you doing?"

"I'm okay," she replied meekly.

I wanted to reach out and hold her. "Sandy has been calling me. She's worried about you and I need to know if you're okay."

From there, I reiterated my conversation with my doctor. "We will come and get you and you can either live with us or we can find you a safe place. It's up to you."

With that, she burst out crying. "Patti, I want you to come and get me."

"When can you be ready?" It was getting close to three o'clock and I did not want to take my little boys. "What time does Mom or Dad get home?"

"Usually around five-thirty."

"I'll try to be there before five. I love you." We hung up.

I wished Rick could have been home or at least reachable so we could have done this together. I called my mother-in-law. Thank God, she answered the phone.

"Diva, I have an emergency. Could you please watch Mark and Duane for a few hours?" There must have been something in my voice that was on alert, for she never hesitated.

"Yes, of course, I can."

I breathed a sigh of relief. It was as if my guardian angels were surrounding me giving me courage and protection. I gathered up my precious boys. "God, I hope I'm doing the right thing, the right way. Protect my children and my sister."

My little boys safely in the back seat, we got to my mother-in-law's house. I could not tell her my mission. I didn't want her to worry or talk me into not going.

I drove through the town of Crete to the long country roads to the house that I had lived in for almost four years, still a reminder of what we had endured. At this point, I had no concept of time. My first concern was to get my sister and take her home. I turned onto Bemis Road. I was almost there. My gnawing pains getting bolder. I approached the large white farmhouse. I looked up at the bay window where I clung for life or maybe not. I won only because the fear of my father was greater than the fear of the fall. I didn't turn into the driveway. I didn't have to for Ginny was standing in front of the driveway holding a small suitcase, her cat and a stuffed toy animal. She looked so young. I had feelings of anger toward my mother for not protecting and dejected resignation for my father.

I had visions of our father seeing Ginny get in my car and chasing after us. That did not happen. For that, I was thankful. My heart was pounding. The gnawing pains were piercing. Is there an existence free of stress? I looked over at my sister. She clung to her stuffed animal and holding her cat close, as the cat was squirming wanting to be released and out of the car. I knew her heart and her thoughts were racing, as were my own. I had to concentrate on driving, but I would interject with "Are you okay?" Ginny would shake her head in reply. I wondered is she was in shock for this was happening so fast. We reached the house of my mother- and father-in-law. When we drove up, Diva approached the car as I got out. My sister was sitting in stone silence.

"Thank you for watching my boys," I said.

Diva looked at Ginny and knew something big had transpired. I gave her a brief summary, which was thankfully all she needed or wanted to know. She offered her house to us, but there was no way that I wanted my in-laws involved. My brother Billy and his wife Shirly had just moved into a new place. We would stay there for a night or two. Ginny and I would have to meet with the proper authorities.

"I'll call you," I told Diva. "We'll be okay. Don't worry."

She watched us depart. We would be okay. I was determined.

We stayed the night at Billy's, for no one knew the address or phone number yet, except Sandy, Rammy and Mary Belle. Mark and Duane accepted this as an adventure. It seemed late when we arrived at their house. I was exhausted. Billy had sleeping bags on the floor for the boys and gave Ginny and me the spare bedroom. The medicine that I had for my pains, the stress was greater. Things would have to calm down to take effect. Did I even sleep that night? Between the pain and the events of the whole day and what was to lie ahead was not conducive for a good night's rest. We only stayed the one night, for in the bright of the new day, things did not seem so foreboding.

I immediately contacted the authorities and Ginny and I met with them. They concurred with what Dr. Parizzi had told me. Ginny was starting to feel more relaxed even though in the heat of our escape, the cat jumped board seeing its own escape. We couldn't find him. Ginny cried about that for a while, but we had bigger concerns ahead. I had no idea how to find a runaway cat, along with everything else. I can't remember if Rick called or if he just came home and I told him about Ginny. He again was accepting. Ginny would take the extra bedroom and Mark and Duane would again share the same room with twin beds.

Also, I did call my mother where she worked at the hospital. Her first job and the same job she held when our father had that terrible accident. She liked going to her little job, the same way I loved going to school. I just wanted her to know that Ginny was safe, but I told her not to tell Dad where she was. I didn't like putting her in that position but I just wanted to relieve her worries. She listened quietly. It seemed she breathed a sigh of relief and said, "Thank you for letting me know." It was what I had to do. Strangely, I didn't hear from our father for maybe a week or more. But the police did give us possible predictions.

One afternoon, of course everything was quiet. Things were getting settled and somewhat normal. The phone rang. I answered. It was Dad. I hoped he hadn't heard the catch in my voice. He sounded too nice, too polite.

"Patti, do you happen to know where Ginny is?"

I tried to sound natural, calm, but with concern also. "No. I'm sorry I haven't any idea."

"Well, if I find the person that has Ginny . . ." Then he started.

I closed my ears, my eyes, my mind to his voice, his words. "I'm sorry. I've got to go. I'm sure when she's ready she'll come home."

The worst part was over. I would not hear from him again. His threats could do nothing for he knew. Not too long after that call, our mother and father would move to Florida.

Ginny would adjust to her new surroundings. She liked being in town and even got a part-time job working at a taco restaurant. She seemed to like working there, but when she came home her hair and clothing smelled so much like tacos that she was like a walking taco herself. She could never smell herself and didn't mind if others told her. When school started, I would have to go to the school to tell them that my sister was living with me now. They asked the appropriate questions, but I'm sure with raised eyebrows. One of the teachers said that he always felt there was something wrong. I wished he would have acted on his instincts as well as many others and stepped in some way. All this hullabaloo did not seem to make much of an impact on my sister. Maybe it was her age—fifteen going on sixteen. So here I was a mother of two little boys, and guardian of my teenage sister. It was a good thing I was young too for I guess I could handle it.

* * * * *

Life was busy and getting busier. Rick was continually moving forward, high praises for his dedication and abilities. The nice thing was back then the wife (homemaker and mother) would also be acknowledged for her role of support and all their hard work keeping the home front running as smoothly as possible.

For they knew that for every successful man was the wife who helped make the successes possible. Can you imagine an up-and-coming executive saying, "I won't be able to finish this project or deadline, because I have to go grocery shopping, clean the house and clean the bathroom, help my children with their homework or it's my turn to fix dinner?" What about those business trips? I hope that it's really worth it. Thank goodness that there is a mother who does all that and more. It is all needed and necessary in order to function. Otherwise, there becomes chaos and disorder. What about when a child gets sick and you're up all night or when they just need some undivided attention?

During this time, Rick did get sick. I was not feeling too well myself. I had some unusual bleeding. We would find that Rick had measles. I went to the doctor myself for this bleeding would not stop.

"What does this mean? Could I possibly be pregnant?" I asked my doctor.

"I doubt it. But if you are, you are very early." He told me I would take the rabbit test and I was not sure how that test worked. Evidently, the test confirmed that I was pregnant with my third child. I started crying for Rick had the measles and I was having this bleeding problem. The doctor gave me a shot, told me not to overdo and to call if things changed.

I would have this problem for the first three months or more and then it stopped. Rick again was happy that we were to have another child. Maybe it would be a girl this time. I didn't want to wish too hard. Mark and Duane were nine and seven. They both were excited at the prospect of their mom having another baby. Mark wanted a baby sister and Duane just wanted a baby but a little brother might be nice. Rick continued to work hard also continued traveling and most weekends would go golfing with his buddies. He had tremendous energy and was proud of it. But when you love what you do and life is good, that energizes. Rick did have a habit that would impact his health for he was prone to bronchitis and occasional bouts of pneumonia as would Mark. Therefore I vacuumed almost every day and I would dust every day. In the children's room I would wipe the furniture and ledges with a damp cloth to remove the dust. That was what the pediatrician recommended. This way the dust would be contained to the damp cloth.

I liked having a clean house and naptime or bedtime toys would be picked up and put away. Because my family was growing, there was always laundry to be done. I did laundry every day for I didn't want anyone complaining they didn't have clean underwear or socks.

Now back to Rick's bad habit: He smoked. As much as he smoked and it was too much, over a pack a day, and it was Lucky Strikes or Camels. I never liked the smell. I never did. If I had a headache, the smell would make me sick. I was constantly cleaning the one ashtray for I didn't want to encourage the habit. Back then, it seemed the majority of people smoked. But I was a rebel in that sense. Just because everyone was doing something that I felt was not healthy or right, I would sometimes be the only one in the crowd. That was okay with me. But I wondered why people could or would take such risks with their health. Rick tried to kick the smoking habit because he was getting sick more frequently. He even tried a pipe. That seemed to be a lot of work and I don't think he was the pipe type. One day, he just quit cold turkey. Gave it up and would not smoke again until several years later.

When I really look back, I realize that I married a high-maintenance man. Things always had to happen on his time and on his terms. Sure, he was accepting of another child, even having my sister live with us. There would be no protest. If anything, that would keep my busier than ever and he wasn't home anyway for his work always took priority. After all, I was the stay-at-home mom that took care of everybody's needs. That was expected. So what if I gave up my life? What life. I didn't live in fear now. I should be grateful, permanently and forever grateful. I would rationalize my reality. I never realized that Rick would be forever and permanently driven and my gratitude was what he depended upon. I would have another child. Through this, taking care of my precious boys. They both were in school that gave me a few hours to myself, which would be devoted to household duties, grocery shopping, etc. If I were super organized, I would find fragments of time to work on painting. Ginny now finally was given a chance to be a typical teenager. She excelled in school for she was book smart. She kept her waitress job at the taco restaurant. She was moving forward. I was grateful for that.

* * * * *

I might as well write about my pregnancy and the birth of Monica, my third child. That was a pivotal time. It was a time that kept Rick and I focused on what was important. The fact that my pregnancy started out a little tenuous made us more aware of this little life that was dependent on me. During this time, as my pregnancy became more secure, it was comforting to have Rick taking more of an interest and concern. Once the bleeding stopped, I felt strong and healthy again. But he would caution me if I was carrying something that he thought was too heavy for me, or if I would walk too fast. He would say, "Patti, you shouldn't be running now." The boys were proud I was going to have another baby. Ginny living with us provided a built-in babysitter, when it worked out.

There were other changes that would be coming about which would require consideration. Rick would continue to impress the people in charge who recognized his abilities and drive. That did not surprise me for I could see for myself that his enthusiasm and confidence kept building. I also knew that I was a big part of his growth, through my encouragement, patience and understanding. I wanted him to be happy in his work. I also knew that our children were the incentive and motivational factor that helped keep Rick focused. It helped me when I was recognized for my part, my contribution. Occasionally, I would receive beautiful bouquets of flowers and a note thanking me for my part in his success. I was the wife and mother who supported her husband in his endeavors. But isn't that what a wife does, wanting the success and happiness to be fulfilled and appreciated? We would attend office parties that included me, that also honored me, the wife and mother, in the process. What an incredible motivating factor for both of us.

Rick was proud of me, telling me I was even more beautiful pregnant. That is so important for a mother to know and hear, especially from her husband. I would gain only seventeen pounds, the same as my second child. That was all but it was better than eleven pounds. Again, I would experience throughout the last month false labor. These would begin when I was up and about and would sometimes stop after a while or if I rested. Rick was out of town on business in South Bend, which took only a couple hours when he drove his car. Sometimes he would drive with a wonderful young co-worker named Al Hopkenson. That lessened the tediousness of the commute. Al would become a good friend to both of us. I remember that time. His friendship was dear and special, but also brief. As he would develop a rare form of throat cancer that quickly spread. When he died, we lost a wonderful gracious friend. I wondered why his life was taken so early, so quickly. It was so unexpected. It was a loss we both felt. I had to believe that such a good man was now in a better place.

Now back to my labor that would begin for real.

Rick was out of town. My contractions started that day. Kids are amazing, much more aware than we want to believe. Little boys have this abundance of energy. They also have a deep love for their mother. They would be concerned when my contractions began. Their little friends would be on hand like the little rascals, waiting to play but knowing that something special was about to happen.

Mark and Duane would check on me and I would reassure them I was fine, that the baby was just practicing to be born. When my pains subsided, I told Ginny that she could go ahead to her job. That this probably still wasn't time for the baby wasn't due for another week. Throughout the evening, the pains continued, just to tell me "be prepared."

Ginny made dinner for herself and the boys before she left for work. I could not eat. I felt anxious. The contractions continued to come when Ginny came home from her taco job, for she only worked a couple hours because of school. I felt that when I went to bed the pains would stop like they usually did. I wasn't too concerned yet.

They continued into the evening. My little boys were tucked into bed, my sister doing her homework and then off to bed. The house was still. Through the pains, I managed to drift into sleep, off and on for a short while. This time, the pains didn't go away. I had a new doctor, one who specialized in pregnancy. He said if my water broke or if I bled to come in. So far I'd just had the contractions. I guess it was innate, or what we call nesting. But I thought as long as I can't sleep and the pains might go away, I might as well do laundry and make sure everything was in order. I would be up all night, folding clothes amid my contractions. I decided to wash my hair. That was a good idea, for then if this were real labor I wouldn't have to worry about my hair.

It wasn't as easy as I thought. The house was still quiet. Everyone was sleeping and I was doing laundry, having serious contractions and just washed my hair and packed my suitcase. It was a little before five in the morning. I started bleeding, which alarmed me. I called my friend Irma. She was the only one who knew would be awake, plus she lived closest to me and the hospital was not too far. Before I left for the hospital, I woke up Ginny and gave her instructions to call Rick in South Bend and let him know I had begun my labor. Irma took me to the hospital. Diva and my friend Susie would be there also. It was like a party, a celebration.

A hospital in some ways is like Las Vegas in the sense that one loses the concept of time. It could be day or night. When I was admitted, I was quickly attended to. While the nurses were checking my vital signs and monitoring my baby, I lay there quietly watching the nurse, her face showing concern.

"I can't get a reading," she said.

It was as if my heart stopped. I started to cry. "My baby. Is there something wrong with my baby?" The baby was always still. I always had to be very quiet to feel the little kicks.

The other nurse took over. As she was intently listening, she finally said to the first nurse, "You've scared her. The baby is fine." From tears to elation in a matter of seconds. As long as my baby was well, I could endure the pain.

Diva stayed with me until Rick came bearing a colorful assortment of flowers. I had not had the baby yet, so I guess he was coming prepared. This again was another long labor. But, since this was my third delivery, Rick was more relaxed and even exhibited a sense of humor. It was August 2. I could feel the heat of this hot summer day. In my delirium, it seemed Rick thought it was rather funny that I begged him to open the window, the window so beguiling to me. I knew if it was open, I would feel cooler and better.

"Please, open the window. It's so hot. I just need to feel the breeze," I begged. My request was simple.

"Patti, I don't know if I can do that."

"Why? Doesn't it open?" I was stymied and frantic.

Rick then looked at the nurse and said, "Well, I don't want you to jump out." Of course, he was trying to be funny. That did not help. The nurse gave Rick a small paper cup of chipped ice. I loved the chipped ice. The sweet coolness provided a momentary relief.

Rick stayed with me, trying to comfort. At least he had a good night's sleep. One of these days, I would too. Finally, they wheeled me into the delivery room where Dr. Pathy would deliver Monica. When my baby was finally born, Dr. Pathy said in his soft accented voice, "Patricia, you have a healthy, baby girl."

"Are you sure?" I could hear bemused laughter before I fell immediately into deep dreamy sleep.

It's a good thing I only had three children because I would have to write about each child! As mothers do at one time or another, we talk about our babies. The whole process. My friend Jill said, "I just loved when after my babies were born, the doctor would put my baby on my stomach. It's amazing having the baby inside and once the baby is born, to see, and feel the baby, on your stomach. There is nothing like it."

"Jill, I don't remember that. I would always fall fast asleep." What did I miss out on?

A baby girl, a beautiful baby girl, the nurse would bring my baby and put her in my arms. My baby was sound asleep, so peaceful.

"You can hold your baby now. But from here she will have to be under the lights. She has jaundice. She'll be okay. It's not unusual for this to occur, but it requires your baby to be under a special light."

I had to think and know that my baby was in good hands. I was still feeling the effects of the delivery. I held my baby daughter close. I didn't want to let her go. I wanted her to sleep in a bassinet next to me like the other new moms. That would not be. At least not in the hospital. Monica would be under the lights for six days. During that time, the first time I stood up, blood poured from my body onto the floor along with a massive blood clot. I was shaken, feeling so weak I could hardly stand. It was not unusual for this to happen. It had been a problem in the past. This time, however, it was more pronounced. At first, I thought it was the blood loss, but I could not understand the lassitude that took hold of me, forcing sleep upon me so readily.

I had a roommate. That was a comfort. She also had a baby girl. When the nurse brought her baby, I would walk to the nursery to look at Monica under the lights. She was a sleepy baby, like her mom. I was so disappointed that I would not be able to hold her during this time. It didn't seem fair. Yet, I was not well myself. I could hardly eat. My roommate looked at me probably the second day after the delivery.

"Why aren't you eating?"

"I really don't know, just don't feel hungry right now. I don't think I feel well."

She looked at me. "Maybe you'll feel better if you brush your hair?"

"Yeah. Maybe that will help." I felt my hair. It was bushy. Full of knots. I stood up to look in the mirror. I resembled a wild woman or child. I still looked so young. The thought of trying to comb or brush this mess seemed impossible. I remembered washing my hair before I went in the hospital. While my hair was still wet, I'd been in a delirium, flailing and thrashing. Now my hair was paying the price. It was a massive bush. What was the cure?

I don't know if it was seeing my wild head of hair or the effort of trying to detangle all the knots, for my temperature spiked to 103. I was not feeling well at all. I would not be able to nurse, for I was on too much medication and too rundown. Rick would come to visit and help me to the nursery to see our new baby, whom we would name Monica Renée. I liked that name and evidently he did too. The sixth day, I was finally able to hold her. When the nurse handed Monica to me, Monica's skin was red with large pieces of dry skin ready to fall from her little body. That was from the intense lights. I would only be able to give her baby oil baths until her skin healed. I was just happy to bring her home to gently heal her body, and for her big brothers to meet their sister.

* * * * *

What I realize now is what a monumental task it takes to be a mother, a homemaker. It seems even more pronounced and blatantly incongruous when there is tremendous success built during that period and in the end the role of mother and homemaker is demeaned, eradicated and devalued. One will be rewarded. The other will be left to defend her worth, her existence and her identity.

I'm sure I've said this, written this in one form or another throughout these writings. But, for me, it is so unbelievable that my marriage could end with such rancorous disregard that I now live my life to defend my worth and position. My sacrifices were greedily absorbed for they were needed to serve the needs of a hungry man, appease his comfort and wellbeing and help build his confidence when overwhelmed with doubt and discouragement. I was there for Rick. Through the years of successes and financial rewards, that was not his alone. He would learn to erase his conscience, forget his family and buy his redemption.

I could continue writing about my life as a young wife and mother, dredging up the past, trying to remedy the injustice with understanding the outrages to the point of having to address the wrongs and restore the dignity that should have been recognized. Why did it happen? Why was it allowed to happen? My husband grew to be a man of position, wealth and power, created in his world of mergers and acquisitions—once known as hostile takeovers. It does not sound people friendly, does it? Well, it isn't. And families are not spared, excluded or given any consideration in the process.

Through the years, while I immersed myself in my family, changes occurred subtle and insidious. Rick traveled early on in our marriage. He would be out of town when I went into labor with our last child. Only to be home for a few days, bringing his work home for he was so diligent. He became unaware of the needs of his family. He could not even recognize the fact that I was still seriously ill, not fully recovered from Monica's birth. He would leave for South Bend to pick up where he left off. He would be gone for five days. In that time, my fever spiked to over 104 degrees. I've written about that so I won't repeat it here.

My daughter would be my last child. I would have severe bleeding problems. I was fortunate that I had my three children. I was still young, so in that respect that would be difficult to accept if I dwelled on my loss. I would focus on my family, my home and my friends. I was fortunate that I had a release through painting, music and dance. So, my life was full. The problem was Rick was rarely home to know his family for his travels never ended. His responsibilities at the office grew and were magnified in their importance and were starting to take its effect on our children and myself. Eventually, we became less important in Rick's life.

By the time, Monica was only fourteen months, we would have made three moves. The first time we moved, I told Ginny that we would eventually move to South Bend. She had one more year before she graduated. The thought of uprooting, leaving her friends and school at this time, was too unsettling for her. She needed more stability and familiar surroundings. Our pretty little bungalow that was so inviting was hardly on the market before we had a buyer. We did not realize how long it would take to sell. We would move several blocks over on Damico Drive renting a light brick rambler with a nice yard for the boys. Mark and Duane attended St. Rocco parochial school, so still in route for the school bus to pick them up. We would have the lease for three- or four-months still waiting for the real moving date to South Bend. As our lease was approaching expiration, Rick decided we might as well buy a house. My sister at this time decided to accept the invitation to stay at the home of friends until graduation.

We found a pretty two-story cape cod with assorted brown and tan stone, the upper part of the house wooden and painted white. The windows were framed with forest green shutters and a cedar roof. There was a row of trees in the small backyard that sloped down into a little creek. The boys loved the creek. We didn't know how long we would be here, but I envisioned building picturesque memories of birthdays, holidays and family gatherings for this was a family home. We no longer settled in when Rick's travels picked up big time. He was hardly ever home during the week. We had great neighbors. The family on the left had two little boys about the ages of Mark and Duane. Monica was eight months and I could hardly believe it but was starting to take her first steps. I wasn't too thrilled about that for she was my baby and I wanted to enjoy her baby stage. But her brothers would always be encouraging her to "Come to Mark" or "Come to Duane."

Our neighbors on the right were interesting and very nice, interesting in the sense that the husband was an ex-priest and his wife and ex-nun. They seemed to enjoy seeing the children play and everyone loved Monica. They were gracious and considerate. In the short time that we were there, the husband noticed that my husband was rarely home. Realizing that Rick traveled so much, and how precious time was he offered to mow our lawn too, since our yards connected. He didn't make a dig deal about it. It was just done, unpretentiously. Not expecting anything in return.

This new complex was complete with a swimming pool and a wading pool for the little ones, all within three blocks. This made those hot summer days refreshingly inviting for the kids, also providing a nice routine that everyone enjoyed. I really had to keep an eye on Monica for she loved water, ever since she learned to love her baths. She was walking really well by the age of nine months and it would not be unusual for her to walk to the ledge and right in the water. The first time she did that, it scared me. I grabbed her up and she just shook her little head, wanting to be right back in the water. After three months of living in this wonderful neighborhood, Rick would come home from the office with news that we now would be moving to South Bend. It would have been very easy to let myself get very attached to this new house and neighbors. But in the back of my mind I knew it was only temporary.

It is always difficult leaving good friends and neighbors. I was trying to think of a way to show my neighbor, who mowed our lawn, our appreciation. I had just completed a painting of a sailboat on choppy water. Soft touches of yellows, greens, pinks and lavender ever so slightly tinted the sky and clouds, reflecting in the waters and the billowing sails. It was all done with a palette knife. It was not a large painting, but it was pretty and special. I decided to offer it as a thank you gift for their act of kindness that did not go unnoticed. Rick later would be upset that I gave it away. "It was one of my favorite paintings," he said. A surprising bit of news to me.

One of the first things I would do when we moved in and settled our new house at 17780 Tally Ho Drive was paint a picture for Rick. This would not be a sailboat though. It was a nice size painting of a clipper ship with lots of sails of all sizes, ropes and ladders, very intricate and challenging. I liked the effect of the waves breaking against the ship, spraying into mist. That painting in those quiet blocks of time was what I needed to create and know that giving the time and incentive, I could do almost anything and with great peace and joy.

When life is good, I want time to move a little slower, just enough that I can savor the moment and hold fast the memories. I do know that life is not perfect, nor will it ever be. But I also feel we all have the capability to do better, be better. To be able to give back to the earth, do our part of humanity, create something beautiful and lasting for our children. Isn't that what we're here for? It's not just for ours alone.

* * * * *

CHAPTER 18

MOVE TO SOUTH BEND

*O*UR MOVE TO *SOUTH BEND* opened up opportunities for all of us in a way that was inviting and plausible. This is where our sons' band experience began, also the strong emphasis in science that heightened my youngest son's interest. Our sons were growing up with intellectual and keen minds, keeping me on my toes. Monica would be a little over a year old when we moved here. Having little ones are the best way to get involved and meet friends and neighbors. For myself, it was like putting all the skills I had learned from everyone in front of me, like a child taking their first step, faltering every so slightly, but with each step also gaining more confidence and independence. I believe during that time our marriage was at its strongest. Rick's career was becoming secure and comfortable. Now that we were in South Bend, his travels were not as frequent. Meanwhile, South Bend was also a Mecca for many great art instructors, so I was constantly in a state of inspiration. I found an incredible dance studio where I would again take jazz and ballet.

I loved taking my dance classes. I loved rhythms and my instructor would say that I had natural rhythm that needed to be expressed. I would do my routines with an added flair or finesse. I could get away with that in the jazz routines, more so than with the more disciplined graceful moves of ballet. But I notice I have learned to cook the same way, adding my own touches of spices, blends or flavor that sometimes pleasantly surprises and occasionally is not appreciated even by myself. So then I try and contain my creative spirit at times, and not go too far astray. My life, my home, was filled with kids, brimming with activity, inside and outside. Music was a big part of our life usually being practiced or played, sung or danced to. I loved that time in my life.

This would also be the time that we would join the local tennis club and our first real country club. The South Bend Country Club, where we fine-tuned our tennis and golf. Our life was full and active but never really seemed stress laden or as hectic as our life would become. Our sons had plenty of friends in the neighborhood. Woods to explore. Open fields of grass where friends would gather to play a game of baseball, sometimes with their younger siblings tagging along with hopes of joining in our just content to watch. This was very much a people friendly and family-oriented neighborhood.

This also would be where I could take a few college courses at the community college. I would take a rather serious subject such as social science. I loved literature and I would treat myself to an art class, drawing class, graphic or graphic art design. With each new subject, I was gaining more confidence and knowledge, an exciting adventure. My neighbor Reecie would watch Monica while I attended classes and I would watch her little ones so she could have a respite. When you have children, time is a precious commodity and it is true, women do tend to do too much, many times multitasking to the point of amazement and exhaustion. Our dreams and our aspirations are suspended, pushed back until all the main necessities taken care of—done either in fragmented or borrowed time, and sometimes not at all. That is when I find that it is important to do what one loves to do in life. For then you are replenished, energized and ready for the next lesson in life.

There was much diversity living in South Bend. We had all the cultural and sports activities so easily accessible and attainable. Since Rick did the auditing for Notre Dame and St. Mary's, we would attend many of the black-tie affairs where I would have opportunities to wear beautiful gowns. I loved getting really dressed up. We would also have front row seats at football games outside in the winter watching Joe Montana. He was pretty cute. Since I was really into the arts, I managed to appreciate the experience of braving the elements in style, depending on the weather. But being surrounded by such great energy and history in the making was an incredible experience in itself. Life was good and it was a treasured span of time.

When we moved, Rick was in auditing and also did yearend taxes. Which is not my favorite thing. For several reasons, but one of them was that my birthday fell on February 1, which by coincidence is very close to Oprah's birthday. We are rather similar in our thinking and ideas, in face I'm a miniature version. At any rate, since everybody knows how taxes are the main topic of conversation, time and thought up until the ninth hour, being in taxes crescendos into a frantic, consuming race against the clock. Obligations are many times put on the back burner. One of these years eventually I would turn thirty. It happened. Rick being so busy, I think his intentions were good and sincere, he said, "Patti, when you turn thirty, I'm going to take you dancing." I couldn't wait for that day. But lo and behold when that time came, he was so busy with those despicable taxes that my birthday just didn't happen. I decided if I was not to have a birthday, then that meant I wasn't a year older. It worked. People still say I look younger than my years.

We would live in South Bend for about six years. Rick from the time of his early successes, building his confidence which thrived on challenges, would ponder his next move. At least back then his family was the main stimulus. This would be a monumental decision that Rick considered heavily. I could not see or quite understand the magnitude at the time. How could I know the real dynamics of a corporate decision? I know I felt uneasy. A small feeling of trepidation that I questioned within. There were other reasons to consider for our life was good and secure here, offering a healthy productive environment. Our sons were now young teenagers. That seemed to both of us another factor to consider. Monica was just starting first grade at a wonderful private school Stanley Clark. It would be difficult leaving our good friends, the music programs, my art and dance classes. How could I start anew in another college? What about my hopes of taking some courses available for me at Notre Dame? There was so much to consider at this precious time of life. I felt Rick's strong pull. As long as we were in this together, we would progress together. Rick would not put his family at risk. We were the mainstay.

I have written about our move to Minneapolis, so I will not repeat it. I wonder though about those deep feelings that I know Rick and I both felt.

* * * * *

CHAPTER 19

SOMETHING'S HAPPENING HERE

NOW IS THE TIME TO address the real issues. There is no easy road or no easy way. How could there be when the wall of silence and avoidance would be the barrier to enlightenment and understanding? How could decisions have been made blindly without consideration or thought of consequences that feeds even greater needs that can only lead to dysfunction and corruption within? There is no accountability. It happened and will continue to happen until both sides are heard without bias or ulterior motive. But sometimes we alone must make that stand. I always wondered why I had such strong convictions that I had to address. And when I didn't address these issues or experiences immediately, they didn't go away. They followed me everywhere affecting every aspect of my life, haunting my dreams and taunting me to do something about it if I dared.

They say the pen is mightier than the sword. I feel that words if heard, read and understood, all sides considered, we all would benefit from the truths, always. I have always questioned those documents or judgments that were to be sealed, not to be heard or understood, with hopes to be eventually forgotten. Time has a way of exposing the results.

* * * * *

When I made my move from the house in Edina, it was with every intention of making a new life. Tucson was a real possibility. I would leave all the bad memories behind and start anew. But my divorce would not be over, for Rick would appeal the settlement. He had the means, connections and the money and definitely the audacity. It did not matter that it was not right or honorable, for he was still in the mindset of power and control. He would test his limits as angry men or children sometimes do. He would be allowed for no other reason other than he could. I would not be given the time or consideration to grieve my loss. Or the fact that along with the big divorce, my last child would be off to college. It did not matter that my divorce in the first place was not fair or equitable, just the sheer fact that the successes including the financial success were built in our marriage. His addiction to money, power and success was as harmful to his family as any addiction to drugs or alcohol. The difference would be as long as he was making millions and not hurting anyone else, his children and I would be overlooked, disregarded.

Time heals, doesn't it?

Emotional cruelty and neglect bear no outward bruises. Continuous stress and trauma provoked over long periods does no damage. Does it? The big question, the unanswered question—this is avoided, never answered—and sometimes not even acknowledged. But it is always there, ready to surface to be finally addressed. The need for closure and dignity is necessary for everyone. There are no exceptions.

I would never make that move to Tucson, for the appeals or a court hearing of some kind that Rick would command or demand—would consume my existence. When my attorney Larry Katz moved into the U.S. Bank building in downtown Minneapolis, he decided to stop working for me. I have written about this. But I will add that I interviewed numerous attorneys. But Rick and his attorney, Ed Weiner, must have been more of a formidable presence than I ever thought. I would not be able to find an attorney. This went on for almost ten years. I was the mother of his children. All the successes were the result of our marriage. We built together. Why would the courts allow this dysfunctional legal extravaganza to torment and erode my financial security? Why didn't they ever stop the legal charade or even question the fact that I was a woman alone and without representation? Rick was a financial expert, a lover of power and money. He hired the same. They held all the cards and made up all the rules. Who would stop them?

It would not matter if it were a holiday or a holy day. Rick would impose his will. He was a man used to getting his way. The meditation that he used helped keep him centered and focused and calm in the process. The combination of the self-hypnosis would remove his conscience. He became cunning and ruthless, with a cold indifference that was felt. His friends fell away. He became a stranger to me. His grown children were not immune. Mostly he was an absent father. He was not a generous man to his family. Isn't that amazing? A man who was blessed with so much and could not even appreciate the real gifts he had before him. He didn't have to try and destroy me in the frenzy. What did this do to his children? Why was this allowed to happen? Why were my children and I the exception to the rule?

I grew up knowing fear. In my marriage, I learned the effects of emotional and verbal abuse as well as neglect. Rick achieved all that he aspired and more in our marriage. I wanted him to excel and be happy. But not at the expense of our family. What would possibly be in the background or nature that would transform him to the extreme? I could understand if he had some traumatic experience, but he had loving parents, a parochial education. He was an altar boy. He was never in the military. There was no real reason for this corrupting change, expect his addiction to more. More money. More power. Never enough.

Meditation can be a good thing. A way to relax your mind and body, but not to excess as the answer to solve all your needs. Rick's world became all about him, his wishes. His needs would always come first. But it was the self-hypnosis that he combined in order not to feel. Eventually, he couldn't discern the difference between family and his world of high finance. Rick would look and treat his family as if we were a business, a commodity.

I could continue this barrage, venting my anguish and frustrations. I gave too much for too long for my husband, Ernst and Young, U.S. Bank. The court system would not even recognize or acknowledge this outrage that was meant to spoil and plunder. It did not matter to them that I was the mother of Rick's children. That alone should have been honored. But even that would not be enough. Rick would use the church to eradicate our existence in his mind, appease his conscience and his shame. Does it help to have those records sealed, never to be known for truth and understanding? Absolution at its highest form. What does it really mean? What does it accomplish or prove?

Because these court hearings would continue for so many years, and me still without representation, pretty much took over my life. Yet before, during and after our divorce, I could see and experience Rick's conflicting emotions. There were times when and if we were alone, he would reach out to me. It would be confusing and unsettling for I never really knew what to expect. I always wanted to believe that he would change, have some remorse. But wait a minute. I always wanted to believe that my father would change, but that never happened until after my mother died. Later, his mind let him be a loving child again in the form of dementia. Is that what it takes?

* * * * *

I remember when my mother died. I had just moved into my house in Shorewood/Excelsior in the fall of 1997. I received a call from my brother Billy. When he told me, I felt an incredible sorrow that held a tight grip that seemed to clutch my heart, leaving an unbelievable emptiness. It had been so long since I had seen her. Before her death, I would call occasionally, for I felt she should know that Rick and I were now divorced.

"Are you going to be okay, Patti?" she worried.

"I'm going to be fine. You don't have to worry about me."

I remembered another time when I told my parents my gift to them was that they never had to worry about me.

I never would have expected such a strong emotional reaction. I wanted to love my mother as the mother that I knew as a small child. I wanted to believe her letters that spoke of her happiness in Florida, her gardens, her church and the wonderful neighbors who seemed to be her family now. She had such a gentle nature, and now I would not experience that gentle care that only a mother can give. For weeks after, for unexplained reasons, I would break out in soulful heart-wrenching sobs. Unexpected. I would be driving the car and the tears would stream down my face, alone in my sorrow.

In my wonderful choir, we were to perform a social awareness concert. One of the pieces had a beautiful poignant poem titled "Letter to Mom" followed by a hauntingly beautiful musical piece called "Songs of Days Now Gone." It was all music that was made by musicians in Buchenwald called the Holocaust Cantata (Songs from the Camps). Anyone who has lost a mother can relate. The tears would come from many in the choir. Since I had just lost my mother, my tears were uncontainable. Bonnie with the most beautiful voice and first alto, singing to the right of me, had recently lost her mother too. Our tears blended in unison. Our director understood, but we knew we had to be professional in concert. I sang for my mother. That was my gift to her, and to me.

Through all this and more, I would continue representing myself in the legal charade that made no sense. I would also learn just before I moved into my house that Rick would be getting married. Not to Janet but to the private secretary of Ed Finn, whom I also knew from dinner parties. She and her husband would even come to the yearly dinner party that we held at our house on Edgebrook. I remember one of the last times I would see her. I had a feeling that Rene would be in my life somehow. I had no idea how. But I had this strong feeling. Maybe we would become good friends.

When my friend Peggy told me the news, I was surprised. Again, I felt a discomfort that Rick would not have the courtesy to tell me himself. It was just another added insult. So I shouldn't be surprised. But I thought at least he was no longer under the influence of Janet. She brought out the very worst in him. I also thought now that Rick was getting married, he would let me get on with my life and forget about these ridiculous legal games. But that would not happen. Rick had a way about him. The skills he learned in the ruthless world of hostile takeovers would carry over in his interaction with everyone. He would close his mind and his heart to any sensitive issue. I could see it in his face, a fleeting look of panic that would quickly turn into stern anger and control. No way would he let himself hear of anything that would touch him deeply. He would not want to know anything about the losses in my life. He learned to completely detach. In order to do that, he would have to erase me from his conscience. The self-hypnosis worked well. I would become an added business to him and nothing more, as long as he didn't have to see me or know anything about me.

To those who knew Rick, they could not understand what was happening. Why all the court hearings? What did you do to make him so angry? You're spending all that money on attorneys? Well, I couldn't get an attorney to represent me.

"Patti, don't you know you should never go to court without representation? Especially against someone like Ed Weiner."

Tell that to the courts, I wanted to scream. Wow, talk about convoluted and confusing. The legal court system was taking over my life. I was not prepared for this. I was a wife and mother, a homemaker with special gifts and talents that I still would not be able to pursue for all this madness.

I lost my mother. For him, it did not matter. He was getting married now to an impressed private secretary. He would spare no expense. It was an elaborate wedding at the Basilica in Minneapolis with a police entourage guarding the doors, just in case I were to show up and disrupt this sacred occasion. I didn't know. Did I really even care? I wanted Rick to have that change of heart and if a good, strong woman could bring a humane quality back into his life that was great. That would be better for everyone. Wasn't he once a good man?

I know about fear and pain. But how could my heart withstand this constant assault? At times, I wished I had no memory. But that would not happen. I guess I was basically too healthy from my natural healthy lifestyle that kept my mind and body capable. I found strength and comfort through my dear friends, my spiritual search for reasons and purpose. I needed to be grounded. I would not mask my experiences no matter how dire. I knew if I did, they would be lying dormant waiting to resurface. I had to face my fears and experiences head on. But I also knew my experiences were too important to be buried or ignored.

Amid the wedding preparations, the wedding itself and of course the grand honeymoon that would announce to the world that he had moved on, found a woman who was worthy. He would spare no expense. I wondered if she knew that he was still taking me to court. If she did know, wouldn't she question his actions? The court hearing would be changed, making a travesty of its very own purpose, and a mockery of marriage while denouncing my existence. The hearing would be moved to accommodate my husband. I would also learn that Rick and his new wife would buy a million-dollar-plus home on Lake Minnetonka in Shorewood. He never wanted to leave the city. He wanted to be close to work. I had my courtyard home in Shorewood during the long continuous legal quagmires created to keep my life in turmoil and unsettled. For this to be allowed was such a waste of time and so hurtful. What was the purpose?

The date could not be moved any longer. The next hearing would be four days before Christmas 1997. I was drained emotionally. The stress was taking its toll on me physically. Healthy me was getting high blood pressure. Yuk. That really scared and upset me. I don't like taking lifetime medicines. They gave me the lowest dosage possible. That still gave me a little cough. But it cured my migraines. Now that was a bonus. Before I go further, I want you to know that I am better now. I am cured. I suppose it could happen again, but I am going to try not to let that happen. Later, I will write about my discovery so you will know.

I was seeing my counselor Karen Nelson to help me through this time. She did not want me to be alone when I went to court.

"Patti, you need to have someone with you," she said.

"I really don't want to ask anyone. I don't want to ruin their Christmas."

"What about your children?"

They were all grown now, but there was no way that I would subject them to this outrage. "No, no. How could I possibly put my children through this? I can't do this to them."

"What about your friends, then? I'm sure they would want to show their support, be there for you."

"Maybe. I'll ask. I'm sure it would be a learning experience." I hoped it would be a good one. I was thinking that maybe I should ask someone whom

Rick and his attorney did not know. Maybe then they would realize I was not completely alone.

Friends are gifts to be treasured. Karen Walker and Gail Nelson didn't even hesitate in helping me. We drove to the courthouse together. This would be the hearing rescheduled after the Judge Brian Moehn conflict of interest, now to be replayed in front of a new judge. This time I would have a female judge, Susan Cochran. To me this was so unbelievable. The hearing had been changed so many times. Each time I would write a letter, giving history, the fact that I could not find an attorney to represent me, background information. I believed that was protocol. We arrived a little early. Hearings are usually pretty punctual. For some reason, we were the only ones seated in this waiting area. The lighting was dim. This all seemed rather unusual.

I was starting to think that maybe we were in the wrong place, when Rick and his attorney, Ed Weiner, with Susan Rhodes, an associate of Ed Weiner's law firm, approached us. Their strides were confident, matter of fact. But the closer they came their gait slowed. I am sure they were questioning who this was with me. They sat at the far end of the waiting area and seemed to be in conference. This was their playing field, their playground, where they felt secure in their turf. Rick had the toughest players. I felt like a female David against a team of Goliaths. They had their heads together in serious discourse. My little team just looked on waiting for a sign of recognition. A friendly sign would have been polite. They all rose from the bench like rehearsed choreography. I wanted to follow them for my curiosity was piqued. Their boorish arrogance so apparent in their demeanor. That should have been enough reason to disbar.

Talk about feeling discounted, left in the dark or a pawn to be used in a game. I was out of my element. The safety net was jerked away and I felt I was free falling. Was I in some perverse movie that embraced cruelty for reasons unknown? What was taking so long? Maybe Rick realized he was married now and this just wasn't right. Before they returned, a tall man approached my friends and me. Was he a security guard? I thought he was going to tell us that this proceeding was called off. But no. He came to tell us this would be a closed hearing. I wasn't quite sure what that meant. I guessed that no one else would be in the room. I didn't question him at that moment. If I'd had the strength, I would have protested. But this was getting eerier by the minute.

I should have been used to this by now but for some weird reason, I felt extremely vulnerable. Maybe it was my high blood pressure kicking in. This certainly would do it. No matter how healthy anyone was. Rick and his gang finally reappeared like cats stalking their prey, reminding me of Sylvester the Cat licking his lips. I looked in Rick's direction, but he would either look away or keep his head down. No eye contact. There still was no one else in this waiting area. We rose from the bench to go inside the courtroom. As we came to the opened door, the security guard stopped Karen and Gail.

"This is a closed hearing. No one is allowed in the chambers."

Scary. Unnerving. What kind of experience were Karen and Gail going to witness sitting in the waiting area where they already had sat too long? Did that mean that this judge wanted Rick and me to herself to observe and question? That was okay with me. But my friends must have looked too intimidating. Rick had his two attorneys at his side. Now tell me, was that fair? There was no valid reason. It was all so senseless. I think in some warped way these hearings would empower him for no one questioned him. How do you explain these hearings that are meant to hurt and humiliate? How does one recover from such experiences that are allowed—for years?!

* * * * *

I went into the large chambers. It was too large for this small hearing. I sat alone in the middle of the one set of pews. Rick and his attorney sat at a long table. I felt like a spectator, uninvited to sit with comrades. Judge Susan Cochran came into the room rather somber. Everybody rose. We sat down when she did. I felt awkward sitting in my pew, but still uninvited. But I would be invited to take the stand. My mind went into a spin when I heard her say, "I received a letter from Patricia. I want you to know that I didn't read it."

Oh my God. I couldn't be hearing this. This can't be happening. I expected Ed Weiner to say, "Well, I received the same letter. So go ahead and read it." She would know nothing about me. I might as well have been a statue or an object.

When I was on the stand, I remember seeing this ridiculous skit of a man representing himself in court, taking the stand, trying to be two people. It was absurd. Ed Weiner would ask me questions that were irrelevant, or that needed further explanation. But I was not allowed to talk. When I tried to explain, Rick would start yelling and screaming like a madman.

"I don't want to ever talk to her. I don't want to ever see her."

What did I do? I had no idea what this was about. But something was terribly wrong. I tried to talk through the mayhem, but I was not allowed. I tried to remain calm. My eyes were wide in disbelief. I would give a brief answer, but if one is representing herself her side has to be heard also. My answers could not always be a simple yes or no. At one point, I was almost in tears. My frustrated state raw and visible. I was determined to be heard.

"Patricia, you must stop. If you can't stop, I will have to hold you in contempt."

"Stop what? Telling the facts? Telling the truth?"

I was living a nightmare, perpetuated by power gone amok. I was so disgusted that I no longer felt fear, definitely not respect. I was resigned to take my punishment for whatever ills Rick and his attorney created for their sadistic and unholy purpose. I really did not know what being in contempt meant. I thought that it meant I had to do and say what they wanted me to do or say, even if it wasn't accurate or correct. I suddenly felt like Joan of Arc. I pulled myself straight as I sat and leaned forward. No longer was I going to be wimpy or afraid of these people. They didn't deserve my fear. I raised both my arms and put my hands together.

"If you are going to put me in contempt, then you better do it now. Go ahead and put the handcuffs on me. I'd rather be in jail than be denied my rights. How is this going to look in the papers, this kangaroo trial?"

Everyone was stunned speechless. Visions of a dozen security guards taking me away to break me into submission came into mind. I was suddenly drained as I looked around me. Everyone was quiet. The judge sank to her chair.

"You're not going to jail. This court is dismissed."

I broke down in tears. Tears that I could not hold back. Rick and his attorneys seemed to slink away. When I walked out into the waiting area, Gail and Karen greeted me with hugs of reassurance, seeing my grief-stricken face.

"Are you okay? What happened in there?"

How could they ever understand the devastation that is brought on by greed and inflated ego?

* * * * *

While writing these pages, my memories and thoughts just spilled out bringing me back to that horrific experience. I wrote until late in the evening again. But what better thing to do when the temperature outside is approaching 100 degrees? The land of extremes, it hasn't changed. I reread these pages this morning feeling a heaviness in my heart. Was this perception accurate? Karen and I are practically neighbors, and manage to get together occasionally amid the busyness of our days. I thought I would call Gail. I hadn't seen her for a few years. If it was meant to be, I would be able to reach her. Gail picked up the phone. Her voice has a melodic quality. In fact, we would meet through the Edina Choral. It was so good to hear her voice. Our lives are busy and full, but so different. When I told her about my book and my purpose, she was interested.

"Gail, do you remember that time when you and Karen went to a court hearing with me for emotional support? It was just before Christmas?"

"Oh, Patti, I remember that day. It was the strangest experience."

"Is there anything about that experience that was out of the ordinary? What was your perception, your feelings?"

"I remember you had already been through so much that Karen and I wanted to be there for you. What I remember is that there was a strong feeling of not being wanted there, not feeling welcomed. It was cold, uncomfortable."

I knew. I could feel it myself. I felt bad that I had subjected my friends to such an experience and just before Christmas.

"Gail, do you remember how dark the waiting area was?"

"There were large windows so there was light, but looking out into the corridors it was dark."

I remembered then. The large windows overlooked the buildings and streets of Minneapolis.

"That is interesting because I remember the waiting area so dim, with no one around."

"There didn't seem to be anyone around. But Rick had put you in a pretty dark place. I'm sure things felt dark and foreboding to you."

That could have been, but also if the sun wasn't shining into the area, it would be rather dark.

"I just remembered how rudely we were treated and how uncomfortable we felt. And then they wouldn't even let us go into the courtroom with you. What was that all about? And was that even legal? We couldn't believe they wouldn't let us in the room to be there for you. So we just sat down and waited."

"When you were sitting out there, did you hear any yelling?"

"No, I can't say that we did. But I just know that you were not treated right and Karen and I felt so bad for you."

"Well, I'm surprised that you didn't hear Rick raging."

But the waiting area was at a distance and the doors and walls were thick.

"Would you mind if I read a few paragraphs? Do you have the time?" I asked.

"Yes, very much. I would like to hear."

During and after my reading we would stop to talk trying to understand how this could even be allowed.

"Did you try to have this reopened or investigated?"

"Actually, I've tried but to no avail. But do you remember that bizarre incident when I dropped off some things of his when he lived across from Lake Harriet?"

"Oh. Yes. That was unbelievable. I can't believe what he has put you through."

"As I was going through these papers, I came across some writing that I had put away, but has come to pass. I guess I had shoved it in the back of my mind for it was so disturbing. When I had dropped off Rick's things, before I left, his girlfriend Janet threatened me, telling me that she and Rick were going to make my life a legal and financial nightmare.

Now I could understand why everywhere I turned legal turmoil was lying in wait.

What I couldn't understand was why he would continue with these legal harassments. Since I haven't been able to get an attorney, I realized my only recourse was to write about this horrendous experience. Last year, Rick and I had occasions when we saw each other because we have children and grandchildren in common. He has changed. At times, I feel sorry for him. I think he knows what he did was wrong. But I don't think he would ever admit it. He has aged and looks older than his years. There also seems to be a sorrow about him.

"Patti, I don't think he is capable. He loves money more than anything. That is his god." I have heard that before and it saddens me. What a terrible price, a fleeting glory all the people and families, my children and myself that would be adversely affected.

"People like that have no boundaries or conscience."

"Well, maybe that is true. But then it is up to the courts to do the right thing and not allow proceedings like this to continue for years. That does nothing but hurt everyone."

For me, the aftershocks of such an experience takes a while to recover. I realized even more the beautiful courtyard home that I built no longer offered me any refuge from Rick or the persons that did his bidding for a price. I remember the short time of unexpected encounters meant to intimidate and shake my reserve. The first time, not too long after I moved in, my friend Cammy came to visit.

It was a beautiful sunny day, towards the end of summer. We completed the tour of the rooms and ended in the office library that looked into the courtyard. I had undertaken a dream and was quietly basking in my accomplishment of such an endeavor of actually building my home. I would have loved to build a family home while married, but that was never a dream of Rick's. Our marriage was the germination of dreams that provided a nourishing environment to see those dreams fulfilled. There would be obstacles of some size or shape to overcome, for life is never smooth. But it was withstanding those obstacles that were part of the process. Sometimes things happen. The excess overlapping, creating an overgrowth needing more of everything not allowing the proper nourishment or space for healthy new growth, consuming and overlooking the delicate beauty of the original design or purpose.

Cammy, so musically gifted, intellectually stimulating, also dedicated herself to giving her best in the business world. She maintained a softness to her character that was recognized and attributed to the successes in her field, a welcome change. As we were catching up, marveling at the turns of life, Cammy looked up.

"Patti, someone's at your door. Are you expecting someone?"

"No, I'm not. But maybe it's the neighborhood welcome wagon."

As I went to the foyer and opened the door, it was a tall man with papers in his hand, serving me legal papers. I was embarrassed and shocked. What was this? Did it have something to do with my house? He handed me the papers and left quickly, his mission accomplished. He didn't have to explain anything. He was doing his job. He would get his pay.

I walked in the library where Cammy sat. She looked at me and said, "Patti, what's wrong?"

"I don't know. I was just given these papers. I have absolutely no idea what this is about."

Cammy besides being a trusted friend had a good head on her shoulders and knows how to keep calm. I sat down to open the document.

"Oh my gosh. Rick is taking me to court again."

"Patti, what is he trying to do to you?"

"I don't know. I thought if I moved away from the city, he would be happy and let me get on with my life." The serenity of my day was unraveling, letting in a sliver of apprehension.

Who knows what these proceedings were to accomplish, accept to instill a certain amount of fear and uncertainty. Many times because Rick was such a busy man with enough money and connections to have his bidding done on his terms and his time. My life would be at the mercy of the courts. I tried not to allow this to dictate my life. I thought eventually Rick and the courts would tire of this game. This would be costly for Rick, at least I think so far he had the most expensive attorney in town, while I could not find one. Who was paying the judges? Where did this money come from? Is it the person insisting on these hearings or is it the unsuspecting taxpayer? I don't know. But one of these days I will find out.

I would live in the courtyard home for almost three years. Until I finally had enough. One day, while returning home sometime after four, just before the traffic going west became too busy, I pulled in on Regents Walk. As I approached the house, I noticed a dilapidated, rusted old car parked off to the side of my driveway and front road. It was not the kind of car that would normally be seen in this gracious neighborhood. I could see a man in the front seat. Maybe he was temporarily lost, checking a map for directions. But my intuition told me not to go in the garage. I drove past the worn down vehicle and circled around the pretty neighborhood. I breathed a sigh of relief when I again approached my house and the old beater was gone. I pulled into the garage and decided to walk to the mailbox to get my mail. As I was going down the driveway, this same battered wreck pulled in my driveway. I stood there almost immobile with fear. Who was this? I didn't know if I should run into my house or run for my life.

The derelict car abruptly stopped and this unkempt man jumped out, coming toward me.

"Are you Patricia Zona?"

"Yes, I am. But what are you doing here?" I shouldn't have asked. Who would have guessed? Papers. I guess that was better than a mugging. I looked at the man, so unkempt and doing the deed of others, who found them too distasteful to do themselves. He was tall and very thin. Almost blending in the earth colors. A good soaking would bring out his true color. I could have felt sorry for him, but he had a Band-Aid across his nose and I questioned to myself how he encountered that blow. He handed me papers that were crumpled and already opened. I didn't want to touch them.

"I'm just doing what I'm told to deliver."

So wrong. Sinking so low. And for what payoff?

I didn't like the fact that the papers were opened. Were they read out of boredom as he lay in ambush for me? Was this acceptable protocol? I wondered if anyone really cared or gave a damn. (Sorry, but sometimes strong language is deserved.) I was resigned to the fact that this too would be ignored, left to reconsider. Rick and his cohorts knew how to test their limits. I wanted to be far away from this nightmare. This was obviously not far enough. I would sell my beautiful courtyard home, searching for peace and refuge.

It was these two incidents and one of the last court hearings that brought me back to the city, for I would sell the courtyard home. At that time, I did not realize that there was no way to flee from the memories or the experiences of the errant proceedings that held my life in legal chaos. It just defied all sensibility, holding me still in bondage. The words of Rick's former girlfriend seemed to ring true: They would make my life a legal and financial nightmare. Was it Rick's idea with her encouragement or was it Janet's idea and in his weakness succumbed. Janet was now out of the picture. Rick was married, but now his assaults were as if he were desperate to conceal his acts.

* * * * *

I still had hopes to move to Tucson. Monica would be getting married in September 2000.

"Mom, why don't you move back to the city until you decide where you want to be? I've looked at the Calhoun Beach Apartments and they really are nice. Why don't you check out those apartments near Lake Calhoun? It would be a great way for you to see what it's like to live closer to the city. I think you might like it."

I wanted to be there for Monica now that she was in preparations for her marriage. I wanted to be part of this very special day. Just knowing that she wanted me close also was enough to make this decision. I must have been a city girl at heart, for I loved my wonderful apartment on the main level looking across the reflecting pond and across the two tennis courts. I could and would walk down the steps that encompassed the water, cascading from the negative edge of the reflecting pond, to the lower level pool of water. I felt like I was on vacation, living a vacation. I was thankful and I wanted to give back.

This was during the time that I would be introduced to volunteer as a *guardian ad litem*. This would also be during the preparations for Monica's wedding. But this would also be the home where I would be living when I learned there would be one last court hearing. A haunting melody replayed one too many times. There were more than a few reasons why this proceeding should never have been considered, but justice is blind, overwhelmed and broken.

Rick was married, living in splendor with his new wife. His daughter was getting married. Who would have time or thoughts of creating more legal turmoil? The fact that it was never warranted doesn't even come to mind, as that never stopped him or the courts before. The precedent was set.

Rick had too much success in the past, especially with the courts. Now he would not know what was right or wrong, fact or fiction. His judgment was obscured. He would be taking me to court for a list of mundane reasons, but one that stood out was that I had talked to Mike Hatch the attorney general. That was what he either believed or was misinformed by someone. At any rate, I had to address this for I didn't know if this was some kind of sordid conspiracy against me. It was bad enough to have Rick and his band of followers, but someone of such reputable character was not possible. I would investigate this myself, for there was just a matter of a few days before the hearing. Mike Hatch validated the fact that he never knew me or talked to me. What was this all about? I gave him a brief history, which was not easy. He simply wrote a letter to the courts, the judge, the president of U.S. Bank Jack Gundhoffer and Ed Weiner, stating the fact that I had never had any conversation or encounter with him.

That was all and good. But I would still go to court. When the judge spoke of the letter that this public official sent, she said she did receive a letter from Mike Hatch informing the courts that we had never talked or met. Then she said, "I'll dismiss this. This time. Anyone can make a mistake." I was astounded. Rick had to make his public apology. I was angry to think that his mistake would be overlooked, but his malicious and intentional actions against me, would be ignored. Rick's actions against a public figure would be noticed. He would take an early retirement with tremendous perks, packages and payoffs. The golden parachute, designed to guarantee financial security without worry or merit.

* * * * *

I knew after that last hearing that it would be the last. It would be for me just another hurdle to try and rebound from. This time my energies would be spread way too thing, for I was still absorbing the trauma of the last hearing. I never realized how vast the demands of a *guardian ad litem*. And now I was thrust in the heart of a serious situation. I would do and give my best. Oppression distresses me. I felt I could make a difference, but it sure would have been easier and nicer too, if there was better communication and support. Plus, the reality that my own daughter was soon to be married that was big enough. But I think all those years of court hearings were taking a toll. But it was in some ways making me feel like super women. I could do it all, but for those quiet moments, and the reality of my situation. I felt the tethered bond of chains that would make claim of my existence, needing attention, a need to be free.

I thought time would heal the wounds, soften the heart and rekindle the bond of respected friendship. Pride would give way to forgiveness and understanding. But when one is taught in the world of high finances that it is all about money, power and control, and to reinforce that lesson with self-hypnosis. There is no getting through the barriers. The mind will not hear of it. Rick and I are still so different. In fact, our experiences have affected us both to the extreme. He was rewarded for his prowess in high finance and high risk with inside knowledge that would be pertinent. Because he will do anything in his power not to hear or know, I am more determined to have my voice heart. I have a strong need to understand how and why things happen. I wonder what happened to our judicial system that can be bought for a price or for special favors.

Even though the legal nightmares were over, the blatant disregard and injustice lay heavy in my thoughts. I knew I needed closure. I realized that I also needed my freedom without the restraints of being held hostage or in servitude. Rick was rewarded in the business world for his loyalty and ruthless ambition. During the height of all these takeovers, the importance of families and the value of the homemaker were put down. The timing was perfect for Rick. His last child would be off to college. I was not necessary in his life anymore. All his needs could be bought, including the women in his life. I would learn firsthand that the people I trusted the most would also disappoint me the most. I did not have the resources or worldly experience that I should have had to be so exposed. I was left to flounder on my own, sink or swim. The rug ripped right from under me. I was on my own now. I didn't like those lessons. Those lessons that could have destroyed me in some form just made me more determined to persevere and restore the dignity and importance of an intact family.

I thought since I was divorced, I would find an attorney to help me gain my freedom. I didn't just want the blood money that was disproportionately doled out with stipulations holding me back. It wasn't fair or humane. Again, no one seemed to want to touch this. At first, they would be interested and outraged. But I had three boxes packed with legal papers that would overwhelm anybody. But the names would instill a certain wariness or caution. To this day, even though Rick at one point said he would give me a lump sum, after consideration he would change his mind. He would not give me a reason other than he held my life in his hands.

I was never taught to numb my feelings or conscience. Nor would I ever want to. But that is what Rick learned and it served him well. I had a conversation with a tormented man who had lost millions during the era of takeovers.

"Patti, your husband made his money when they were thought of as kings. They reaped the benefits that came from the masses. They were made to feel entitled. Now we are all paying for it."

That was a startling statement. I realized that I would have to write a book. I decided to call Rick. I wanted him to know, to give him an opportunity to do the right thing. He was pleasant. When I asked him if we could meet for coffee or tea, he seemed interested but then he questioned me.

"What is so important that you can't tell me on the phone?"

"I wanted you to know what it going on in my life." I wanted to tell him about my book and I wanted to give him an opportunity to address some of these issues. Offer his thoughts. I wanted to show a positive change in attitude.

"I can't do that," he said. "I can see no reason to meet with you."

"Okay. That's fine. I just thought it has been so long that now was the time to have better communication. But if that is what you want." I would continue my writing with the knowledge that I have always tried to do what was right.

Because of all the biased court hearings, I realized that the only way to make a difference was if my story were written to enlighten those who would never understand the magnitude of injustice. I was compelled to write for my experiences were too important to be ignored. My story is about the importance and value of family, being the reason and purpose that seems to be forgotten. Women who do too much, who give up too much and their role or contribution discounted so disgracefully. What has happened to the men who can't seem to grow up and take responsibility? And when they are industrious, turning into extreme forgetting their own reason, purpose and families, too busy to take time to cherish or know their own family, but turning to the trophies at hand. It seems we have perpetuated the attitude in our society that the bottom line is the most important entity even if it means sacrificing our most precious—families, children and friends in the process. Time is never enough for the burdens trickle down. Cries needing to be heard and attended to. But the bottom line entices for there is never enough to satisfy the hunger or thirst, forgetting that the greed is costly to those who really do not have enough to feed, or clothe or shelter their own. What has happened to the family when both are forced to work for not a living wage, stretching their meager wages to meet the rising inflated costs? While the wealthy consume, exploiting and flaunting their wealth without a thought or regard. When will we all recognize there is a problem here and that we can do better?

If not questioned, how they come to their power and glory—do they eventually stumble and fall one too many times, becoming the pawn in their own games? Why do we wait so long?

* * * * *

CHAPTER 20

FINAL REMARKS: AUGUST 2006

I'm concluding with my final remarks. Since I've moved to my ivory tower, I have found there are still lessons to learn.

It is now August 2006. I have lived here since March 2000. The first year savoring the simplicity that soothed my thoughts that allowed my creativity to flow once again. I loved the large windows in surround, capturing the beauty of the sunsets, or watching the storms roll in or the dramatic streaks of lightning that streaks across the sky somehow making me feel part of the spectacle, yet removed just enough to feel safe and secure. To see the reflection of the lights on wet, rainy nights draws me to the glistening vista below. Sometimes I go on my balcony to experience firsthand the cleansing rain, gently breathing in the softness or coolness of the gift from the heavens. The snow comes softly, quietly transforming the world below into a magical place. All the seasons displayed in their brilliance that one wants to share with that special person. So in many ways I have been fortunate. I treasure those times.

One Tuesday morning in September, I would be leaving for my bible study group. I was still getting acclimated to condo living, starting to get exciting ideas for furnishings that would accommodate the wall space and large windows. I wanted the views to be the main focal point. But I could imagine a few murals on designated walls that would add interest and not take away from the views. When I'm in the creative mode, I rarely put on television or the radio. I might put on a CD for background, depending on what I'm working on. If I'm in that thought process mode, I like the stillness, the quiet that take me into deep reverie or a contemplative state. I can lose track of time, so the mornings go quickly. If I'm deep in a project, I like music that suits the subject matter. When I did my works of design, when completed the design would have a dancelike quality, fluid with movement, whichever way the picture was turned.

Since I had not put on the news of any kind, I was unaware of the 9/11 terrorist attacks. It would be my neighbor in the elevator who would tell me.

But when Pat Lyons told me how awful it was, I thought she was talking about the new renovation of the hallway. I shook my head.

"Well, yes, it is. But I guess it had to be done," I pleasantly replied. I was trying to be diplomatic about the renovation.

There was a look of shock on her face, which didn't make sense. "You are talking about the hallways, aren't you?" I said.

"Haven't you heard?" she exclaimed.

"No. What?" For some reason I had been too busy to watch news that day. I was getting ready for bible study, going over the lesson plans of the books of Exodus. We were studying Moses.

"Some terrorists took two planes and flew them into the New York World Trade Center."

The elevator we were riding landed at ground level. I could not comprehend the magnitude of the whole thing. I could not imagine anyone deliberately flying into a building. It made no sense. We continued discussing the attacks all the way to our cars.

When we parted ways, the first thing I did was put on my radio to catch the news. That was not difficult to do. I was glad I was going to be going to my B.S.F. group. There, I knew, would be hundreds of women who would have heard this news about the same time. As I drove through the side streets and onto the 394 West highway, I noticed people in cars around me driving pensively, fully absorbed by the words they heard on the radio. It was surreal. The somberness of the morning commute pervaded every car. Ears were glued to the news. The occupants in the cars were in deep concentration. But one could feel the stunned disbelief, sorrow and shock. I knew our world would never be the same.

When I got to the bible study, the church was packed as always. But this time a respectful silence and questioning pervaded the rooms. I don't think anyone really knew at this time the magnitude of the attack. It was just too unfathomable. We were all united in prayer, wanting to believe that our world was safe and secure. After our prayers, we continued as usual to break off into little groups to study Moses. I loved learning about Moses. He was amazing. He wasn't perfect by any stretch. But God knew that when he selected him. He knew of Moses' heart and strength and he wasn't going to give up on Moses. I loved the fact that Moses had this very special relationship with God, disagreeing, pleading, falling down, torn between his great love for God the Father and loving his people too, sins and all, and he would beg God to forgive his people. It is a great study of the deep love of God, human frailty, obedience and disobedience and most of all of teaching and not giving up. It's a great study. If you haven't had this lesson, it is well worth it. So I hope you will one of these days. Being in that study almost took me away from the morning news, still not quite understanding the impact that those two planes would make.

The first thing I did was turn on the news when I got home. Everyone knows the devastation that will be forever imprinted on our minds. Hundreds of innocent lives so callously taken for reasons that we will never understand for it runs too deep and has for too long. I believe when people live in oppression and hopelessness, not seeing a way out of the bleakness of their existence with no hope of anything different, they begin to live their lives in simmering rage. Not finding peace or happiness in this existence. They don't value this life. Desperate, unhappy people do desperate things. When many people are oppressed, they will unite for the end sometimes is their glory or only hope for anything better. It really is sad when we turn our backs on understanding the real problem, ignoring the deep-rooted issues or the cause and effects. We don't have all the answers. How could we when we are so oblivious to what we have done to our own?

The weapons of mass destruction that is what we all were fed day after day, month after month. Until the real weapons of mass destruction became fear itself. I lived in fear all my life. I know fear prevents rational thinking and immobilizes productivity. We are waiting in fear for someone to tell us what to do next. Not wanting to really know, just going along with the people in power, for they have our best interest at heart, don't they?

Why am I writing about this? I am not a politician. To me, it is about the most qualified person in office, but it seems to be the one who has the most money to run on. Now that makes me nervous. Look at how the majority of these politicians acquired their wealth? Usually not honorably.

So, since I moved to my ivory tower, the shockwaves are still evident in the way business is done or progress is made or not made. The aftermath permeates our thoughts and decisions, clouding our judgment combined with murky transactions meant to complicate and conceal.

I was talking to a friend and tax advisor who has been trying to help sort out my financial worries and woes. I know things will be fine, but I know too that it is a known fact that divorced women eventually suffer financially especially when the outcome is severely inequitable. For some reason, although my area of expertise is more in the creative aspect of life, I could still see my value and contribution equally important and probably even more so.

* * * *

During my divorce and the ongoing unnecessary court proceedings for all those years, I was provoked into action and a need to address my experience to help enlighten women and men, people of position and influence. There is a responsibility in their important positions in knowing the cause and effect that shape their decisions will help or hurt those who are vulnerable and trusting. The homemakers who are truly needed. Families. We are the reason and purpose and should be valued as equally important as any career. We depend on honesty and integrity in those who dole out the judgments. We are at the mercy of the trusted professionals. What happens when those virtues no longer exist?

The aftermath of 9/11 played out big time in the financial sector, causing greed to raise its ugly head in all directions. Those with the right connections would be spared while the trusting and vulnerable were used to make up the difference.

"Patti, are you going to write about your experience with Merrill Lynch or your Florida home that you invested in?"

Well, actually I wasn't. But I guess it should be told for I certainly learned a lot of hard lessons there also. Maybe I should. Then others can learn from my experience. Here I go.

Once I was divorced, I would be made to feel invisible. Maybe an afterthought that would be discouraged and pushed away. Ernst and Young would not offer any of their expertise or tax guidance. I was just a casualty. U.S. Bank could care less about my circumstances and the role that they played. I lost the country club lifestyle. That was okay. Too many shallow people who golf their cares away and use the clubs to impress, sometimes as a front. It's all about being seen and connecting with the right sources. No perks or benefits for me. I would become a commodity and business to Rick. I get my maintenance, but I pay high taxes to the government, also depleting my maintenance to taxes and unnecessary insurance, paying off my high mortgage. Meanwhile, he is qualified for he works for the bank special exemptions and etc. Meanwhile, I am a tax write-off for Rick. Since I am now divorced, marriage is now a tax write-off. Every one knows that it costs more to be single. But, *"Asi es la vida."* Or, such is life.

Since I was not getting any guidance from Rick, Ernst and Young or U.S. Bank, I was left to find my own way. I found a wonderful woman Judy Rummler who would help me with my financial portfolio until she and her husband retired to Florida. Because my financial situation was still uncertain with Rick's appeals, I eventually would turn to Merrill Lynch.

Tom D. contacted me and was interested in having my business. In the beginning, 1994 until 2000, things were looking sound and secure, until I bought a condo. The biggest role of course was 9/11. The other eroding factor was panic and neglect, people trying to be creative in making up differences. I started losing so much money that I had thoughts of trying to use my money in something tangible. I didn't have a vacation home, or cabin up north. I didn't like the complications of owning two homes, especially when some people had not home or were struggling to make payments on their home. That bothered me. I was thinking about my financial future. I didn't want to be a financial burden to my children or society. But I had to be realistic also.

In 2003, I made a difficult and rather bold beginning move for me to invest in some property. Actually, it was with a friend that I met in choir, very talented and intelligent. A take-charge personality, accommodating and capable. I had sung in this choir throughout my marriage, also during the whole sordid divorce and appeals process. It was something in my life that was a constant and a positive reinforcement.

My financial portfolio was taking tremendous dips. Meanwhile my advisor Tom D. told me not to panic and to be patient. Things would turn around, especially if people didn't panic. Well, I didn't want to be part of the problem. I would be a little more patient. But I could see by 2003 things were not getting any better. I called to talk to Tom D. and the secretary said he was no longer working for me.

"What? When did that happen?" I said, "Incredulous. Why didn't he call? Why didn't anyone call me? What happened to him?"

Choosing her words carefully, she replied, "Tom is now working in another capacity and your portfolio had been given to Chad E. Don't worry. I'm sure once you meet Chad, you'll feel better."

Amazing. I did meet young Chad. He was very professionally groomed, willing and wanting to impress. He reassured me that things would turn around.

Eventually, my losses were too big to be ignored. My life was becoming uncertain. Jim A. and I became friends, based on our creative interests. We occasionally might have lunch or talk during breaks at choir, becoming friends and confidants. We both could express our problems and fears, along with encouragement. He was going to move to Florida with his partner Jim B. I wished him well and felt that is was good for him to make that leap.

I was surprised that Jim kept in contact with me. He missed the choir. But he loved Florida. Eventually, the house that he was renting would be sold. He needed a place.

"Patti, I have a thought. How would you like to live in Florida?"

"I love Florida," I told him. "But Rick has a place in Naples. I've actually been thinking of a getting a place in Tucson." I was trying to justify owning two homes. It felt complicated to me as a single person. I didn't want to leave a place empty. The renting aspect seemed another problem in itself.

"Patti, Florida is a big place. You could get a place in Miami or Fort Lauderdale. And Jim and I can rent it for you."

I'd met his partner Jim B. He was a soft-spoken, gentle man. He was also a pharmacist. "Patti, if you buy a house, I will be the caretaker," said Jim A. "I will pay rent and if you decide to sell we would like first option to buy."

Since my portfolio was dwindling to despair, I decided this would be the opportunity to put some of my money into something tangible. To me it seemed it would be the solution that could help everyone. This would be my first venture stating my savvy new independence. People do business negotiating all the time. But this was more than business. It was helping each other, trusting each other to do their part. My portfolio was still on a steady decline. I decided to sell my condo. I would learn during a possible transaction that Merrill Lynch or Tom D. had put the sale of my courtyard home into stocks of various natures, seeming to be a hodgepodge mix, just thrown in the pot randomly. He lost it all. This would leave me very little to reinvest in another house. I was sickened. What I have found when corporations or anything becomes too big, it then becomes too easy to move those problem areas around, giving them time to find ways of complicating and convoluting the trail of deception.

By the end of 2004, I would take everything out of Merrill Lynch. I found their arrogance appalling when I told them I had no recourse but to take whatever money I still had out. They snidely informed me that I would have to pay heavy penalties. Also, since they had everything of mine, including checking and my mortgage to my house, I would not have any help from Merrill Lynch relinquishing these funds. This was December 2004, creating a most distressful holiday. I have learned that ethics and standards have changed to accommodate the bottom line. Many times the client used merely as a pawn when their grand schemes go awry.

I would also sell my Florida home for Jim and his partner weren't paying rent, making it financially difficult to cover two mortgages plus paying two property taxes and everything else. People say that Jim knew how to use the system. That must be. He would move to Vermont, leaving me with a nine thousand dollars' moving bill, also taking the furnishing since he was now in a new state. There was nothing that could be done. Consider it a loss and lesson learned. The criminal does seem to have more rights and protection than their victim. I wonder who makes these rules and laws that encourage such behavior. I've sold my Florida home. A corporate friend of mind said, "Patti, you were trying to help someone. There is nothing wrong with that. That if anything should be commended. Don't be so hard on yourself. We all have made mistakes or erred in our judgment."

Sometimes, we have to consider the loss and learn. But do we just move on or do we address these issues somehow, some way. That not only do we learn but others learn from our mistakes.

* * * * *

Believe it or not, I am learning. I was telling a good friend of mine that was in disbelief on hearing of my past misadventures during and after my divorce. Because Rick and I were married for so long and whatever real successes, including the financial success, was built in our marriage. I felt that Ernst and Young would offer some kind of help, maybe with my taxes or financial guidance. I felt that U.S. Bank would also offer some kind of plan that would reassure me of my financial future. After all, they now had my husband's complete attention and loyalty. But instead they would turn their backs, enforcing Rick's wayward path against me. He vented his frustrations and anger toward me, and it would be allowed and rewarded, when what he really needed was help from himself. What does that say to society on how we regard our children, our families and marriage itself?

Our divorce was done intentionally to undermine my worth and contribution in our marriage, my role as a wife, mother and homemaker would be totally discounted. It would not matter that Rick did sacrifice his family for his own career. It did not matter that I sacrificed my own life for the needs of my husband, who in the end would not appreciate but expect, would not value but try and destroy. He worked himself into a frenzy of greed that generated a distorted view of himself through his world of special entitlement, exemptions, privileges and excess. He was not alone during this period, where homemakers would be discounted. Who would take care of the children? When is there a stop to the consumption of more money, more stuff meant to impress, bigger to the point of imposing on others' space and rights that only feeds their inflated egos while flaunting their toys and trophies while ignoring the plight and conditions of others around them.

Not too long ago, maybe it was last summer, Rick and I had a relatively civil conversation. Our conversations are always guarded on his part, wanting to feel that I have finally accepted the conditions and terms of our divorce. Meanwhile, in order not to provoke him, I have to choose my words cautiously not to offend or anger him. Has he changed? I want to think so. But his guardedness makes it difficult to converse freely. If I request something like maybe an opportunity to talk to him about a family issue or myself, his tone and demeanor changes. He becomes sharp and threatening. He would not want to hear for then he would have to acknowledge his own part.

"Rick, I need to talk to you about my life and how the changes have affected me. My life has so many restrictions. I never thought it would be like this. I was supposed to get life maintenance, but I heard that it wasn't my life. It was your life. If something should happen to you, my maintenance stops. Do you think that is fair? You didn't want me to work. I have no financial security or guarantees in my life. You know our divorce wasn't fair. I know you don't want to hear this, but I am the mother of your children. You and your wife live a very extravagant life. I can't do this any longer. I'm exhausted mentally, emotionally and physically."

I wanted to tell him about my book. But he would not hear of it. He controls my life. I want him to know and the courts to know that I want my dignity back. I want my freedom. He has no right to control my life and the courts have no right to give him that decision to make.

I would continue with my book. But, believe me, it was as if I were reliving it all. I would get sick. So tired that I thought I would just expire. Could I even complete this book? I remembered my daughter when she went to an acupuncturist for treatment, when she was trying to get pregnant. Through her acupuncture treatments, her allergies were cured. I thought maybe I should get acupuncture. At least have a consultation. I called Dr. Hu. She wanted to know about my medical history. She listened intently. She then wanted to know what was going on in my life. I breathed deeply. My body felt weary. I touched as briefly as I could on the critical aspects of the divorce, appeals and annulment that were forced upon me for so long. I then told her about my book. That I was in the process of writing, and how emotionally draining that was. I told her of my concern about writing my book with the right intent, not to offend but to enlighten. I told her how it affected my whole being, that at times it was so painful that I didn't know if I would expire once this book was completed from sheer emotional and physical exhaustion.

She looked at me with great consideration. She looked for any vital signs of problems and took my wrist to feel my pulse. She was having difficulty monitoring my pulse.

"Patti, your pulse is very weak," she said.

"What does that mean?"

"It means you're very weak and rundown. That is why when you get sick it takes so long to get better. Your resistance is so low that it makes you susceptible and also takes you longer to recover."

"What can be done? I've got so much to do. And my daughter is going to have another baby. I want to be able to help her. Plus, I've got to finish my book."

Dr. Hu gently looked at me. "I can help you and you will finish your book. It is too important not to do."

The fact that she understood the gravity of my situation and was encouraging also gave me renewed hope and reassurance. I would see Dr. Hu once a week for an acupuncture treatment for ten weeks. My first treatment, I felt totally relaxed falling in and out of sleep. Even after the first treatment, my head felt clearer. I felt a lightness and I knew I would get better. I liked the fact that the acupuncture was non-invasive, painless and had no side effect. A gentle healing. Thank you. Thank you. How can I ever repay or acknowledge such a gracious act of care.

"You will be okay and you will finish your book," Dr. Hu had said. Those wonderful words of reassurance will always stay with me. Because my book has been quite the project for me, along with the stresses of daily life and unresolved issues that resurface needing attendance to be put to rest. I still continue with my acupuncture treatments to help heal my body and easy my weary mind.

I had a conversation with Duane about my book. I wanted to reassure him. He understood. At one point as the seriousness lifted, he gentled laughed and said, "Now, Mom, when you write a book like yours, sometimes it's difficult to end. As you know, life continues and it can go on forever. It's a lifelong project."

"Oh no. I certainly don't want this to be my life. But I do want it to be helpful in many ways for others."

I love the wisdom of my younger son. My biggest regret is that our divorce did not have to happen. But it did. It was the way that it was allowed to continue to the point of great anguish and disbelief that affected not only myself but also our children. I do not want this to be the standard or the precedent. We all have the capability to do better and if not, dysfunction should be nipped immediately, not encouraged to be used to confuse and traumatize eventually turning to corruption disguised as progress.

* * * * *

It is now August 2006. I am leaving my beautiful ivory tower that has offered me so much. But now it is time to relinquish and move on once more. It will not be Tucson, at least not yet. So I am savoring my last few weeks, in between all the busyness that moving entails. These last few months have been almost relentless with knowledge of other big changes to come. This morning, I awoke, went to my balcony and decided to spray my flowers with my balcony hose. What a wonderful invention. I love my moss roses. They have done especially well this year. I have an assortment of colorful flowers in flowerboxes and big pots. I have planted two different types of zinnias of all colors. I found a pretty little white flowered plant that drapes down the railing of the balcony and down the big pots, looking fragile but has withstood the heaviest of winds and storms. My frog sculpture and wise and fearless owl to scare away the big black crows. As I am pruning and then gently spraying my flowers, I start to sing: "Wrap up all my cares and woes. Here I go, singing low. Bye, bye blackbird . . . " I hadn't thought of that song in years. It was sweet and lighthearted.

I was thinking about the past week. I sold my house and bought a wonderful cottage house not too far from here and a little closer to my daughter, her husband and of course, little Lucia. I want to be in my house before the new baby boy is born. We are all so excited! My house will have English gardens and inviting walkways, walkways to friends gathering for impromptu little dinners, family and friends around the piano and eventually when this book is done—I can paint beautiful picture, take up dancing in some healthy magical form, and sing to my heart is happy and content. I hope that is not too much to ask for. May God bless all with a happy and loving home.

I wanted to tell my artist friend Susan about my move. At first she was dismayed for she was such a big part of this transition and transformation, helping to create a very unique and beautiful living space. I understood how Susan felt. Change is always difficult anyway, but to compound it knowing that this place could never be duplicated or replaced. Or would it really be valued in its' gift. I felt the same way. Leaving something beautiful and going into the unknown is not easy—ever. I wanted to reassure her and myself too. We were both fortunate in that we could create and make beautiful things happen.

"Susan, let's set a date when you can come over. I'll make a little dinner and we can talk about doing something creative and wonderful for my new place."

She liked that idea very much. There is something about that energy of enthusiasm and passion that is contagious in a positive way.

"Patti, I love your place. But your new place will be as wonderful. So I am happy for you." And then she added, "An artist and musician friend of mine lives just behind you. It's too bad you're moving because his is doing some great things to his place that you will be able to see from your windows on the Cedar Lake side of your condo. I've been telling my friend Scott about your place and since you're moving, would it be okay if he comes over to see your views and all the paintings?"

"Sure, that's great. It's always nice to meet new artists and musicians."

She called Scott from her cell phone and he said, "I'll just run right over." And he did in record time high energy, creative wheels turning, sparking life and vitality around him.

What a wonderful end of the day! It's great seeing and experiencing appreciation for whatever is accomplished or achieved. The skies were threatening storms all day. After the tour and much animated conversation, we gathered around my table overlooking Cedar Lake. It was funny because Scott started talking about food, his favorite restaurants. Then we started talking about cooking. Then we adjourned to the living room, taking in the views of Lake Calhoun. Susan and Scott agreed that we should all get some dinner. That was fine with me. But as I looked farther to the west, I could tell a brilliant storm was brewing.

"You know, it looks like there is going to be quite the storm. Maybe I should prepare something for us here. I've got lots of vegetables and different cheeses that I should use up."

They thought that was a mighty fine idea.

"Let me help you," Susan offered.

"That's okay. This is very simple. You and Scott can sit at the table and take in the views and watch the storm roll in."

I was happily fixing the simple meal for my friends and listening to the conversation. There was much to take in between the stern, dark, stormy clouds rolling in above me, while the demolition of several buildings below me had just taken place, leaving large spacious mounds of earth, giant craters with mechanical Caterpillars at halt with various other machinery that is used for such big projects.

"Look at the huge crane," Susan remarked.

Briefly, I stopped my preparations of our meal to look out at the storm and the large crane below. "Susan, this is so strange to me, all this construction everywhere. And I just wrote months ago, before all this began, about my father when he was on a catwalk. I think that is what you call them. He was working on a tall building in Chicago when a crane larger than that one, by accident, happened to pick him up and swung him in the air."

"Oh my gosh! How awful."

I realized as I was saying this I was also seeing this in my mind once more. "The operator of the crane never heard his cries, until eventually he discovered to his horror himself. Everyone thought he was dead. But he lived. His malaria came back, though. He was in the hospital for nine months."

I shook off the memory and walked back to the kitchen. As I was turning the roasted artichokes and tomatoes, Susan came toward me with her arms outstretched. I looked up at her and she gave me a comforting hug.

"Susan, how sweet you are," I said in surprise. "How come you did that?"

"When you were telling your story, you just looked so sad."

"Oh. It's just that I have all these coincidences. I guess in a way it is like closure. How often does that happen to one's father and how often does one have giant cranes beneath them in their own home even if it is a condo?"

I was okay. That was probably a good sign.

My simple dinner was well appreciated. The storm lifted.

"How would you like to see my place?" Scott asked me.

"Wow. I'd love that."

Scott ran like the wind to his place between Sunset and Depot. I followed Susan in her car, but would not get very far for the streets and the parkways were flooded with water, looking like another lake. Minnesota can never have enough lakes! Susan and I both took pictures. Taking a detour to Scott's wonderfully enchanting, magical and mystical house—what a wonderful surprise! There is nothing better than unlimited creativity and actually being brave and bold enough to live your dream. That inspires and delights. I was thankful for the gift of life.

Hopefully, I can offer something of inspiration and hope, forgiveness and enlightenment.

* * * *

CHAPTER 21

THE DECISION

*H*OW CAN *I* POSSIBLY GO back once more and make sense of it all? Too many months have passed since I have written but in rereading the manuscript I realize that the writing I lost was needed and necessary for better understanding. During this time, the day turned gray. The warmth of the morning left and brought a gentle coolness in its place. My plans were changed and I would use this soft and much needed rain to help bring me back to the time and place where I would finally take a stand and address the issues that had such a stranglehold on me. How could I do this without causing even more heartache? Not just for myself, but for our family, our friends and all that had been part of our life for so many years. Would there be any sensitive way to approach this without further pain and sorrow? But I'd rather do something than nothing at all. Maybe expressing the depth of my concern to my husband is what I needed to do. Maybe then Rick would realize our marriage was worth saving. That he still loved me. That he loved our family, our home, our life together for twenty-eight years, too important to be dismissed and way too important to be broken. I was in such mental and emotional anguish for so long it actually affected my health. I knew I didn't have any alternative.

I had written a five-page letter to my husband. It was a loving message sensitively worded to convey thoughts that there was never enough time to express to each other, as his work and other commitments always intruded. I wrote of my hopes and dreams, the years together, our family growing up, all the struggles and the happier and good times also. I wrote of my love for our children and the importance of parenting, especially how important a father is to his children and always will be. In that respect, we were truly fortunate. I did not want to hurt him. But I felt that I wasn't important or necessary in his life anymore. For so many years, the high demands of Rick's career had taken way too much time from our family. Now our last child would be going off to college, and I felt that I didn't know my husband any longer. How could I possibly feel a connection when Rick did not seem to value his family or me any longer? His needs and his career would always come first. I didn't want to write about the arrogance that he acquired through those many years of successes. I didn't write of his demands that were never satisfied or his continuous insults that came with the inflated, albeit fragile, ego. That all came subtly, mixed messages meant to confuse, hurt or give false hope.

I did not put any blame in my letter. Maybe I should have. I just know that I did not want to see Rick in any kind of pain or sorrow. Just the fact that I needed some reassurance of my own and letting Rick know that we needed to step back, take some time to re-evaluate what was really important to both of us. I wanted a strong, solid and loving marriage. I wanted him to take some time away from all the pressure and endless demands that had forever permeated our marriage in one form or another, taking way too much from all of us. I wanted to wake him up to the reality of our situation. If only I could snap my fingers, waken Rick from the hypnotic state that held him to his mission making sure nothing would come in his way. However, nothing or nobody would deter him from his lofty ambitions. Through those years of climbing the corporate ladder, he was now at the top and totally lost sight of his family. I painfully realized there was no hope for our marriage as long as he was so obsessed that he could not appreciate what was of most importance. Our last child would be going off to college and I could foresee and feel the emptiness ahead—already. Maybe, he was not capable or could not see for the delirium of all the success that would rob his family—and he could not even see or comprehend his part any longer. I knew, I had no recourse but to address this matter of contention. I felt I was being submerged and did I even have the strength to survive—sink or swim . . .

* * * * *

It was a Sunday. Our house was quiet. We had begun the empty nest syndrome. I put the letter on the freshly polished table in the den. I felt numb. Too many days had been spent waiting for my husband to come home. I could not keep up with his travels where he would be was unknown to me. Many times his business trips were combined with pleasure, such as golfing at a posh country club or resort. Several years before, the wives or spouses would also attend. But the corporate elite decided to eliminate that practice to save expenses. Which meant that there was even less time with my husband. The corporate demands and expectations isolated Rick from his family, especially from me. This was during the time when homemakers were not valued and it was obvious in Rick's attitude and demeanor that he bought into that trap. I thought we had something bigger and better than that. I was wrong.

I had made my decision. Yet, I would always leave an opening for a change of heart. In the past, I would be the one to make amends. The one to acquiesce. This time it would be up to Rick. In some strange way I felt strengthened once I made that decision. I did not want my marriage to be based on shallow pretense. I wanted a marriage of substance, a marriage that was mutual in every way, which brought out the best and offered the best to each, and was not one sided.

When Rick came home, I greeted him in the foyer. I wasn't angry, nor was he. I know he wasn't expecting this, but part of me felt he wanted to provoke me into making this move, like a game of chess maybe even a game of checkers.

"I need to talk to you. It's a matter of importance," I softly said. I was so saddened. I could hardly speak.

"What's it about?" Rick started to say in his business tone. But there must have been something in my expression. He sensed something monumental in the moment.

I told him I felt we should separate. I also told him of my letter that would explain my feelings better. He got angry.

"I'm not going to read any letter," he stormed.

"That's up to you, if that is what you choose to do."

We stood there face to face. Nothing between us. Our eyes searched out the other for a sign, a sign of hope, of remorse, of forgiveness. Something that would give us a strong will to persevere against the odds.

"I'm going to my office," he said at last, breaking the moment. "Give me the letter. But I won't read it."

The letter was his. He could do with it what he wished. I watched him as he left, tearing down the flagstone steps to his car. The sky brooded with storm clouds. I felt the heavens wept.

I can't really remember what I did until Rick's return. I was saddened he hadn't wanted to read the letter. The letter that might possibly save our marriage. If he'd only read it. Or if not, at least he would have some understanding that might promote a positive change, some enlightenment. The clouds parted. Rains poured from the spilt, a billion tears. Tears we were too proud to shed ourselves.

I sat on the chaise overlooking the Mill Pond below me. The waters churned with the torrential rain. The storm's power mesmerized me. I was thankful for the cleansing and release. Something Rick and I could not do.

I heard Rick's car pull in the drive, bringing me out of my reverie. I wanted desperately to see him, to know he was okay. I rushed to the door as he was coming in. My heart ached when he stumbled into the foyer. He was soaking wet, drenched, water puddling on the floor. His eyes were red from crying. I ached for him. I wanted to take away his pain. He fell into my arms and I held him. Here was my husband and all his pain.

"I have really lost you this time," he cried over and over.

"No, Rick. No, you haven't lost me. I will always be here for you. This doesn't have to be the end. I love you. I will always love you."

We went into the den. Rick sank to the armchair, literally exhausted as I caressed and his kissed his tear-stained face. We held each other. We consoled and reassured with our arms. Slowly, Rick regained his composure.

"Rick, I thought you were going to the office. How did you get so wet?" I asked.

"I did go. I was going to do some work, but I started reading your letter. As I was reading the letter, I couldn't help it but I started to cry."

My breath caught. I understood his pain. I hugged him closer. Again, he spoke. I knew it wasn't easy for him to do.

"As I sat at my desk with your letter in my hand, I tried to control my emotions but I couldn't. I left the office and I ran around the lake in the storm."

"My God, Rick. The rain's so cold and heavy. I'm so sorry. I don't want you to get sick."

"I won't," he said. "I just didn't want anyone to see me like this and since it was raining so hard . . . No one would know the difference."

How could love hurt so much? I asked myself.

This was the man I married twenty-eight years before. Once, he'd been a good man. Good men stumble and fall, especially when they are never satisfied with enough.

I should have barricaded the doors. I should have thrown a tremendous tantrum. Anything that would have prevented him from returning to his office at U.S. Bank. I could picture him falling back to the same pattern, meditating first thing in the morning and doing his self-hypnosis. He didn't want to feel. He never would allow himself to feel so deeply again. He would always be in control of any and all situations.

One day, shortly after Ricks' visit, I had a call from a woman in Chicago. She and her husband at one time lived in Minneapolis. In fact, the husband had been a partner at Ernst and Young. She told me of a woman Rick was seeing. She said she felt I ought to know. I was sickened.

When I confronted Rick, he told me he wanted a divorce. He was angry. He told me he had ripped up my letter. It was as if he'd ripped out my heart. This was the writing I lost and had to try to reproduce.

We would be divorced. But that would not be enough for Rick.

* * * *

CHAPTER 22

A Need to Be

I feel the courts have allowed:
Emotionally I feel a prisoner—chained and shackled
By a man/ex-husband that is bankrupt—morally
Not letting go his prisoner for pride/ego
Long forgotten his reason or his feelings—but,
What he has been taught . . .

I am his property/business—
To do as he wishes

He doles out his crumbs—in his arrogance
Oblivious to his cruelty/negligence
Rewarded by his entitlements—through his so called
Financial success, becoming "his alone?"
That is his armor now—replacing
The man he once was . . .

I want to be free of this man
Who hates me so—for I am
A reminder of the best of him/until he became
The worst of him
Not wanting to let go of his first prize/for I am
His possession to do what he wished—flaunting his
Mistresses and his ostentatious wealth . . .

While his family looks on—
Bewildered and shamed—
What kind of legacy has he left/taught
His own—
When money becomes the god—
Replacing his soul/conscience

Not wanting to look back or be reminded
Of what he sacrificed for a price . . .
And was/is—rewarded
But does not have to see/or hear of his
Destruction, brought by—the trail of his
Greed
I want to be free—to be . . .

CHAPTER 23

SACRIFICE

*H*E WAS A MAN AND father who sacrificed himself for his career. Although, in the courtroom for the world to hear, he stated, "I sacrificed my family for my career." To hear those words coming from her husband's mouth was beyond comprehension. She felt sickened and ashamed, wanting not to hear, wanting to flee the courtroom and hear no more. Suddenly, she felt the impact of those words and felt a chilling fear that gripped her. What would be the ramification of such a horrendous statement that even the people in the courtroom gasped in disbelief that anyone in their right mind would utter such a reckless and immoral statement. She wanted desperately to forget the ugliness of those words. Yet, they were said.

Her attorney gently put his hand on hers to offer a show of compassion, reassurance and understanding. Her emotions were jumbled, and she was visibly shaken, but she knew she had to stay strong and composed. She felt she might break down, but she dared not, for then she might not stop. And this man, whom she once knew so well and loved for so long, was now so cold and indifferent, like a hardened stranger. She mourned the loss of her husband, for he was now someone she no longer knew.

There was no turning back. He was unreachable. She knew then his world would not include her. Nor did she want to be part of it. It was excessive. Values were misplaced. The arrogance shameless, the entitlements were for a few alone. And at the cost of integrity, honor and honesty. Now her husband seemed to be devoid of feeling, as if he had been programmed and was determined not to be deterred by sentimentality. Maybe he thought those words would gain sympathy for his sacrifice. His distorted mind was now his reality.

He climbed the corporate ladder. When he stayed totally focused, it became a steady climb, never looking back, never faltering or questioning. He learned to be tough and detached when he made those difficult decisions others dared not make, regardless of who would be hurt or dismissed in the process. He became driven, obsessed, discarding those in his path. He would not rest and his wrath would fall on anyone who questioned or stood in his way. He lost his true friends. His family suffered and would be discarded in his fury, for he knew no boundaries. He had not conscience or compassion; he was now a man with special privileges and the incentives that enhanced his decisions and position for the corporate cause. He became a man of arrogance with his special entitlements. All the money and power became his mistress and addiction. No one would stop him or question his actions. He was too important in his firm, making millions that impressed many. His firm had much to gain from this man who was willing to sacrifice himself until needed no longer, just to prove that he was deserving. He could not recognize the cost.

She knew she had to leave to avoid losing herself; to regain her self-respect and restore her dignity, and try to pick up the pieces and mend the years of emotional pain and neglect for herself and her children. The damage was far-reaching and it would take time to mend mind, body and spirit. Little did she know that the hidden rage of her husband would continue for years, and she would be a woman alone, against a corporate giant, who would become determined to control her and to break her into submission.

* * * * *

Some people who do not know me might look at me and say, "What are you complaining about? You are fortunate. Most people cannot identify with your problem. Get over it." But they are only seeing the surface. The people who know me can understand my search, my quest and my outrage at the injustice that has been done to me, affecting my children as well as others. They understand the importance of having closure, acknowledgement and restitution, and my growing need for independence, freedom to be my own person before it becomes meaningless to me. I want the freedom to be able to pursue and accomplish my dreams on my own terms, with no restrictions or barriers put upon me by a biased court system that is controlled by a man who has the power to extort and manipulate the laws in his favor. He has the money, position, influence and connections to control. He will continue to use every angle and person who is willing to compromise their integrity until the damage extends too far, for too long, and is too blatant to be ignored.

When I write about this, I feel disturbed. It is not something I wish to dwell on. It drains me emotionally. Unfortunately, the magnitude of the injustice is not mine alone, for others have been affected also. The awareness of this creates a tremendous responsibility for her—and accountability. That is not an easy matter to be addressed or encouraged, so I have to tread lightly, knowing that egos are frail. I want these issues to be looked at, addressed and amended to restore our basic human values and the trust that instills human dignity and acknowledges the value of keeping families intact.

Unless the corporate demands, exclusions and numerous entitlements are recognizes for what they truly represent, these problems will continue to be more pronounced and the problems will spill over and become everyone's problem. When the legal system can be bought and is allowed to play the harshest role by creating loopholes and designer laws, then the courts become the playground of deceptive collaboration for wealthy clients, like a bully on the playground, testing their limitations and boundaries by using tactics of intimidation and exaggerations, distorting the truth for their own purpose. Now it is not about integrity or honor. Justice becomes a forgotten word. It has lost it's true meaning and purpose.

There will be people who want to read and know what goes on behind the scenes, and question certain actions and decisions. That is everyone's right and should be encouraged and valued. There will also be those who couldn't care less, for they are indifferent until they are touched in some by a decision or law that takes away one of their rights, privileges or freedoms, which are precious to them.

I have written many letters of plea to be heard. But what I have learned is that when there has been an act of deception, many people do not want to know. They just want it to go away, especially when it involves consequential matters that they prefer to keep neatly unwraps, unspoken.

CHAPTER 24

A GAME OF LOVE

*I*WAS NEVER KNOWN AS an athlete growing up. I loved the arts, music, dance, creating anything that inspired me. In school I was either known as the artist or the singer. Music truly was my passion to be expressed in many ways. I loved hearing a beautiful melody or hearing the perfect harmony that would make me stop and listen so keenly that I would feel transformed to another place, maybe even another time. To hear the rhythms that draw me like a magnet to its pulsating beat that captivates and captures my inhibitions to respond to its enticing resound is to energize my body and restore my spirit that releases joy that can no longer be contained but expressed and shared.

Music moves me. It inspires me, also heals me and for that I am grateful. It is a magnificent gift that has done so much for me. When I started painting seriously, my children were young. It seems I was my most creative at that time in my life. They loved to see the paintings progress, each stage completed. I painted landscapes, scenes that ranged from floral to leafy wood with all its rich texture and capturing the way the light played with shadow, bring out the depth. That interplay is mysteriously effective. I'd become lost in the world I was creating. I learned to paint by reproducing the master, from Monet and Renoir to Picasso's "The Lovers." That was one of my favorites. I also tried my hand at some of Van Gogh's earlier works. I loved portraiture, and nautical pieces—ships and colorful sailboats. Trying to capture the water, be they placid or the exciting grandeur of crashing waves, all was truly challenging to my imagination.

One of my favorite paintings I created with music playing in the background. It was a majestic seascape that I had to reproduce for painting class. I can't remember the artist's name. It was the painting itself that captured me. It was an attempt to duplicate a master painter, and turned out to be a great teaching tool. There was the beautiful sunset peeking through misty clouds in shades of gold, amber, purple, azure and aqua green, meeting the edge of ocean somewhere.

The waters from a distance looked vast and serene, but as the water neared the shore, you could see the beginnings of a small whitecaps, rippling in poetic splendor. The whitecaps expanded into larger waves crashing into giant rocks on the beach. The sand's texture asked to be experienced. Felt. The indentation by the force of each wave left small pockets of ocean water that cleansed the earth.

I loved that painting. It was as if I were there. My children were sleeping and my husband was on a business trip. Many times when I was so inspired, it was my real time to create. Many times I would listen to music, maybe rock or classical. By this time, it called for "Jesus Christ Superstar." This time I was in my element, feeling at peace and thankful. I had worked on the sky and the beginning stages of the water, and was eager to bring the water to life with all the vibrant energy. The passionate music inspired my paintbrushes.

I started out delicately and then added thicker paint on my brushes for the giant waves. I did the giant rocks with a palette knife that could help me bring out the reflection of the heavens. The contrast from the gradation of delicate touches in the background to the heavier paint of the waves to the massiveness of the boulders and then now working on the sand. Pretty tricky. But the music inspired me. I gently worked my medium. I adopted a squared brush for the sand and its edges.

I worked on that painting until after three in the morning, feeling a welcoming sense of quiet peace and serenity, and had a very restful sleep afterwards. It was always great to hear and see my children's responses, as they inspired me also. When I brought my painting to class, my instructor Carla Bullaro was somewhat impressed. She wanted to know how I managed to create the effects. I told her it was listening to "Jesus Christ Superstar." So that was the secret of my inspiration.

I was known as the artist in Chicago and South Bend. My family's move to Minneapolis brought a very different element and focus to each of us. I had to put my painting in the background, as this move was more challenging. I wanted to incorporate my background in the arts to my tennis game. But I'm getting too tired, as again I am working way too late. Tennis is a game of love. Yet my world of the arts can never be replaced or forgotten.

* * * * *

Writer's Block

Right now I have writer's block. I feel overwhelmed and frustrated by the turn of events that have affected my life adversely. I am at a place where I feel I am rebelling against myself. I realize that no one can be at their best or make the best decision when there is a constant reminder of the inequitable outcome that changes one's life so profoundly. These experiences have contradicted what we all have been taught or valued and believed to be true.

At times I feel as if there has been an exception to the rule for me. I know I am not alone but it does anger me to think that people will say and sometimes with that wry little smile. Well, you know life isn't always fair? When I hear that ignorant phrase I want to scream. But what do they know for they are either incapable of understanding or too complacent in their own small realm of contentment to dare rock their own comfort zone to raise a question of doubt or uncertainty in the decision.

Unfortunately, most people will be apathetic or indifferent to others' misfortunes as they will never understand unless they have experienced the effect of years of devastation that has been thrust upon them relentlessly and deliberately. What one learns in this or these disquieting lessons that have continued for years as if a game of power or amusement is far-reaching for everyone involved.

For me, I learned that too much money can become a person's first love, and too much power in the wrong hands can become merciless and voracious, with special exemptions and entitlements that create the need for more. I learned that money and power can buy people of position to erase or eradicate their mistakes. I learned that people are impressed with money and position, no matter how acquired or who has hurt or discarded in the process. I learned that too much money and power left unchecked and misdirected can become an addiction as strong as alcohol or drugs. The difference is that certain addiction is rewarded and encouraged by those in power, for they will gain from this obsession, regardless of the destruction it creates. Why is that?

* * * * *

I could see the effects of the years of climbing the corporate ladder, becoming the banking expert. His area of expertise became mergers and acquisitions and in the beginning of this success, the formidable phrase of hostile takeover was used—until that phrase sounded too harsh and they changed to be more people friendly. But it wasn't friendly at all or kind or compassionate. It was all about acquiring, taking advantage of a weakened situation. Many lost their jobs callously, with cold determination and detachment. It did not matter the longevity, loyalty or position, friend or foe. There was no reason for consideration. It was all about becoming the biggest, the most powerful and the impressive bottom line was the big incentive.

I saw him change from a loving and devoted husband and father to someone I no longer knew. He would do meditation morning and evening to relax, for in his new world there was no relief or reprieve. When he needed to be more focused and detached from his hard decisions, he started doing self-hypnosis to numb his conscience and his feelings. It was a difficult time for many, and now his own family would feel the brunt of his addiction. If he would have been an alcoholic, his peers would have insisted on treatment. Instead, he was rewarded with more money, incredible perks and incentives that he could not refuse in his exhausted delirium.

Insidiously, his world would take hold with a grasp so tight that there was no reaching him. I feared his practice of self-hypnosis, for his eyes became cold and hard. It was as if he was consumed by his conquests, which were endless.

Her children were growing up, witnessing the change in their father but not understanding and wanting to avoid him when possible, for he was cold and quick to anger. His sense of humor was forgotten and replaced by arrogance. She made the agonizing decision to separate from her husband to somehow maybe awaken the seriousness of their situation. At first he seemed devastated. She felt a faint hope that their marriage could be saved. That he would realize that they had shared too much together to just walk away. She wanted to believe her marriage and their children were his main priority.

He returned to the office for a few days. He seemed more affectionate, a sweetness returned but also a slight awkward hesitancy, as if holding something back. She wondered if all their years together could be mended or broken. But it was not for her to decide. He was cool and calm in his professional manner stating that he did not want a separation but a divorce.

From that moment, she became another business for her husband to weaken and conquer. Within two years, they were divorced. But that was not the end of it. For he was angry in his mixed obsession. After the divorce, he waited as long as possible and then he started the appeals and endless court battles, lasting for almost ten years, eroding her financial security bit by bit, having strict stipulations in the divorce decree that would keep her dependent and restricted. She thought the courts were there to protect her and instead they became her husband's own personal playground where he could challenge the system to his advantage and wield his power of connections and influence.

May 2008

Am I going to drown in a sea of memories that keep resurfacing, keeping me submerged but still clinging for rescue, some hope, a promise of something better that makes life worth all those trials and tribulations? For there is something greater. Through it all, I am grateful that I have a purpose. Maybe, because I have experienced and survived it all, intact—relatively, at least, fro now—I believe in order to move forward, remove those chains, forgive and offer the gift of dignity as an enduring friendship—for we have lost too much already. I do need to talk to you . . .

This is my last letter,
Patti

May 28, 2008

Dear Rick,

Thank you for sending the divorce decree. I made the mistake of rereading those papers. Thinking, maybe there was something that I missed—something that would help bring closure or a better understanding. It did neither. What those papers did do was create further distress and anguish that is almost in possible to bear. But, I did have a revelation. Actually, several.

The first revelation: Was it possible that you never read the decree? The second revelation: Was there a second decree after your appeals? If so, we should probably sit down and go over these matters—for peace of mind, respect for each other and our children. And for trust that maybe we can rebuild through understanding. Is that possible? Now this is important in so many ways, therefore . . .

Would you please, think of this as reading an important dissertation that will help provide a more meaningful perception? I don't want my life to be like this. Every day is a reminder of my loss . . . my losses. Every transaction is a reminder also; the broken promises gives into disillusionment, too many opportunities surrounding me—*professional people that were not what they seemed just an opportunity to gain something of value. It is not easy being "suddenly" alone. I had an empty nest and a divorce at the same time. I had no family here, except for our now grown children. They were struggling along with me. I had no one to turn to for guidance. The only people that were to protect me—or my assets—had their own best interests at heart. There would be no one in my corner. The people that wanted to help seemed to have their hands tied, or insurmountable problems of their own. Sometimes, simply not having the right connections or know how—or they knew how but did not want to risk getting involved with the big boys.*

I have learned some very valuable lessons in very hard ways. I think the broken trusts and disappointments were the most disheartening. Every year of the appeals presented unseen and unknown challenges within itself. But outside of the appeals, life continued and ended. You would not know. You didn't want that burden. You would not know, shortly after our divorce, my sister, Mary Belle, lost her only son. You lost your father. I'm sorry. Yet, you did not want me to know. He was like a father to me, too. That loss seemed to unleash a furor in you, directed at me. My brother, Billy, lost his wife, Shirley, to breast cancer, leaving three wonderful teenage sons and a beautiful daughter, Kim. Billy was and is living in Texas now. But recently, his son, Kenny, died in a tragic accident. When Shirley died, my sister, Mary Belle and I went to Texas for several weeks to help our brother. During this time, I really got to know my nieces and nephews quite well. Candice was four, and she loved me. She would fall asleep with her little head in my lap as I read or sang to her. My sister and I would cook, clean and organize their little house, wanting to help in very way possible for our brother and his young family. I brought tennis rackets for the older kids and they showed me how to play basketball, We played a game called HORSE. In that time, I saw a side of my own family that made a wonderful impression on me and it was very difficult to leave. It's a long way—Texas to Minnesota.

I don't think you know that my mother died. When I learned of her death, it hit so hard, leaving an unbearable sadness and another form of emptiness. My dear sister Mary Belle and her husband would take in our father for the rest of his duration for he was becoming disoriented after our mothers' death. He grew to have dementia and became childlike. I feel that at one time he was a loving child but never had a loving or nurturing home and when he grew up, he never had those skills or lessons. I feared my father. I kept my distance. That is sad and should not be—ever. But, I could understand, when I learned that he lost his mother at an early age, tragically, He would join the army at the age of fifteen. Of course, he lied about his age, but the army offered him something that was lacking in his own life. I know your father was in the service too. He was a good man. You were fortunate to have known him and so was I.

My sister took care of my father, but during this care, her husband had his own problems that eroded his health. Our father would die a peaceful death. But it probably seemed peaceful to me from a distance. Not knowing where I belong or my real purpose any longer.

I now you have had your own losses. For some reason, I would not know until after the fact. Susie would usually call me and keep me informed. I felt for Aunt Elda when she lost her husband, John. But my sorrow was also mixed with a sadness far removed, undetected, unfelt and unseen. My sister, Mary Belle, a few years ago lost her husband as well. I won't burden you of the details. She remarried a very nice man last August. It was when my niece Melanie was getting married that we learned my dear sister, Sandy, had drowned. What we learned was that she died about the same time as Kenny did. It was beyond comprehension. I'm tired of doing this life alone. I'm tired of carrying the whole burden myself. I want somebody in my corner to fight for me, to care about me, to love me unconditionally, respect and cherish me, someone to once again laugh and play little dance a little. I want to have some joy in my life.

Now, I want to add a few more details. Everything in this letter, with the exception of Kenny and Sandy's death would occur during all those appeals. As you know, I could not get representation, but that is a moot point at this stage. You were not aware. Ernst and Young took so much of you for all those years. First Bank, now U.S. Bank replaced your priorities big time. As very one knows, the world of mergers and acquisitions have never been family friendly. All your travels, big business, and all your added interest—kept us apart for so long that we did become strangers. That was also during an era when homemakers were devalued and secretaries were prized. I knew my worth. I knew what I contributed not only to my family but also to my community and society itself.

But, you would learn to disregard me, and eventually replace me. You were not easy to love back then for I felt your cold indifference. I'm sure, I was not very lovable myself, as remember, I had that terrible virus, that low grade fever, horrible cough and weakness for six months. And, on top of that, I had the injury to my quads that left me in terrible pain. I would have that pain, although each year it would lessen. Pilates and acupuncture actually healed and strengthened my legs, for which I am thankful.

You and Rene are married now. I find it strange that our own home seemed to mean very little to you. Your time with us was very little, filled with stress and bordered on neglect. Correct me if my words are too harsh or wrong. I need to know if you really ever cared enough. I met you in your typing class. I'm a pretty good typist now. I've known you for almost my whole life, well—since I was fifteen. You and your children were my whole life. it's not what I planned—I was going to be a singer, dancer, artist, and missionary. I did a little of it all, on borrowed time with limitations. I accepted my role, but I never knew for certain that I could give up my dreams to be a wife, mother, homemaker, etc. Fortunately, I would eventually realize that combination was a gift that would enhance our marriage—in fact any ones. It was not easy, but that experience can never be replaced or erased. But evidently, it cannot be recognized or honored in your world.

I hope you and Rene are happy together. I hope that your marriage is based on love and not just for the appearance only with the monetary package as the agreement. I wonder if your wife ever questioned the purpose of the hearings that were going on before and after your marriage. I wonder and hope that if she did not, the truth be known.

Remember when our daughter fell down the stairs while carrying baby Vinnie? He was only three months old. I moved into my little cottage house October 2nd and Vinnie was born October 5th. I tell you, that was a tremendous experience. I had very little help, and more times than not, I did most things myself. Because Lucia was not yet two, and would not be until February 3. Lucia was almost my birthday present. I would be unpacking my little house, trying to settle in, but mainly helping Monica for still was still healing. I will never forget that afternoon of January 16 when Monica fell down the stairs holding the baby. Her instincts were to protect her baby and she did.

When she called, I dropped everything and rushed to be with her, praying that she was safe, but I knew by the frantic fear in her voice that I could not escape her pain. I found her on the floor cradling and trying to comfort Vinnie. He was unhurt from what I could see. But I still didn't know if there was anything that I could not detect. It was unbearable, to see our daughter in so much pain, and even worse, so afraid. The fear of what could have happened. I did not know if I could take any more. Why did this happen? Especially when Monica seemed to be getting stronger. I called 911 for an ambulance and the rest is history. You were there, later.

What you did not notice was seeing the impact on me. During that time, I had very little sleep or rest, I rarely had time to even eat a meal. I would take care of Monica and the babies. I would do her laundry, I would go home and do my laundry and what ever else I could do. There would be all the meals, taking care of everyone else's needs. There would be very little reserve left for myself. But, I knew this also would pass. Monica's knee would heal. This gave me an incredible bonding experience with the babies. It was hard on Monica to be do immobile. That also made it difficult for me. It was an exhausting time. During this time, I became hyperallergic—to almost anything and everything that I ate, breathed, or touched. The doctor gave me an Epi-pen, and I do not like needles. Fortunately, I haven't had to use it. I did go to am allergy specialist in La Crosse, Wisconsin. He was very thorough.

Not only did he want to know about my medical history, but my whole history. It was interesting and fascinating at the same time. It made sense. The doctor told me that I was stressed to the max, on overload, exhausted for so long that my body could mot take any more, and was reacting. He said, "Think of a pot of oil that has been boiling for too long and someone walking by and carelessly throws a lighted match. The pot bursts into flames." I realized he understood. I needed to take care of myself. I had some tests taken and was allergic to practically everything. I never had been before. He gave me a remedy to build up my resistance, just three drops a day. It took almost a year. My allergies aren't quite as severe now, but it is clear that the stress has taken their toll.

Life has not been easy and I don't know if it is meant for me to be here in Minnesota. I do have concerns that don't or won't go away. I want a normal life with some happiness. Remember when we all were leaving Lucia's little dance recital. I asked if we could talk. We could even meet at my house. Rene walked up and I said, "Rene, you're welcome too." You looked as if I insulted you. You did not want to take the time to hear or try to understand or know me—for you never knew me. For if you did, you would have recognized and appreciated the incredible gifts before you and you would have cherished those gifts. But, your rewards and trophies were your importance.

Did you or Rene not recognize me pain? You son did. He tried to console me while you and your wife ignored me. I don't want to be part of anyone who wants me as a business or a tax write off. How can I forget when I am constantly reminded of the inequities every time you and Rene flaunt your wealth? Why did you marry me, if you were going to try to take everything from me—while I gave you everything that was good and decent and most precious—your children and your grandchildren.

I talked to Rene briefly at Michael's confirmation celebration, I apologized, saying "I can't believe I did that." "For what?" she said, and I could not believe she could be so oblivious. What is worse—knowledge but apathy, passion or indifference? Once again. I was insulted, disregarded for it did not matter to her. Her world is secure. She has what is rightfully mine. Don't you realize that your financial success was built in our marriage? She wasn't even your private secretary, but Ed Finn's. What are we going to do about this situation?

I'm exhausted. I want my freedom. You took the best years of my life. I gave you the best and it showed in all your successes. The more I gave the more you took. Eventually you could not even appreciate but just expected. Our divorce wasn't even fair. You got the savings account and I got the high maintenance house, with high taxes and memories in every nook and corner. Didn't anyone ever tell you that I was the mother of your children? You don't want to try to destroy their mother, do you? What about what you refer to as "my" grandchildren? Do you want them to know the truth about what their grandfather did to their grandmother? Is he an honorable man? I cannot go with this madness. I deserve some happiness. If you cannot treat me with consideration, respect, some dignity, then I cannot have you controlling my life—like a prisoner.

I am your tax write off. I also pay high taxes on my alimony. So, you win and the government does, too. I've had a high mortgage ever since the big D-thanks to you. You and your wife have several multi million-dollar homes, expensive cars, country clubs, and a very luxurious lifestyle—that would impress anybody. Or make one wonder. How did you do it? Why is my life filled with financial struggles that the disparity is so obvious? Enough of this, you don't want to hear it and I'm sick of the whole thing. Now you are probably going to forget about reading this as a dissertation. In fact, you probably aren't reading this at all, but delegating it to your secretary or your infamous attorney. I don't' care what you do. Regardless of what happened, what has transpired through these years—of the aftermath. I still care enough to care about you to give you the chance to make amends and do the right thing for it is time. So please, just let me be —free. Let's talk and work something out that if fair and right for both of us.

Patti

I started the second part of this letter yesterday, late afternoon. I wrote until almost four in the morning—searching for the right words, the right way to reach that part of you that you avoid—your humaneness. Monica called early this morning needing my help. She was not feeling well. Of course, I again rushed to be with my daughter to help her in any way with the little ones. I was relived to see that she was standing. A faint smile appeared on her beautiful face but I could also see a weariness that touched me for I understood. "Mom, thanks for coming over. I'm okay, but I'm exhausted and feeling sick to my stomach. I think I'm pregnant—again." I wanted to reassure her, "Monica, a baby is a blessing, a gift. You will be fine and I will help you as much as I can." She replied, "Yes, I know that Mom, but after Vinnie when I broke my knee, Phil said that we would not have any more children." I remembered those words. I also remembered that they saddened our daughter. That saddened me. "Monica, Phil is a good man and he loves you and the children very much. He was feeling overwhelmed at the time and worried about you. Your children bring so much joy. They are a gift." I probably said more, for that is how I am.

By now, you probably must know. I will be there for my daughter, for our sons. For that also is the way I am. I know this once more will require a tremendous amount of energy. I always say, "God, give me strength, give me wisdom to do what is right." Sometimes I would also need to ask for courage. Now, I want to add along with the strength and wisdom, and still a little courage, some peace, joy and contentment. I want to be excited about life once more, inspired each morning, with a life rich and fulfilled with all that is good. I want to add, I want to forgive and be forgiven. Can we make that happen?

Patti

* * * * *

What does it take to rebuild the bridge to communication? Without communication there will never be any understanding, just an empty meaningless void, filled with unnecessary and unwarranted struggles beyond comprehension. You were taught and were rewarded not to feel. That became your right. You earned it. When did you cross that line? Did you do it knowingly, up until the very end, or was this part of you deeply engrained and finally surfaced? I thought it was over. We would recover from our loss and all the hurt. We could have, but you wouldn't allow it. You held all the cards in the game. You knew all the rules and how to manipulate to your advantage, never playing fair. You never took time to see the results of your actions. You never had to for you didn't want to know. You hurt me. You hurt yourself and our children but you want to pretend all is well. But it is not.

These unanswered questions that never were allowed to be addressed r even mentioned—this was your armor of defense against your conscience. The thought of such an awakening must have horrified you, for you did everything and used every means and defense in order not to know or acknowledge. Do you now what it is like to be betrayed, to be trusting and innocent but set adrift to the unknown, unprepared—to defend against people that should have protected and supported you? Instead, to be tormented for years for no reason except that it is what you wanted and it was allowed. Separated, divorced, appealed and annulled. And after the divorce, I could not find anyone to represent me. What was that? Why was it allowed to continue—for ten years!? Am I just to accept the injustice and indignity as if I was of no worth or value? You know better. I know I do. You used the courts to execute your plan. I was a woman alone, going through this terrible nightmare that never ended and would come back to taunt me. What was the purpose of the ultimate betrayal? Was it a test for you to see how much you could get away with, or was it a test for me—how much could I endure? Is there a breaking point that diminishes or strengthens? I wonder if it's even possible, maybe with fierce determination, or better yet, an offer of the olive branch of peace, to get through this phase of life with both of us having our dignity intact? Is that possible?

* * * * *

Sorry, but I do tend to get distracted by what I see, hear and experience. But I also still believe that we all can do and be better, even through all the distractions of life and some times the chaos that might surround us. I can do my small part, but we all have a certain responsibility is what we choose, how we behave, and what we accept. Sometimes the people who come into my life or that I will meet will quietly impress me with bringing hope and inspiration. These will be at the times that the expectations seem to be too great to be addressed or even acknowledged. I wonder then, if it is arrogance or fear that is not able to meet and embrace the moment of truth.

Now is the time of change. We all have made some kind of mistake or misjudgment. But the important thing is to learn and correct these problems that hurt and erode, and replace with solid values that will build a better foundation for all and in future generations. We can do that, if we know that we have that capacity or ability and it is shared.

* * * * *

7/17/08

Recently, while going through documents in search of my divorce decree—I would need once more to provide my financial income . . . . Because of my move and all the renovating that needed to be done, dredging through all the files, amidst the dust . . I felt once more degraded . . . put in my place. Memories of all the injustice and humiliation, Filtering through the process, as if a flood that wants to consume and ravish. I won't let it this time. While searching for the decree, I came across a beautifully designed file, covered with an array of roses of various color and size, nesting in leafy greens with sprinkles of tiny blue and white flowers, almost like baby tears. Inside that file were my writings, handwritten of a previous time. I realized, this would be the catalyst—the genesis and making of my story. My book.

Patti

Now is the time to break the silence, communication is the utmost importance—the time for compassion, enlightenment for understanding and to heal . . . and to finally move forward, for this has been ignored for too long.
Show details 11/7/08 Reply

(FALL 2008)
To the attention of Ed Winer,

There needs to be a change of heart and how can that be when there is no communication or understanding of the depth of the emotional pain that has been inflicted on me and my family. The mind does not forget emotional trauma, especially when inflicted over a matter of years. I am speaking of my ex-husband Rick Zona. You would not know any thing about me and it would not matter that I could not get representation here in Minnesota—you didn't question, the courts didn't question or hear my anguish. I learned you were a powerful and ruthless attorney that Rick would hire. I could not understand why Rick would appeal when our original divorce was unfair. I could have lived with that, I just wanted to move on with my life that was on hold for all those years. I also could not understand why he would need an attorney that specialized in the financial side, "that was your expertise," while Rick himself, " his expertise was mergers and acquisition and eventually "the banking expert." I was a homemaker, a wife and mother at the age of seventeen. We would have three beautiful children together. He was once a good man. I gave him his reason and purpose also the quality of time and an atmosphere to focus and achieve his dreams . . . and he did. I gave him the best, and he grew to be tremendously successful, until one day. "that was not enough" His arrogance grew with each success of the takeovers. He also meditated twice a day to stay calm under the constant demands and he incorporated "self hypnosis" in order not to feel in the difficult decisions that he would have to inflict on those that he would use to achieve his purpose. . . at any cost . . . He was driven.

I could see a terrible transformation in my husband at the time. There became a hardness to him. He became critical and demanding, nothing was ever good enough. He became a cold, hard and indifferent stranger in our home to our now grown children and me. That was the price of the success on our family. He made so much money but resented the fact that now his children were growing up needing college education . . . But, where was he during those formative years??? Now, it was as if he looked at his own children and me as another business . . . and were we an asset or a liability. Ernst and Young and U.S. Bank would replace his family. The first time, we went to court and Bob Zalk was Ricks' attorney back then, Rick stated . . . "He sacrificed his family for his career." And, he did and he would be rewarded. It made me sick to hear those words. What happened to him that he was so willing to sacrifice and not give a thought to those words. Was it all the meditation, combined with the self hypnosis that he felt so removed, entitled and deserving that he was above the law, he felt he was entitled—all those hefty bonuses and golden parachutes that protected his wealth would become his inclusively. Rick was a jealous man, a possessive man that did not like to share or compromise or listen. He would strike with a vengeance, relentless—using others to help do his dirty work for he had the means.

He did sacrifice his family. He's hurt his family in ways that is now unspeakable and he wants to forget his cruelty—for . . . now we do have grandchildren. It is not possible not to see or speak that is unrealistic. We can't pretend, but we can forgive and do the right thing for our children and for ourselves. You know, I sacrificed my "life" for my family. My family always came first. On borrowed time—I would paint and my paintings were beautiful, I loved to dance—that came naturally, the love of music and good books will always be, but my family and friends cannot be replaced. I gave Rick his time to grow. I never had that. During the divorce that cruelty in Rick surfaced over and over . . . saddened and confused me. The hardened changes were gradual and insidious, but I began to wonder, "Was that the real Rick Zona that I never knew but now has emerged.

I am and always have been patient, probably too much so. I want to believe that Rick would awaken from all that self-hypnosis and realize the damage that he has done . . . to me and his children. I don't want our grandchildren to grow up knowing what their grandfather did for the love of power, control and money. . . That will happen. What does this teach our children and future generations. Right now, we are seeing and many of us living and experiencing the aftermath of all the dysfunction and corruption that has been allowed to grow from the negligence, misdeeds and apathy that has been left unchecked for too long . . . that finally has to be addressed. And. you know—what I learned from my own experience was . . . if this could happen to me and my family what is the corporate world, or the courts real purpose or role? Is it always about the bottom line? . . . Secrecy and avoidance? When the legal system purpose works only for the select few with hidden agendas, when the church looks away, hides and denies and when our government becomes so dysfunctional because of power in the wrong hands awarded, unchecked and ignored—becomes the norm . . . Then we have a system that is broken. What Rick did to his family and me was and is a shame. What he was allowed to do with the help of the courts was and is a travesty. When the corporate world permeated/intruded into our home and eventually replaced Ricks' family it was beyond comprehension. That sadness permeates the thoughts and memories and intrudes on every holiday, recital, birthday, or holy day . . . Welcome to the world of divorce—Minnesota style.

Rick does not want to see me or talk to me. That saddens me, but I could live with that if there was a reason. But, he just cannot face himself or hear the truth and he certainly does not want to feel the hurt or pain that he has caused so many. Only, because he has the money and the means is he able to manipulate to his advantage. He does not care who he uses or hurts in the process. That is really rather pathetic. Where is the courage to do the right thing?

Ed, You've sent me several pieces of correspondence, stating not to talk to Rick.

He just won't wake up to the reality to the damage he has done and doesn't want to do what is right—because, he wants to control my life. Plus I am a tax write off for him and then I pay higher taxes on my alimony "maintenance." Rick left me with a tremendous financial hardship from the beginning, yet, he and his trophy wife have a very lavish lifestyle, flaunting his wealth and excessive life style.

Before Rick married his current wife he was seeing a career woman. She told me—that she and Rick would see that I had" all kinds" of financial and legal problems. That is the type of people that Rick would now let into his life. you've helped him accomplish some more of his goals. And, one wonders why our world has so many problems.

I gave too much for too long and to be treated and held back by this man that only wants to control my life and degrade me by his shallowness and disregard. What do I have to do to get "my" life back.

I do not want to be his property. I do not want to be his business or his tax write-off. I want my freedom. Either we can sit down and talk like civil human beings or you can approach Rick with an offer that is fair to me that I can live with. I also need to know what to expect from him or you. It is time for accountability and restitution. I want to forgive and forget, but, Rick has to look at himself and rise above his actions and finally "wake up" for he has created a terrible nightmare for too many. I need to know specifics about my future monetary expectations—like a retirement settlement. Did you know that when Rick and I got divorced, he got the savings account and much more—I got the house with high taxes. I would learn that Rick never paid on the principle. He made sure that he would have no financial worries.

What I want is to be free and clear. I want to know what to expect. I want my dignity back and I want to be free to remarry if I decide. Rick can do this in several ways ... He can give me a lump sum that will provide for me for the next thirty years ... Or, he can pay off my little cottage house and continue giving me the alimony/maintenance as is but without the restrictions that have been put on me. The maintenance continues even if I should remarry and if I have a little career—I like that better than a job—the money would not be reduced. Also, I need to know if Rick has honored the life insurance to me—what is the dynamics of that policy. And one of these years my social security will kick in. I'm exhausted from all this. I'm not a businesswoman, I'm not an attorney but I can do many things. If I would have had the same opportunities as my ex-husband, I could have been all of the above—if I chose. What ever I do, it is to make and be a positive difference.

Patti Zzzz
a little tired

SEC Response - File HO1280859 SEC Response - File HO1280859 New U.S. Securities and Exchange Commission 9/17/08

Dear Ms. Zona: This is to follow-up on your telephone call on September 15. I . . . show details 9/25/08 Reply It is rather interesting

U.S. Securities and Exchange Commission does sound rather impressive. I was a homemaker, thrust into situations beyond comprehension, that could shatter anyone's' belief and trust in corporate, the legal system, our government, that turns their back and allows dishonest acts, does nothing to protect the innocent but will benefit from their inexperience or naïveté without a hint of remorse and they don't have to—for that is the normal procedure and the dishonest never have to take responsibility or pay back but they will be bailed out and once again at our expense. I have written a book, about all the opportunist that lay await to strike and take what ever they could so cleverly, deceptively get away with. I am so sick of the bottom line, the greed that is so rampant and destructive and never enough to the point of blatant dishonest acts, laws, loopholes, golden parachutes for the so called entitled and "deserving?" it goes on and on, bigger, more, to the point of ugly and obnoxious and shallow in every form. I am tired of being surrounded by opportunist in every direction and it has been like this ever since my divorce. In fact, it began with my divorce "when my husband of twenty-eight years, three children said in court: "He sacrificed his family for his career" and he did and he was allowed. His corporate girlfriend at the time, said: "We will make sure that you have all kinds of financial and legal problems." and you know, my life has not been easy. I was the mother of his children, tremendous financial success built in our marriage. He was the merger and acquisition specialist for corporations and became the banking expert. He waited as long as possible and appealed the settlement of our divorce, even though it was not equitable. My attorney stopped working for me when he moved into the same bank building as my ex-husband. I was left without an attorney and none to be found for me. Why was that allowed to happen? He treated our divorce like I was a business to be destroyed . . . and he was allowed. This went on for ten years. During that time, opportunists were waiting in the wings Merrill Lynch was one of them. Where and how does this end. Am I suppose to accept injustice, deceit, and callousness. Is this "now" going to be my life defending myself from predators that use their professionalism as a front. And, people that know and see but do nothing. Is it fear? Are they so impressed? Are they so oppressed themselves that they have nothing left to give. I'm sorry, but I cannot accept this blatant act of dishonesty to be ignored and swept under the rugs and I will not pay for their mistakes that came from their greed that was continually being fed. We all make mistakes, but we only learn when we acknowledge that mistake and make restitution to those we have offended, hurt or taken advantage. We can't put Band-Aids on cancer and our country needs to get back to reclaiming and restoring our dignity and trust. Again, I will say, I am sorry I cannot accept this. This has taken way too much of my time. It really is a simple thing when you do the right thing. But, corporate, government, legal, etc., needs and likes to complicate and convolute to their advantage. Enough said for now.

Patti Z

-Show quoted text-
Reply Forward to Securities
Patti Zona
show details 9/28/08 Reply

This is the response to the letter sent from Paul Giappone, director-senior counsel—also at the Litigation Department. So, is he an attorney representing Merrill Lynch? If so that explains a lot. He has no interest in helping me but his corporate client. This letter also states that it is from the office of General Counsel ... How dare Mr. Giappone writes that I did not complain about this! I trusted Merrill Lynch, Tom Drees and I gave Chad Ellman a chance to fix this mess. Because, I was told "if I everyone took their money out-it would create tremendous problems-cause a crash. I've never wanted to be part of any kind of problem. Merrill Lynch misled innocent and trusting people down a path that would only give them valuable time to hide and conceal and plan their monetary exits. When I confronted them, they were arrogant and rude, telling me "They would not make it easy for me if I took my monies out. It would be a long expensive process." And, it was. It is bad enough that they used me and the money that I entrusted to them, but to insult me and pretend that they to Securities
Patti Zona
Merger Acquisition »U.S. Securities and Exchange Commission 9/17/08

1/19/09 5:47 PM
Gmail - SEC Response - File HO1280859 - patianz@gmail.com

Paul Giappone, youre telling me Merrill Lynch did nothing wrong? Who are you kidding? For once, do the right and moral thing and stop denying, distorting, convoluting, complicating and confusing the real issue. Stop making matters worse. I've learned valuable lessons here. What about you?

Patti Z

- Show quoted text -
Reply Forward
show details 9/28/08 Reply

Please send this previous e-mail to Paul Giappone and let him know I expect a reply and an explanation of his and Merrill Lynchs' erroneous action and I don't want them to plead the fifth.

Patti Z

- Show quoted text -
to Securities Exchange Commission
Patti Zona

Index